# > > > *Running Money*

ALSO BY ANDY KESSLER

*Wall Street Meat*

# > > > Running Money

## Hedge Fund Honchos, Monster Markets and My Hunt for the Big Score

**Andy Kessler**

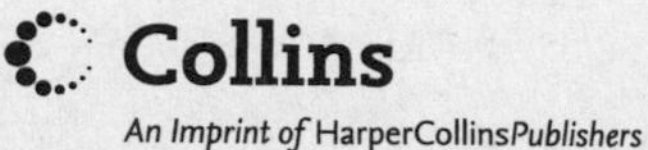

HarperCollins books may be purchased for educational, business, or sales promotional use. For information, please write to: Special Markets Department, HarperCollins Publishers, 10 East 53rd Street, New York, NY 10022.

FIRST COLLINS PAPERBACK EDITION 2005.

*Designed by Nancy Singer*

The Library of Congress has catalogued the hardcover edition as follows:

Library of Congress Cataloging-in-Publication Data

Kessler, Andy.
Running money: hedge fund honchos, monster markets and my hunt for the big score/Andy Kessler.—1st ed.
p. cm.
ISBN 0-06-074064-7
1. Hedge funds. I. Title.

HG4530.K47 2004
332.64'5'092—dc22
[B] 2004047585

ISBN-10: 0-06-074065-5 (paperback) ISBN-13: 978-0-06-074065-8

05 06 07 08 09 ❖/RRD 10 9 8 7 6 5 4 3 2 1

For Nancy

and our bookends, Kyle and Brett,

and our books, Kurt and Ryan

> > > **Contents**

# > > > Ssangyong Sweat

This market really sucks. It's the fall of 1998, and things are banging around so much, my head hurts. Just like that, our gains from the last few years have vanished. Poof. You can't ever forget how precarious and humbling running money really is.

Some funny currency crisis is going on in the Far East. I'm not sure if this makes any difference at all to Silicon Valley, where most of our investments are based. We didn't need this shit, as we're still scrambling around, raising money. Without decent numbers, we're just two nobodies above an art supplies store in Palo Alto. I desperately need a day to sort out what is really going on and to figure out which way is up.

In reality, I'm looking forward to a day of doing absolutely nothing. It's midmorning, and just as my Monday-Night-Football-at-the-Oasis-Bar–induced throbbing is beginning to fade, the phone rings, making my head hurt even more.

After fifteen years as a piece of Wall Street meat—first as a research analyst, then as a lousy investment banker—I find myself running a real live hedge fund. It has been two years since my partner, Fred Kittler, and I started scraping together a tiny sum of money, mostly from old friends and a few moneyed folks willing to take a risk on a pair of refugees from Wall Street. It's not a lot—hardly enough to make us respectable, despite our first-year numbers being pretty good, up 50 something percent.

Until two weeks ago that is. Korea and Russia and Malaysia have just collapsed under the weight of their respective foreign debts, and they took our gains down with them. Now we're break-even for the year—all that hard work down the drain in a few ticks of the tape.

No wonder I'm in such a foul mood.

"Can you make it down to the company for a lunch today?" the voice on the phone asked. "We have something of mutual interest to discuss."

Andy Rappaport was a partner at August Capital, a B+ venture firm in the valley. A few months earlier, our fund had invested in a private company where Rappaport sat on the board, keeping an eye on August's stake. The company sold chips for $5 that cost them $1 to make in Taiwan, which allowed LCD monitors to display sharper images and disk drives to connect faster. Pretty neat stuff.

"What's it about?" I asked.

"I can't tell you."

"I'm kinda busy."

"This is important," he said with a half-pleading, half-excited tone in his voice. "Trust me."

"Who's going be there?" I asked.

"Myself and another board member. Just us, not management." There was that tone again. (I didn't know him well enough—maybe he always sounded this way.) "There's an interesting opportunity here."

I happened to like the management team, a big reason why we had invested in the first place. But "interesting opportunity." Hmmmm. Those are always the magic words.

"OK, fine, see you at noon," I said.

I made Fred come along. We were running our fund out of a dumpy office above an arts store in Palo Alto (low overhead). Anyone who visited probably thought we were running some investment-scam bucket shop instead of a hedge fund. I dunno, some days I wondered if we weren't. Our fund was different from most. We were buy and hold—stocks only. I'd rather eat pork bellies than trade them. We invested mostly in small public companies and a few interesting private companies.

I wasn't so sure about this one. I'd had no plans to go anywhere that day, so I was wearing jeans and, I'm pretty sure, a clean shirt. Fred and I hit Sunnyvale and parked close to a nondescript steel-

and-glass box like those that house every company in the Valley. We were ushered into a conference room that could probably seat 20, with the standard fare of slightly smushed multicolored tortilla wraps sitting uninvitingly on a platter. After almost 15 years in the investment business, I had learned never to trust anyone or anything (let alone eat wraps), so my cynicism was busting out today.

Rappaport didn't waste any time. "There is a group who invested in an earlier round, and they want to sell their shares."

"So?" I blurted out. "Wouldn't we all."

"Well, there seems to be a sense of urgency here."

Now my ears perked up. "Urgency? Who is it?"

"Well, the investor is Ssangyong . . ."

"Who?" I interrupted.

The other board member, a guy from VentureStar, a fund with money mostly out of Taiwan, jumped in, "Ssangyong. They are a Korean company that makes everything from diesel engines to cement. They are spending a lot on LCD monitors, and invested here, hoping to get a jump on some of the technology that could add value."

This was starting to make sense. Korea was drowning in a sea of foreign debt built up in the '90s, but Korean companies didn't make enough profit to pay back the debt. As other Asian countries began defaulting on their debt in '98, investors panicked and called in Korean loans. Anything that wasn't tied down was for sale in Korea. Ssangyong was something like the sixth largest corporation in Korea, not that I had ever heard of it.

"So let me guess," I said. "They need cash quickly."

"I think so."

"Sounds like a distressed sale. Let's lowball them."

"Well, it's not that easy," Rappaport replied. "They know things are going well here, and that CS First Boston is interested in taking this company public in the next year."

Our fund had just invested a slug of dough at $4, and if all went well, we figured an IPO run by Frank Quattrone would be priced at around $16–$18 next summer.

"Ssangyong thinks the shares are worth seven or eight bucks today."

"Why doesn't August just do the whole thing itself?" I asked, putting Rappaport on the spot. "You guys have deep pockets. You don't need us."

"Well, um, er, we own a lot of this thing, and I'm not sure my partners want to add that much."

Now I really didn't trust him. I didn't want Fred and me to be the suckers here. We had invested only a few months ago, nothing had changed really and I wasn't all that interested in getting more exposed. The company had a lot to do before CSFB would take them out—not-so-easy things like doubling their sales. If it didn't work, we would be stuck with worthless stock. It's the worst place you could possibly be running a hedge fund—long and wrong.

I leaned over to Fred, and before I could ask him what he thought, he whispered that we should take the stock. He thought the company was going to be a home run.

I wasn't so sure. Fred is ten years older than I am, with light-years more market savvy. I make judgments much too quickly. But when Fred comes up against a difficult problem, he just reaches back into his long-term cranial memory storage and does a little pattern recognition until he can say, "I've seen this before." We were the yin and the yang of rash and rational, which is why the partnership worked so well.

"We'll pay $2.50," I said with more confidence than I thought I had in me.

"That's only slightly more than what Ssangyong paid a year ago, and they know we just did a round at $4."

"That's why they call it distressed," I said.

I was in completely over my head, my hangover hurt and our fund's performance was like an erratic yo-yo. I would have been happy to go back to my office and stare at my screen. "They need the money, and they're going to make a small profit on their investment, even at $2.50. Sounds like we are doing them a favor."

We batted it around for another 20 minutes. I watched my untouched bean sprouts and avocado wrap wilt into itself, then got up and took a nature break.

"OK, so we agree on $2.50?" Rappaport said as I walked back into the room.

"Yes," I said, then turned to go.

Over my shoulder I added, "We'll do half of the shares, and you guys split the other half."

"Great," Rappaport said, perhaps too easily. "But there's one more thing—we took a straw poll while you were in the bathroom and decided that you've got to tell him."

"Tell who?" I asked, whipping around again. I had been so close to the door and freedom.

"Mr. Shim from Ssangyong. He's in the next room."

"Oh, great," I thought. "I had to miss that vote." I heard myself say instead, "No way."

"No one else wants to."

"Fine. I'll tell him." I really didn't care—I just wanted to get the hell out of there.

On cue, the CEO of the company whose shares are being sold by Ssangyong walked into the conference room, looked at me and asked, "Ready?"

I followed him into a smaller conference room where a short man was sitting alone at a table for five, thankfully without wilting wraps. The CEO introduced me to Sang Win Shim, a Korean gentleman in an ill-fitting off-the-rack brown suit, white overstarched shirt and cheap tie, who was nervously sucking on a lit cigarette like it was connected to his air supply.

When the CEO left, Mr. Shim stared at me with one eyebrow arched in anticipation of bad news. I also noted a few beads of sweat above his lip. He surveyed me, unshaven, wearing a short-sleeve polo shirt, Wrangler jeans and slightly used ASICS sneakers that were made in Korea, probably in the next town over. He must have thought, "What the fuck is it with these silly Americans? Can't they even wear a suit?"

Neither of us spoke for a minute or two, so I decided to break the ice.

"I understand you have some shares of the company you would like to sell."

"Yes, yes," he said, and his arched eyebrow eased slightly.

"Well, we met in the other room and discussed your situation, and we would like to buy your shares."

A crooked smile came over his face, as if I had made his day. He asked, Yoda-like, "Yes, yes. How much pay you for shares?"

"We are prepared to pay you $2.50 for your shares."

I watched as his lips parted, his teeth clenched and he sucked in what seemed like all the air in the room in this reverse hissing sound that could be heard for blocks. The sweat spread to his forehead, sideburns and shirt. He lit another Marlboro and dragged on it so many times, so quickly, that the room became a thick cloud of smoke. I thought I was in a police interrogation scene from a bad black-and-white movie.

"No, no, not enough. We pay that before—stock now eight dolla."

"Well, that is all we are willing to offer. There's a lot of uncertainty, your shares have less rights and based on our risk discount calculations"—I didn't know where that line came from—"we can only offer you $2.50."

A few more giant sucking sounds and Bogart cigarette-sucking imitations and his sweat grew so heavy he looked like I had pushed him into the Pacific Ocean. Perhaps I had. He kept muttering, "No, no. No good. I need much more. People want more."

"Sorry, that's all we can do."

Finally, shaking his head so hard that the conference table was getting soaked, he mumbled almost under his breath, "I no able to accept. I must talk with my chief."

I suppose I knew the negotiations were over and he was just saving face, even to a sloppily dressed bozo like me. I just said, "OK, just let us know, thanks."

I ran out of the building as if I had seen a ghost. I told Fred on the drive back to our office that these guys didn't have any other buyers and my guess was we would get a call tomorrow saying that we could have the shares for $2.50.

And sure enough, the next morning, we did.

# > > > Part I

# Raising Funds

## > > > No Homa

KOWLOON, HONG KONG—EARLY 1996

The doors of the marble-lined elevator opened on the 32nd floor. I walked out, looking for a receptionist to direct me to William Kaye, a money manager I was set to meet at 10:00 a.m. Back in 1986, Kaye ran the deal arbitrage desk at PaineWebber. Now, 10 years later, he is running money out of Hong Kong, and I was trying to get him to invest in our fund or point me to others in Asia who might be interested.

But something wasn't right. There was no receptionist, just a giant room filled with Chinese men and women bustling about, jabbering away, passing pieces of yellow and red and orange plastic around the room. Boxes filled with wires and screws and nuts and bolts were on every table. Against the wall, a stack of shrink-wrapped boxes looked ready to ship out. This was all very odd for a classy office building in Kowloon. I made eye contact with a woman scurrying by.

"William Kaye?" I asked.

"No homa."

"He's not in?"

"No, he homa."

"So he is in?"

"No. Homa. Homa Sim-san." She pointed to the finished boxes.

She was right. The boxes were of Homer Simpson figures. A giant arrow on the box told me to push his exposed belly, which I did and heard, "D'oh!"

• • •

I checked my calendar. William Kaye was on the 33rd floor. D'oh.

I rode the elevator up one more floor, and the doors opened to a completely different world. Cherry wood–lined walls, modern furniture, a sign that said Pacific Group, under which sat a blond receptionist who greeted me by name.

"Mr. Kessler, Mr. Kaye will be with you in a moment. He is on a conference call with the management of a Thai cement company. May I invite you to wait in our conference room? Tea for you?"

I stood and stared in amazement out the conference room window overlooking Kowloon and Hong Kong Island and the port of Hong Kong. What seemed like hundreds of container ships stacked high with, well, probably with Homer Simpson figures, shuffled along, while a few junk ships and motorboats darted in and out.

I guess you can run a hedge fund anywhere—they come in lots of different flavors. Some come up with complicated strategies to speculate on the rise of Malaysian currencies versus pork belly futures. Or to take down the Bank of England.

In 1949, a guy named Alfred Winslow Jones figured out he could improve his investment returns by simultaneously borrowing money to buy stocks with one hand and selling stocks he didn't actually own with the other hand. If he constructed the right transaction, he could make money in a rising or falling market. That's how Jones discovered a "hedge." Ever since, smart guys who wanted to be rich began creating complicated hedges and getting rich people who weren't as smart to invest in them. How do I know this? I tripped across the name "A. W. Jones" on a door at One Rockefeller Plaza in New York years back and asked.

A few years into the evolution of hedge funds, in the late 1960s, you started to recognize the names. Guys like George Soros and Michael Steinhardt and even Warren Buffet ran some of the 200 hedge funds that popped up. You must be a millionaire to invest in a hedge fund—an "accredited investor," in regulator-speak. The Feds, focused on the downside, figure it's OK to let rich people be stupid—after all, they can afford to lose it all. But all that really does is keep ordinary folks from getting great returns.

By the 1990s, a couple hundred funds had become thousands, most of them fast-money operations eking out tiny returns on each trade but buying and selling so much stuff day in and day out that it eventually added up to real money. That's what Julian Robertson at Tiger and the Nobel laureates at Long Term Capital Management did. They ran huge pots of capital through monster trading floors filled with computer monitors covered in dancing green and red prices. These folks hedged anything that moved. I was trying to raise money to get in the game.

"You Andy? Yeah, I remember you. Chips or something like that. You sat back there with Jack Grubman."

Seeing Kaye brought the '80s flying back. I had spent five years at PaineWebber and another five years at Morgan Stanley as a semiconductor analyst. I was the poor slob that had to say Buy or Sell on stocks like Intel and Motorola and Texas Instruments. These stocks loved to bob when everyone else weaved.

Technology was volatile, but stocks of companies that made chips were like hyperactive kids munching on cotton candy: they'd fly high until they crashed hard, and my job was to figure out when the sugar high would begin and end. I always figured I would end up with gray hair and ulcers. My clients were big money firms—Fidelity, JP Morgan and increasingly lots of fast-money hedge funds that liked to play where things were moving.

I had hopped off that roller coaster still sporting a head of dark brown hair, but now I was getting into running money or at least I hoped I could if someone like William Kaye would give us enough money.

Kaye was a reasonably slight, very New York–looking guy, with black hair and eyes set a little close together, which gave him both a serious and mysterious, almost sinister look at the same time. He was also smart as shit. At PaineWebber, he had made the firm and its clients tons of money (I assume he did well himself too). Courtesy of Michael Milken and Drexel Burnham and hot money in junk bonds, the late '80s saw mergers announced almost daily. If a stock was trading at $45 and a deal was announced at $60, the stock might jump to $57. You could still make $3, not much, but in only three months, which was a 21% return, even higher if you borrowed money. Kaye and his team would figure out how solid the deal was, chase down deal documents, figure out if the price might even go up and then put the "arb on."

"That's me, nice to see you again." I ended my sightseeing and leaned over to shake his hand.

"Please sit."

"Thanks. I'm out raising money for a fund to invest in communications technology companies, public and private. I figure there might be interest from folks out here in the Far East." I started to give him the pitch, but he waved me off.

"I've got a couple of guys in New York who might be interested. Out here, we are still in the industrial age."

"What do you mean?" I asked.

"Look, you guys in Silicon Valley are so far ahead of the curve, you have no idea. The Industrial Revolution is just hitting around here. It's decades behind you, maybe more."

"Are you really investing in cement companies?" Not only was I curious, but I still had 50 minutes to kill until my next meeting. He'd turned down my pitch to invest in our fund pretty quickly, and it wasn't like I was coming back to Hong Kong anytime soon, so I might as well learn something.

"Investing in the U.S. is so advanced," Kaye went on. "There's technology and biotech and all this highly valued stuff. Around here, they are still building roads and putting in telephone wires and putting up office buildings and chemical plants and factories. I can just look at what worked in the U.S. 30 years ago or 80 years ago and then go find similar industries and companies around here."

"Really?" I asked.

"Yeah sure, I've been in more lumberyards and ethylene plants and shoe assemblers than I care to remember. But that's the easy part."

"What do you mean?" I asked.

"Accounting is a joke. I don't trust anyone. The Japanese are the worst. They say they make money, but they really don't. Almost every Chinese company I know is a not-for-profit entity. In other countries, like, I don't know, Singapore maybe, they say they don't make money, but really do."

"I take it they don't do 10-Q filings like they do in the U.S."

"You'd be lucky to get some of these companies to say anything. I'm on a plane most of the time, visiting management to figure out how much money they are making. Then I've got to figure out what they are going to tell everyone else who *doesn't* visit. The banks are mostly crooked, the governments not much better. You've got to watch them both as closely as the companies, make sure the whole damn system is solvent. The biggest question is how the U.S. trade deficit is going to work out. But I love it."

"Why? It sounds hard."

"Not really. It's like living in 18th- and 19th-century England and knowing ahead of time how the whole Industrial Revolution ends up. You guys have to sit in Silicon Valley and try to figure out what the world is going to look like in 20 years. Good luck. Around here, I've seen this movie already. I get to cheat. I know how it ends."

"Isn't it maturing faster than the West did?"

"You'd think. But they do all the same stupid things—bad laws, protectionist policies, full employment instead of quality employment. When I do find someone making money, I've got to worry about banks in the country overlending."

"Why does that matter?" I asked.

"The U.S. trade deficit means dollars pile up around here. If the banks lend too much, foreign money pulls out, the currency starts dropping, interest rates go up to keep money in the country and my little moneymaker gets sucked into a nasty depression and becomes worthless."

"Wow."

"To be honest, it's a lot like the deal arb days back at Paine-Webber. You try to figure out if management is honest. Most governments aren't. Their central banks use dollars instead of gold, but they still make bad loans like banks for all time have done, and then they cover it up. But if you find anything that smells like an American or British model, you can make lots of money. That's why I'm here."

I took one last glance at his spectacular view of Hong Kong harbor, thanked him for his time and headed back into the swamp of Hong Kong. I always hated meetings like that, hearing from someone who actually knew what he was doing. The future was a giant fog bank to me, and here is a guy who has a spectacular view and a script to follow. I made a note to buy a Homer Simpson doll at the airport.

# > > > You Need an Edge

NEW YORK, NEW YORK—EARLY 1996

"Let me show you into the conference room. Mr. Nash will be with you in one moment."

"Thank you so much," I said.

The receptionist led me and Fred Kittler into your standard-issue New York City conference room—a round table with six chairs, a leafy green potted plant in the corner and cheap blotchy nondescript prints that was some office manager's attempt at soothing art. The only difference from every other conference room I had ever been in was a giant monitor, maybe a 50-inch diagonal screen, looming over the conference room table.

"Mr. Nash has just one request. He would like you two to sit in these two seats." She pointed to two chairs directly under the massive monitor. "He will sit over here. He does this every meeting, don't worry about it."

My partner and I exchanged a that's-weird glance.

"OK, got it."

Jack Nash was a Wall Street legend. He was on the top five list of greatest hedge fund managers along with George Soros, Julian Robertson and I'm not sure who the other two might be. I think I remember seeing him on the *Forbes* billionaire list.

Fred and I were out raising money for our fund, and one of our investors, Jim Torrey, mentioned that Jack Nash was liquidating his Odyssey Partners hedge fund. Something like $3 billion was going back to investors, and a lot of that was Jack's personal dough. He was hanging up his cleats and looking for others to manage some of his fortune. Torrey set up this meeting, and despite working on Wall Street for almost 15 years, I was intimidated as hell to meet and pitch a living legend. We had a few small investors in our fund, but nailing Jack Nash would be big, I figured, since everyone he knew would then call us begging to invest in our fund. (I could be quite delusional when I put my mind to it.)

"OK, hello there, please sit down," Jack Nash said as he waddled in. He looked like a classic aging New Yorker, short, slightly stooped over, a white mop of hair straggling from his head. He gave us a half smile and waved us to be seated.

"Thanks for meeting with us," I started.

"Yeah, yeah," he mumbled.

"We are based out in Silicon Valley, and our fund is focused on communication technology and . . ."

I kept babbling on about our background and what we were going to do. I tried to make eye contact, but old Jack was staring over my head, shaking his head and muttering something incomprehensible every couple of seconds. He would occasionally look at me and nod, a go-on-I'm-paying-attention nod, and then go back to staring above my head at the screen. It was hard to hold a thought and keep talking, but I kept going. This was nothing. I've pitched to investors who have fallen asleep on me. When Nash was as warmed up as he was going to get, I passed the baton to Fred, who told him how we would find long-run value in technology land.

We were pitching pretty well, but Jack Nash kept staring above our heads. I couldn't take it anymore. I leaned forward to see what was on the screen. Of course, I said to myself, it was a Quotron screen. The entire 50-inch diagonal monitor was filled with itty-bitty quotes, hundreds of them. And the stock prices were flashing—IBM, GE, AT&T, Merck—the entire S&P 500 must have been up there. Green ones were stocks going up; red ones were stocks going down. Jack was scanning the screen a hundred times a second, looking for . . . What the hell *was* he looking for? Investing by staring at screens? That was so . . . so yesterday. Since the invention of the stock ticker, there had been legions of traders who could "read the tape" and figure out when someone else was buying or selling a particular stock. That smart guy would step into the middle of the trade and make money. But now the action was in options and futures. You needed advanced calculus to figure out the value of those. But Nash wasn't thinking about puts and calls. Here was an old-fashioned trader looking to get in the flow. He was clearly a guy who couldn't let go.

I'm used to the "roving eye" at meetings. One guy in Denver was trading interest rate swaps for his own account while we talked. He checked the quote screen in his office so often, I thought his eyeballs would pop out. But even he was an amateur compared to this. Fred finished up and there was a long silence.

I jumped in. "Thanks again for taking the time to meet with us. We would be honored to have you involved in our fund."

"Yes, yes, but you haven't told me what makes you unique," Jack admonished.

"Unique?" I asked.

"Yeah, your edge."

"Edge?" I asked.

"Yeah. What do you know that no one else knows? What's your little secret? What's your insight? You gotta have something or else you're just chicken feed like everyone else on the Street."

This guy was staring at flashing numbers, but he was listening. We hadn't told him anything worth hearing. It was all, "This is who we are; this is what we want to do."

"Well, we are in the heart of Silicon Valley."

"So?"

"We understand technology."

"So does my neighbor's 12-year-old kid."

"There is an economic engine to all this."

"Like what?" Jack asked.

"I don't know."

"You don't know?"

"Well, we do, it's just hard to articulate."

"Try me." Jack had stopped looking at the green and red flashes above us.

"I used to buy DEC VAXs for half a million bucks."

"That piece-of-crap company blew up a decade ago."

"Yeah, but now you can buy that same VAX, the speed anyway, for 50 cents."

"OK?" Jack was losing patience and was back to staring at the monitor.

"But now there are billions sold."

"And you can make money doing that?"

"Sure, every time Intel cuts prices, they make more money," I said.

"OK, I know that. Intel has been a great stock. You going to buy that?"

"No." Fred jumped in. "But there are lots of small companies that have the same model and can grow to become big companies. We are going to find a bunch of them every year."

"It's been picked clean."

"Maybe," I argued. "But that's just computers. There is other stuff."

"Stuff?"

"Uh . . ." I started stammering like Ralph Kramden. "Humminah, humminah, humminah."

"Turn stuff into a way to find great stock picks, and you've got an edge," Jack said.

"We have a list of . . ."

"I'm not sure I want any U.S. exposure anyway. The dollar is going to get crushed until the trade deficit starts shrinking."

"I, um . . ."

It was too late. Our time with Jack Nash was up. He stood and headed out. I assume it was back to his desk with larger monitors and even more stock quotes. I think I figured out why he was getting out of the business. Tough way to make a living, staring at each tick of the stock market tape. Maybe you can make money that way—Jack Nash obviously did—but what a way to spend your day.

On the elevator ride down I said to Fred, "Please promise me that's not how we end up, slaves to the last stock tick."

"Don't worry about it. That's not investing. He's obviously done well, but we're not going to get a penny from him. He is right though."

"Right about what?" I asked.

"We need an edge. Something to hang onto."

"This ain't easy, is it, Fred?"

"It will be. It shouldn't be that hard to outthink guys like that."

## > > > H & Screw Conference

SAN FRANCISCO, CALIFORNIA—SPRING 1996

"This place is a zoo," I said as I rushed passed.

"It's just unclear which side of the cage we are on," Nick Moore quickly shot back.

I'm late as usual. I've just run through Union Square, dodging pigeons and lots of smelly homeless bums, to get to the lobby of the St. Francis, which is packed. I've never seen more people dressed in khakis with cell phones surgically attached to their ears, standing around in one small place.

I'm just in time to catch a presentation by one of the companies in our portfolio, but I didn't count on having to fight the crowds. I need a machete to cut a path to the main ballroom, but I make do with elbows, shin kicks and the occasional head nod of hello across the sea of bodies.

Welcome to the H&Q Tech Conference. Every brokerage firm runs a technology conference of some sort or other, but this is considered the granddaddy of them all. I suppose it's like the Rose Bowl. Hundreds of CEOs and CFOs show up to give 25-minute presentations followed by 25 minutes in a "breakout session" upstairs. As in high school, you get five minutes between meetings. Also as in high school, I learn what a bizarre world the investment business is.

Despite hundreds of seats in the room, I stood in the back. I'd already heard this presentation a few times. I was listening for the "news"—you quickly learn the trick of focusing on what has changed from the last presentation, that was the news—and the only thing the stock market cared about. I didn't hear anything new, so I headed out to the hallway to find my way to the next meeting.

"You coming from Bill Larceny's presentation?"

"Excuse me?" I thought I recognized the voice, but I wasn't sure where it was coming from.

"Bill Larson. Network Associates. It's amazing what he gets away with. His honey pots and cookie jars, the guy practically admits he cooks the books."

Standing behind me was my buddy, Nick Moore, who has done just about everything in this business, from being an analyst, a portfolio manager of mutual funds to running a hedge fund.

"What a zoo," I said, repeating myself.

"H & Zoo. More like the H & Screw Conference," Nick quickly replied.

"Who are all these people?" I asked.

"Well, it takes all types. See that guy drooling orange juice who looks like he just got out of high school? He runs the Fidelity Select Software fund. And those two guys over there . . ."

"With the preppy tortoiseshell eyeglass frames?"

"Yeah. They're from Janus or Invesco or one of those Denver momentum funds."

"What about that guy?" I asked.

"With the Ca-cheese-io shoes?"

"If that's what you want to call them," I replied.

"He's one of those popcorn hedgies," Nick told me.

"A what?"

"Yeah, one of those guys that just pops around, looking for some quick idea. See, watch this. He's walking up to Kipp. Let's go listen."

Kipp Bedard is the investor relations guy for Micron Technology out of Boise. Micron is one of the only memory makers left in the U.S. and is a proxy for how the chip business is doing. Kipp looks like an old track star and usually tells it like it is: what he sees demand looking like, what pricing trends are. Nick and I join the "scrum" around him.

"How's business, Kipp?" the popcorn dude asks.

"Pretty good. We're seeing decent demand from all geographies. Asia is a little stronger than Europe," Kip answers.

"PCs leading the way?" Popcorn asks.

"We are seeing even stronger demand from communications. I think we are designed into some routers."

"And what about pricing?"

"About what you'd expect. Sixteen meg prices are about what we thought, but the new 64 meg prices are dropping faster, which is great for us. The crossover will be right on schedule." This is normal and means that one 64-meg chip will soon be cheaper than four 16-meg chips and then everyone uses them.

As the popcorn guy strolls away, Nick leans over to me and whispers, "My-cram's stock is going down."

"Really? Sounded good to me." I was confused.

"You'll see. Let's go over to the Quotron."

A group was gathered around the quote screens. You see it all the time, some poor schmuck plugging in his favorite stock and hitting the return key again and again hoping it goes up. Nick yelled out, "Put in MU. I think it's gonna move."

Sure enough, the stock was down a buck and a half.

"Any news?" one of the quote junkies asked.

"You hear any?" Nick asked him.

"Something about pricing. Not sure."

Another guy walked past. "Stories going around that Kipp lowered guidance. Disappointing prices."

"I heard from my trader that Europe is weak, there are problems with PCs and prices are cratering. And Micron hasn't even given their presentation yet," another investor added.

"Nick, what just happened?" I asked incredulously.

"That guy probably called into Moron Stanley or Worst Boston and shorted Micron's stock, and then told them he heard straight from their investor relations that things are a disaster, PC makers have stopped buying, prices are collapsing, the fab is on fire, who knows."

"The stock is now down two and three quarters."

"That's probably it. He's now covering his short and will move on to the next company."

"Hell of a way to make a buck."

You'd think it would be impossible to do this, but investors are so nervous about how business really is tracking and how the quarter is going to come out that just whispering something that sounds like news can move a stock several points.

Companies announce earnings once a quarter—that's it. High-growth companies are especially vulnerable to bad news, and even the hint of problems creates a shoot-first-ask-questions-later response. If Micron really missed their profit estimates, their stock price might halve, so you can appreciate how sensitive traders are to any news. That the popcorn dude, who probably has never been to Boise let alone knows how to spell DRAM, can spin an investor relations guy's words into a magnified and basically bogus stock call speaks loudly to how bizarre and hypersensitive short-term investing is.

"I think that's about the only way that guy can do it. He's not smart enough to actually figure out if a stock is going to go up tomorrow or next month or next year," Nick said.

"Who is?" I asked.

"Good question. Probably no one," Nick said with a sour note to his voice.

"I gotta go," I said.

"Who you going to see next? Mis-informed-ix? Creeple-soft?"

"No."

"Crapple Computer? Fraudvision? Strata-con? Net-mangle?"

"No. And you've got to stop."

"So, who?"

"I'm not going tell you, or you'll come up with some silly yet oddly appropriate name and I'll never be able to invest."

My perception of investing was pretty simple. You invest in companies with great long-term prospects. As usual, I am famous for overstating the obvious, with lots of conviction, no less. But that line is so stupid as to be meaningless. It is kind of like movie studios saying they like to produce hit movies, or book imprints saying they like to publish bestsellers. The stock market is all-knowing and all-humiliating. You can invest real money in real stocks and watch them go up or down or sideways or all of the above, causing an endless personal parade of jubilation and disappointment, yet still be clueless on how the stock market works.

Which companies? What is *long term*? What does *prospects*

even mean? What price do you pay? I spent the rest of the time at the H&Q Tech Conference asking everyone who would talk one simple question: "How do you invest?"

No two people answered the question the same way.

"We are business momentum investors."

"We look for earnings surprises."

"Growth at a reasonable price."

"Trailing 12-month earnings multiple."

"There are no great companies, only great stocks. Don't ever forget that."

"I like to focus on margins."

"I only look at one thing, and that's management. A lousy management team can run the greatest company in the greatest industry into the toilet. And a great management team can profit selling ice cubes to Eskimos. When I find a great team, I stick with them forever."

"I just watch interest rates. When they go down, I buy stocks."

"Currency rates tell you everything you need to know."

"The second derivative of the change in industrial production numbers."

"Marginal flows into gold."

"I check the difference between personal income and consumer credit until it flashes bullish."

"Jobless claims lead interest rates, which lead consumer cylicals. 'Nuff said."

"It all works on the Greater Fool theory."

The most honest: "We're indexed."

One guy, Jim Burkhardt from Chicago, gave me the best line:

"Yeah, sure, I check all the stats, economic indicators, earnings numbers, all that garbage. Everyone has them, so they don't provide much of an edge."

"What does?" I asked.

"I just try to know the headlines before they appear."

"You what?" I asked incredulously.

"There are a bunch of long-term trends. I just pick a few I really believe in and then extend them far enough out that I can write next year's headlines today."

"Today?"

"I'm not always right. But I usually get pretty close. It makes all the noise go away."

I wanted the noise to go away too.

# > > > Hedgies

After a dozen years of working on Wall Street, I find myself running a hedge fund. I'm not even sure how that happened—I've either reached the top or the bottom of my profession. If I screw up, it certainly will be the basement. If that wasn't enough, I am completely and utterly lost—clueless. About the only thing I really know is "Buy low, sell high."

But buy and sell what? There are thousands of different stocks and bonds and currencies and commodities. As an analyst on Wall Street, you just say Buy or Sell, but someone else actually does it. Your call is just a concept. Now it's real money. Actually, it's still someone else's money, but I am now personally responsible for it. If I can make the stake go up in value, I get 20% of the upside (oh yeah, that's why I'm doing this). If it goes down, I get nada. Jack Nash was right, I need an edge. But what?

Everybody I meet in the business seems to have an edge, or so they think. It's like senior year in college, when I'd meet these self-assured and overconfident types who knew exactly what they were going to be doing for the rest of their lives. "I'm going to law school and then will join a New York law firm and probably make partner in six years." "After med school, I'm going to intern at Mt. Sinai and then set up a cardiology practice on Long Island." "My MBA will get me a job at Salomon, where I'll probably trade medium-term govvies." Those bastards—I had no clue what I would be doing, but not for lack of thinking about it. It was what I didn't know about that always seemed more interesting.

As an analyst at Morgan Stanley—a job I didn't even know existed when I was in college—I met just about everyone who ran money around the world. That was my job—they were my clients.

I've known hedge fund types for way too long. Now I am one, and I realize I haven't the foggiest idea what they really do.

The folks that ran hedge funds were always the weirdest. Sometimes seedy, they were usually way too bright. But what struck me again and again is that they were, almost to a person, very unemotional. Cold.

And they were not just cold. Hedgies stuck me as incredibly detached as well. Apart from the real world. On another planet, almost. Actually, a lot of people on Wall Street are this way. They reside in a different layer from the rest of the world. I suppose it is how the financial system is set up; they can buy and sell companies all day without really caring what they actually do.

I once met a Hollywood director who referred to actors as "meat puppets," to be manipulated as he saw fit. I think hedgies have a similar detachment. It wouldn't matter if General Motors made cars or candy bars, as long as the company beat the forecasts and the stock went up.

Author Michael Lewis picked up on this in his book *Liar's Poker,* when he talked about ways his clients made money in the Chernobyl disaster or a Japanese earthquake. He basically said that folks who run hedge funds are different from you and me. A headline says a hurricane has hit. Most people would feel bad for the people who had to evacuate their homes, while someone who runs a hedge fund would immediately think that he needs to buy construction companies and short insurance stocks.

Mayer Rothschild, the patriarch of the European House of Rothschild, gets credit for the adage "Buy when there is blood in the streets." When everyone else is in panic and chaos, fleeing the scene, you step in. Rothschild also gets credit for shorting the market in Paris when he learned the news of Napoleon's defeat before anyone else.

Unemotional, most hedge funds will take either side of a trade.

Change is the key. Things that stay constant or grow too slowly are way too dull to invest in. The economy grows 3%, 4%. Bonds yield 5%. Ho hum. Why bother? Change, change, change. Lots of it. All the time. That's what hedge funds thrive on, something you can make money on.

But it's not just change. If everyone thinks Cisco is growing by 30%, and the company reports earnings showing they are growing by 30%, there is a loud sigh heard throughout Wall Street. They just *met* their numbers? Where is the fun in that? There are legions of people sweating away, trying to figure out if the company will beat the numbers or blow the numbers.

My problem? I'm too damn lazy for these short-term moves.

Well, not lazy. It's just impossible anymore to take advantage of these short-term shifts. There are traders with massive workstations that feed trades down to the New York Stock Exchange or to the options pits and move millions, sometimes billions, before you can blink an eye.

In January 1991, then Secretary of State James Baker met in Geneva with Iraqi Foreign Minister Tariq Aziz to find a peaceful solution to Iraq's occupation of Kuwait. Baker stepped out of the meeting and said, "Regrettably . . ." Before he finished his sentence, oil prices spiked 30% and stock markets sold off.

I can't move that fast. Entire trading floors at Goldman Sachs are set up to do this stuff. I had to find some other way to run a hedge fund. Could we make money thinking out long-term ideas? That was almost heresy in the hedge fund world, but I suppose I had no choice.

I had heard that in the 1970s, the Rothschilds—yes, the same "blood in the streets" Rothschilds—had bought tons of real estate in Albany, New York. Their rationale was that sometime in the next 50 years, high-speed light rail would connect Albany and New York City in under an hour. OK, so someone in the family has taken a bullet waiting on that bullet train, but even the family that invented trading was now investing ahead of the market. It just helps to be right.

The guy who told me he looked at only the second derivative of industrial production was onto something. Because information is distributed in milliseconds, there is no time advantage anymore. You have to be ahead of news. You have to look not at change but at how fast change is changing. Your old calculus teacher would remind you, the first derivative is speed. The second derivative is acceleration.

There are so many barriers to change. Some are technical, some are based on silly government regulations. But who cares—barriers are barriers. As long as you can find a barrier to invest against, you can make money when the barrier breaks, when change accelerates.

Most hedge fund guys take the other side of a trade when they know something no one else does, i.e., investing because others don't know. That's their edge.

When you think long-term, the edge is really investing because others *can't* know. I suppose others could know if they thought hard enough, but, oddly, no one does. It's not the actual declining cost of power or transportation, chips or bandwidth, etc., that is hard to figure out. It's the change they enable.

These concepts are hard to grasp.

It's that nasty second derivative stuff. It's not the amount of change, but the change in the rate of change. Confused? Me too. It's why there are few physicists and why people quit science after high school. It's just too hard to think about.

From the side of the highway, you can't tell which cars are going a constant speed and which are accelerating. But from inside the car, you can feel the seat press against you when you gun it. That's probably the first lesson I learned: to do well, you've got to be in the car, not on the sidelines watching.

But in reality, second derivative stuff is quite simple. If you can figure out what is getting cheaper, year by year, you can start to imagine the change to the status quo into the future. And, I think, you only have to be close.

That's the beauty of Silicon Valley. It is about only one thing—change. Maybe I could find pockets of change. Then I wouldn't just be looking for a 30% move in the value of construction stocks after a hurricane; instead, I'd be trying to anticipate huge moves of 500% or 1000% that take place after a barrier collapses.

Peter Lynch, Fidelity's legendary fund manager, called these stock moves five-baggers or ten-baggers. He espoused the idea that ordinary investors could find ten-baggers by themselves: "Do you like shopping at Toys 'R' Us? Gee, golly, maybe you should buy the stock." I wish it were that easy.

So, what is it? Are there still barriers? How can I make sense of the sea of economic data, earnings announcements and noise on the Street? What is it that others *can't* know because second derivatives are hard to conceptualize? Could I find a grand unifying theory of how the world works? If so, while others are sweating out and trading around short-term changes, I could sit back and think out the big moves. Or die trying.

# > > > *Making Your Month*

SAN FRANCISCO, CALIFORNIA—FALL 1996

"Thanks for coming, everybody," Jim Torrey said, calling his unruly lunch companions to order. Jim runs a fund of funds. This means he doesn't invest in companies—he runs a fund that places money into other hedge funds. I'm not sure whose job is tougher. "I thought it would be a good idea to get all you guys together. We are investors in each of your funds, so I thought it would be interesting to sit down and swap war stories."

Jim had been a great help to us, setting us up with Jack Nash, investing in our fund and introducing us to anyone who would listen.

I looked around, and you probably couldn't have put together a stranger mix of people in one room. One bearded guy looked like a college professor, another a little too slick was overdressed in an Armani suit. There was a guy who made me nervous just looking at him—he was constantly turning his head from side to side, looking around and twitching his eyes and mouth. Then there was Fred and me—Fred had the decency to wear a blazer, I was in my trademark jeans and a pullover shirt. The others were all in San Francisco, trying to raise money at a Montgomery Securities Hedge Fund conference and dressed to impress. Our fund was not yet on that radar screen, so we just came as we were.

"Our guy in Moscow was supposed to be here, but he is having some, how should I put this, depreciation issues." Lots of hot money had flowed into Russia in the last few years, and the market there had taken off like a jackrabbit, attracting lots of 27-year-old money managers. But it was rough over there.

"Joe, why don't you go first. You have the steadiest numbers," Jim Torrey requested.

Joe was the Armani man. "Thanks, Jim. Yeah, I spent about a decade on the convertible arb desk at First Boston and set out about a year or so ago to do it for myself."

"Can you explain what that means?" Jim asked.

"Oh, sure, I guess there probably are still a few who don't know about convertible arb." I was one of those. "Companies issue debt. But instead of just bonds, they issue these things called convertible bonds, which are really part bond, part stock. They pay interest, say 6%, but if the stock does well, goes up maybe 30–35%, the instrument converts into stock at a predetermined ratio. It's a way for companies to issue bonds, but since they give investors some of the upside as if it were a stock, they can pay a lower coupon."

"You mean interest rate?" Jim asked somewhat rhetorically, probably for my benefit since I looked confused.

"Yeah, a lower interest rate. Some investors love these things. Fido has a whole group of funds that just buy converts." He meant Fidelity Investments in Boston. "But we love these converts even more. You see, we can buy the converts and then short the exact amount of stock that it would convert into. That's why whenever you see companies announce converts, their stock goes down. It's us shorting the shit out of it."

"So it's risk free?" I asked.

"More or less. You see, if the stock goes down, we just cover the short but still collect the coupon every quarter. If the stock goes up, the thing converts into stock, which covers our short, and we just collect the coupon all that time for free."

"What kind of returns?" Jim asked.

"Converts are pretty volatile, the Fed is banging rates around, companies report earnings, that kind of stuff. If we trade these puppies right, we can make 2% pretty quickly and we've made our month."

"Made their month?" I whispered to Fred. I wasn't sure why our portfolio went up or down each day, month or year. This guy was saying he had a sure thing.

"Once we hit 2%, we go flat, so we hit our 24% annual return targets."

"Can anything go wrong?" Jim asked.

"Not really. Well, I guess, maybe, but it's rare. Converts can get called early by the company, which is no fun. Or sometimes, companies go out of business, which whacks the stock and the convert. Or Fido is blowing out a position, and these things go down. And there is the 100-year flood thing. But we think we can make our month every month."

"And you have. OK, who's next?" I wanted to ask about the 100-year flood, but Jim was moving things along. "How about you, Doug?" Jim ran a good lunch.

"Hi, hi," said the twitcher. This was going to be interesting.

"I run a REIT fund." He talked really fast and in a squeaky, high-pitched voice. "REITs are Real Estate Investment Trusts. It's a bunch of real estate piled together. The REITs don't pay taxes, as long as they pay out all their profits after operating expenses. They are pretty cool." I don't think he had taken a breath yet.

"What kind of returns?" Jim asked.

"Well," Doug said as his eyes blinked about 100 times a minute, "they pay dividends of 6–8% nominally, and as long as you are mindful of geographic perturbations, and"—he coughed and almost swallowed the next three words—"use heavy leverage." He returned to his normal, fingernails-on-chalkboard voice, "You can make 20–25% returns."

"Any risk?"

"We don't think so. They're not making any more of it, are they? Heh-heh. We are bullish on real estate pricing—it's hard not to be. I mean, if real estate prices went down, REIT prices would get hit more, which would wipe out the dividend, but hey, c'mon, that's not a big possibility. Things are a little dicey in the last month or two, but we are still bullish."

"OK, thanks, Doug. You've turned in good numbers. Keep it up."

"If anyone is interested, speak to me afterward." Squeaky was always pitching away.

"I've got some land in Florida to sell him," I whispered to Fred, who just shook his head.

"Let's see, how about you, Professor?"

"Thanks, Jim," said the bearded one who I thought was a professor. "I run an international arb fund. That sounds fancier than it really is. We look at entire countries, at their currency, government officials, debt, wage rates, politics, bad loan ratios, everything we can get our hands on and decide whether to go long or short each country. Then we construct a portfolio of these things, pairing countries off on the long and the short side to minimize exposure. Not much leverage, only where we see real funny stuff going on."

"Travel a lot?" I asked.

"Constantly. I've got multimillion-mile accounts at most airlines. Probably three out of every four weeks I'm somewhere else. You have to be on the ground, asking questions, visiting management, government officials when you can."

"What kind of returns?" Jim asked.

"I couldn't tell you. It's pretty volatile. Things work when they work, both on the long side and on the short side. The biggest problem we see for many of these countries is that they suck dollars from U.S. consumers into their central banks, and then their regional banks dole it out like it's candy. They overbuild hotels and shopping malls and factories, and then the whole damn thing collapses into an ash heap. Happens every time."

"So, how do you know when it's a good time to buy?" Jim asked.

"We always wait for the puke," the professor answered.

"OK, *that* you'll have to explain," Jim told him.

"Oh, sorry, sure. Look, people are always selling. You can find some cement company in Indonesia whose stock is under pressure for months at a time, but we hold off. A cheap stock is not the time to buy, because it will always get cheaper. We just wait for the puke."

"Which is what, exactly?" Jim prodded.

"It's when there are no bids. Some guy at Fidelity has fund redemptions or maybe some leveraged-up hedge fund has a margin call. These guys not only want to sell, but they have to sell. An involuntary impulse. They puke it up. You can take it off their hands at almost any price. They are just glad to get rid of it."

"I get it," Jim said.

"Yeah, it's hard to sit around and wait for these things, but you know it when you see it. When someone pukes up a stock, it's not hard to miss. Mispriced securities all over the table. And we are there with a barf bag, collecting all we can."

"It takes deep pockets?" Jim asked.

"It sure does. That's why we are here."

"OK, glad you told us that before dessert."

"Finally, I have my special situation guys, Fred and Andy, out here in Silicon Valley. Tell them a little about what you guys do."

"We buy companies with great long-term prospects," I said. I'm pretty sure I heard snickering all around the table.

## > > > Gimme Half Your Firm

NEW YORK, NEW YORK—FALL 1996

"I can get you all the money you need."

So said a smarmy-looking guy sitting across from us at II Nido restaurant on the east side in Manhattan. II Nido was my idea. It was one of my favorite spots in New York, Old-World charm, just enough tacky mirrors to know it was a real Italian restaurant. And it was the only place I ever ordered angel hair pasta, which I had a hankering for that afternoon.

Fred and I had just spent three days in New York, calling on old friends and whoever they pointed us to, trying to raise money for our fund. Trying but not succeeding. I think I would volunteer for a colonoscopy before I sign up to raise money ever again. I felt like a Fuller Brush salesman, with virtual doors closing in our faces everywhere we went. Time not spent begging for money was spent haggling with our bill-by-the-hour lawyers over the language in our documents. And now someone had just said the magic words: "All the money you need."

"Really?"

"Sure, sure, sure."

"Wow. That's great. We think we have a unique story, but we have gotten a lot of pushbacks. And even more folks that stop returning our calls. It's gratifying to hear someone who shares our outlook."

"Sure, sure, sure. I mostly talk to timers, but you guys are different. Seems a little more volatile, but maybe more upside."

"We like to say that it works when it works. We can't guarantee any given month," I said.

"I can make a number of introductions. I have a network of folks that would be very interested in a fund like yours."

"That's great. I look forward to getting started," I said.

"I think we can do well marketing to a number of sources I have. Our long-term prospects thing is quite appealing."

Did he just say "our"? This guy is jumping right into this project. All right, finally someone gets our story.

"Are you talking about Europe? The Far East?"

"Sure, sure, sure. We can go into all these avenues when we settle on a few things."

"OK. What range are we talking about?" I asked.

"Oh, whatever seems right. A hundred million? A hundred fifty million? That's about what you are talking about?"

"Yeah, that would do it. We can't get much bigger than that. We want to focus on small cap, which means we need to keep it small."

"That's no problem."

"Great."

"That would lead to the appropriate consideration."

"Huh?"

"Naturally, there would be a consideration for access to my network."

"Consideration?"

"Sure, sure, sure. Fairly standard stuff. I think you guys are onto something, and the proper consideration would be in some form of modest equity participation."

"Equity? I had assumed that your network is looking to put capital to work in technology and we were a good fit, that you were helping them get exposure."

"Sure, sure, sure. But I still need a consideration." He got up to head to the bathroom.

"Andy, we've got to go," Fred said rather adamantly.

"I know," I whispered back. "But this could end our fundraising hassles."

"No it wouldn't. It would create a bunch more."

"Let's hear out what his idea of consideration is. A couple of percent won't kill us."

"We won't like it."

"Let's see."

"Plus it will be all fast money—he's probably also getting paid on the other side of the transaction."

What a dumb shit I am. I forgot the golden rule: on Wall Street, everybody gets paid. This guy had his hand out, a little more bluntly than most.

Mr. All-the-money-you-want sat back down at the table.

"We just want some more details on what you consider a consideration," I said. I wasn't even sure what I was asking.

"Sure, sure, sure. Typical terms. I wouldn't ask for more than half." Whew, I was relieved. A half a percent. I can live with that. I was thinking about how I was going to needle Fred for wanting to go.

Then the guy said, "Some funding sources like to take 80%, but I think that is a bit greedy. Fifty percent seems more appropriate to me. You guys don't look like fund-raisers to me, you want to spend your time running money. I can parachute $100 mill in pretty quickly. We can have a great partnership."

F-f-f-f-fifty percent? I really am a dumb shit. This guy was trying to steal our firm, and it didn't really even exist yet. I just sat there with my mouth open, staring at a mirror across the room.

Fred jumped in. "You know, that is an interesting offer. But I think we would like to build some value in our firm before we consider selling off a part of it. We really are just starting out. Perhaps we can talk again in a few years."

"Sure, sure, sure . . ."

"Thank you for dinner. We've got to head over to our lawyers to try to get them to stop billing us for the evening. It was very enlightening meeting you," I said as we ran out of Il Nido.

# Part II

# Revolution

# > > > Meeting Mr. Zed

*Sorry to do this, but I need to take you back to an important day in this story.*

AMERICAN AIRLINES FLIGHT—1991

Once again, and it never fails, I had about three minutes to make my flight. Luckily, I had only a briefcase in one hand and a stack of reading material in the other.

In what would be my last year as an analyst following dysfunctional chip companies for Morgan Stanley, I was trying to make my way back east from Silicon Valley. American Airlines was like the Pan Am shuttle to Boston for me, except the flight was six hours instead of one.

The 3:30 flight to New York was always at the same gate, number 63, which, unfortunately, was at the goddamn far end of Terminal 3 at SFO. I was here just last week, and the week before that. Life is a blur. I ran like the wind, doing my best O.J. imitation, hurdling baby strollers and other less frequent fliers who didn't know enough to get the hell out of the way.

After three days of scouring the Valley for interesting companies, I was looking forward to settling into my seat, skimming a few trade rags, downing as many gin and tonics as it took to fall asleep and then waking up as the wheels hit the runway at JFK.

"Hewe yuvv gwo," I said to the flight attendant. I was holding my boarding pass in my teeth, but I think she got the message.

"You just made it. You should leave more time," she scolded me.

"Sorry about the teeth marks. I'll be early next time."

I zipped down the jetway, stowed my briefcase and plopped

into my seat—1B. Thank god for Morgan Stanley's policy of flying first class. It made getting yelled at by almost everyone there a little easier. I leaned back in my seat, with just a stack of magazines and company literature on my lap. I closed my eyes, looking forward to 5 hours and 42 minutes of rest and relaxation.

"Looks like we are in the same business." Where was that voice coming from? It sounded European. I opened my eyes and looked to my left, and there was a pleasant-looking, slightly rounded man, probably around 60, balding on top, wearing khaki pants and a blue blazer with a yellow handkerchief in his breast pocket. "Oh great," I thought, "some lonely duffer is going to chat my ear off about how his son works at Hewlett Packard in France and he was out visiting Napa Valley or playing a round at Spyglass."

"I'm sorry?" I said.

"I can see from your stack of reading that we have similar interests." I looked down at the stack of reading—a couple of *Upside* magazines on the top, a *Forbes, Electronic Engineering Times, IEEE Spectrum* and the sports page from the *San Francisco Chronicle.*

"Oh, yes, of course, well, it is a funny mix. I browse all these things."

"Yes, me too."

"I know these guys at *Upside,* and they run some things I've written every once in a while."

"Oh, really, which one are you?" he asked.

"Here, let's see if this issue has something. Oh, here we go, page 18, a piece that says 'PC channels are going to change, from dealers to direct, like stereos did.' "

"Yes, I read that one, very astute."

"Oh, well, thanks. Here is another one—'Standards are great but can hold back innovation.' "

"That was a few issues ago. I liked that one too." Hey, maybe this guy wasn't so bad after all. I wasn't sure anyone read my drivel.

We talked and talked. This guy knew more about Silicon Valley than I did. I was so used to getting stuck next to some brainless investment banker from Robertson or Goldman talking about some boring-ass disk drive company. It was nice to talk to someone without an altitude problem.

"So, what do you think it is?"

"What *what* is?" I asked.

"What it is that makes Silicon Valley so special?" he asked.

"I don't know. I've been coming out here for years—on these stupid American Airlines flights, I'm so sick of them. All I know is that every time I come out, whatever I figured out on the last trip is now cheaper."

"That's it," he said.

"It's annoying. Investors love things that go up in price. Tobacco and beverage stocks are the rage now, because they just raise prices and earnings follow."

"So?"

"Well . . ."

"Well, what?"

"Well, Intel cut prices on their 386 last week. The stock got clipped—it was down 15%, I think," I said.

"Happens every time."

"Yeah, but . . ."

"It's always a 'yeah, but . . . ' " said my rowmate.

"Yeah, but . . ." I laughed. "I think Intel will sell twice as many processors at this lower price, maybe three times as many. Every time they cut prices or memory prices get banged, some new application opens up to take advantage of the cheaper functionality."

"That's it."

"I remember spending $12,000 on a laser printer back in my days at Bell Labs."

"Yes?"

"Well, a fast processor and a couple of megs of memory and the same damn machine, four pages per minute, goes for $799 at Fry's."

"That's it."

"What's it?"

"What makes the Valley special."

"Maybe," I said.

"Not maybe."

"OK, I think so too. It's just hard to explain to investors. Prices down. No worries."

"But that's right."

"It's just unnerving. What if it doesn't work?"

"It always works, throughout the ages," he said reassuringly. "You should go prove that to yourself. I call it scale."

I know what he's talking about. Economists call this elasticity. Not that I ever trust economists. But elasticity, when it works, is something like: prices go down, stimulating new demand. High elasticity means that unit output goes up more than prices went down, so you get a growth business.

"But you just have to close your eyes and hope it works?" I asked.

"That's called conviction. That is the real secret to investing that nobody knows. Find something you know is right and that you believe in. Fire in the belly, I've heard the American expression."

"Yeah, but when the stocks get whacked, it's more like 'fire in the hole' for me."

"You watch too many Hollywood movies."

"Stuck on these flights . . . I'm sorry, now that we've talked for most of the flight, I don't know your name or where you're from."

"If you are ever in Zurich, please stop by."

"Zurich?"

"Yes. I must come to the U.S. to do my investing. I just came from Sequoia's annual meeting. You know Don Valentine?"

"I've met him once or twice."

"Tough SOB, but he has a nose for scale."

"But why come all this way? Aren't there decent investments closer to home?" I asked.

"Europe has great food and lousy technology. No scale."

"Great wine."

"Yes, but you don't get wealthy squeezing grapes."

He went on to lecture me, that only the British could figure out how to get really rich, but that they lost the formula along the way. They industrialized the world economy, but that's long over. There is some new model. Technology has a new formula or maybe just one borrowed from the old Industrial Revolution. It was too early to tell, but whoever figured it out would have a real edge.

"Ladies and gentlemen, please fasten your seat belts for an on-time arrival at New York's John F. Kennedy International Airport."

"Wow, that was fast," I said. "Well, I enjoyed it. Perhaps I'll see you on another one of these long flights. It beats *Teen Wolf* or whatever excuse for a movie they are showing."

"Keep figuring out what makes Silicon Valley work. You will do well by that."

The stack of magazines had gone unread, and I had forgotten my thirst for a g and t or three. Even so, I was headed back to Wall Street with more questions than answers.

## > > > Monster Markets

*One more flashback:*

SAN FRANCISCO, CALIFORNIA—SPRING 1994

I was stuck at the adult table at the closing dinner for C-Cube. The best part of taking a company public is the closing dinner, a lavish affair with all the bankers, lawyers, accountants and management of the company celebrating a successful IPO. And even sweeter, the dinner is charged to the deal, meaning the new public investors get one last expense—pâté and steaks and fine wine and limos. I was involved in the C-Cube–Microsystems deal, but just barely. The male-relative bankers, Lehman Brothers and Alex Brown and Sons, did everything they could to throw me out of the deal, but I snuck in. I had known founder Alex Balkanski for a lot of years; he was my go-to source whenever I needed an update on digital video. C-Cube owned the market for chips that compressed video, selling to everyone from Comcast to Sony.

But Alex was sitting at another table, and it looked a lot more fun than mine. They seemed to go through three times as many bottles of wine and were now flipping rolls from one side of the table to the other with soup spoons. I was stuck with the hitters. I suppose I should have been flattered, but I preferred the adolescents. I was chatting with C-Cube's CEO, Bill O'Meara, who I had also known over a few of his jobs, but Lehman banker Stu Francis and Alex Brown banker Andy Sheehan kept interrupting.

"So, I did enjoy how you positioned C-Cube," Bill told me.

"Bill, since this deal is over, I'll let you in on a little secret, if you keep it to yourself."

"Sure."

"I'm pretty lazy."

"I'm not so sure of that."

"Look, I spent a few too many years at Morgan Stanley working with Frank Quattrone."

"I remember."

"I would get calls in the middle of the night, on weekends, on vacation, demanding input on positioning companies for IPOs."

"So?"

"Well, getting tired of this, I finally figured out that you can position every company the same way."

"The same?"

"Sure. You remember my suggestion for C-Cube."

"Of course, you told me that a salesman or broker has 30 seconds and three bullet points to pitch our deal. So we need to provide that in our positioning."

"Right. But I figured out that the bullet points are always the same."

"Always?"

"Sure. Bullet one is a large market, as Don Valentine says." Don Valentine ran Sequoia Ventures and first made his mark funding Apple Computer. His golden touch didn't stop—he funded Cisco and Sierra Semiconductor. He was also chairman of C-Cube and sitting across the table.

"Bullet two is an unfair competitive advantage, and bullet three is a business model leveraging that unfair advantage. I just fill in the details company by company."

"It's 'monster market,'" Don Valentine threw in. Shit, I didn't realize he was listening.

"Excuse me?"

"Listen, if you are going to quote me, at least get it right. It's 'monster market,' that's what I look for. Puny little $100 million markets don't interest me; I like the ones that are monster in size."

"Bill, what I meant to say is bullet one is a monster market, as Don Valentine says," I corrected myself.

"That's better." Don Valentine endorsed my stealing his words, with attribution, of course.

While not even dreamt of when Valentine invested seven years earlier, C-Cube was making a killing selling video chips into the

Chinese market in 1994. They had a $40 chip that turned a Sony or Panasonic CD player into a $100 video CD player that you plugged into your television. They sold five million of them in the first year, and as prices dropped, they sold 20 million plus the next year. In China, you can buy most any movie for a buck or two, all of them pirated. Stores that looked like Blockbuster Video were popping up in every Chinese city, filled with copies of first-run movies on CD. Chinese intellectual property rights laws were enforced like jaywalking is enforced in Manhattan. A $40 chip and almost free movies, that's about as monster a market as you can imagine.

# > > > Homework for Mr. Zed

PALO ALTO, CALIFORNIA—FALL 1996

"Good morning. It's not too early for you?" It was the Swiss gentleman I had met on the American Airlines flight. We had kept in touch over the years. He was from Zurich, so I called him Mr. Zed, but not to his face.

"Of course it's too early. Anytime before lunch is too early. But I am here by 6:30. Coffee is pulsing through my veins. The market opens in New York, so I'm here, raring to go."

"So I can call?"

"The stoplights are still flashing in Palo Alto at this hour. It must be, what, three in the afternoon in Zurich?"

"I think it's four."

"A full day," I said. I enjoyed talking with Mr. Zed—he always pushed me in the right direction. Over the years, I figured out that Mr. Zed was one of those elusive Swiss billionaires whose names you don't find in the *Forbes* Richest lists. When Fred and I started our fund, I did my usual passive-aggressive marketing pitch of "Gee, I'm sure you really don't want to, but just to let you know we are starting a fund, and if you are interested, we'd love to have you as an investor."

"So, I will invest in your fund," Mr. Zed blurted out. I was floored. We were having a hard time scraping up money for our fund, and this came out of the blue.

"Wow, thanks, that's great."

"Just a second, my friend. I'm going to put money in your fund, a nice amount too, but you have to tell me how you are going to invest."

"That's easy—we look for companies with great long-term prospects."

"Yeah, I've heard that. But how are you going to find them?"

"You know, growth markets, great management."

"That just makes you ordinary. I want extraordinary."

"In what way?"

"You have some work to do in figuring this all out."

"That I know."

"Well, find somewhere to start. Find something that has worked in the past."

"Like a company."

"That's OK, but really a system. Something that scaled. Then you can figure out how your system will scale."

"It's not easy, is it?" I asked.

"Of course not. If it were easy, everyone would figure it out and there wouldn't be any decent returns left for guys like me."

I started laughing.

"What's so funny?" Mr. Zed asked.

"Well, we are out raising money and were in Hong Kong."

"Lots of money in Hong Kong, but no investors."

"Well put. Anyway, I met with a guy that I knew back in my days at Paine Webber, a Bill Kaye."

"Haven't heard of him."

"He runs some Asia investment fund and seems to have it easy. I guess I've been depressed about how hard it is since I talked with him."

"Why is that?" Mr. Zed asked.

"Well, he had it all figured out. He said that I had the hard job, figuring out the future, and that in Asia, it was just the Industrial Revolution movie playing over again, and you could just find countries and companies in different stages of development and place them in the Industrial Revolution timeline and figure out whether to invest. So, why do I always pick the hard stuff to do, instead of just sitting in some marble building and eating Peking duck all day, picking stocks from a script from some already played-out movie."

"Well, you've got the easy job."

"How's that?" I asked.

"Because you can find the next Industrial Revolution."

"I don't understand."

"You will. Go find that movie and play it. Find the parts you need, and then make your own. Then you will tell me how you will invest."

"I thought I stopped doing homework when I graduated college."

"Surely you have figured out that you never graduate."

"Never?"

"Get back to me, you have some work to do. In the meantime, I'm going to wire $5 million into your fund tomorrow morning. But your hard work is just starting, not ending."

Hey, Mr. Zed is in. I didn't tell him, but he is about half of our fund. Fred's old employer, JP Morgan, came in for a couple, and with some other dogs and cats—and I mean that in the nicest way—we were in business. We put a five-year life on the fund, with the ability to extend it year by year. Fred's line: "Let's be able to declare victory." I wasn't sure what that meant, but I went along.

We had hoped to raise $100 million and be off to the races investing. Instead, we were forced to start small and keep up the "pubic begging" for funds. The 1% we charged on the puny $11 million we now managed didn't quite cover our office and travel expenses, let alone permit us to draw a salary. We stepped into a hole, and now we had to dig deeper to get out.

I did have a lot of work to do.

## > > > *Wilkinson and Watt*

The Industrial Revolution movie. Hmmm. Like everyone else, I must have slept through 10th-grade history. It had something to do with steam engines and workers covered in soot and Mary Poppins and Victorian England and all that tea sipping, stiff upper lip, Empire stuff. But somewhere in that story is massive growth. Every loose piece of gold not tied down around the world flowed into English banks. As far as I can tell, they didn't steal it on the high seas, not in the 19th century anyway. So what was it that caused that massive growth? If I could figure it out, maybe I could figure out how the world works today and put some money to work. But where to start?

Toward the end of my days of pretending to be an investment banker, I was given the task of raising money for the video game company Activision. The CEO, Bobby Kotick, looked about 12 years old but was a pretty savvy dude. He had just taken over by lending the company a pot of dough, some of it from Steve Wynn, the Vegas casino king. In a conference room at the Treasure Island casino, we gathered a bunch of big institutional investors who were in Vegas for the Consumer Electronics Show. Bobby insisted the meeting start at 3:15 and be done by 4:00. I protested, but Bobby just said, "Trust me."

The meeting went well. Steve Wynn popped in for the last 15 minutes and said Bobby was the smartest kid he'd ever met. This was going to be an easy deal.

At 4:00, Bobby asked everyone to step out onto a terrace just off the conference room. Below us there was a battle on the Strip, between a British frigate and a pirate ship that was part of a tacky casino attraction. The explosions, and there were a lot of pyrotechnics, were anything but tacky: I thought my hair was going to catch fire. The British frigate eventually sank, captain and all.

"There is no way this would have happened," a short, balding, British investor screamed in my ear.

"Why not?" I didn't like anyone bursting my childhood pirate fantasies.

"Because we Brits had Wilkinson cannons."

"You mean Wilkinson swords."

"You Americans watch too much TV. Wilkinson, the Iron Master. The Board of Ordnance loved Wilkinson. He was the great hero of the British Empire."

I was about to ask why, but my right ear was temporarily deaf from the big finale.

It didn't take me long to figure out that John Wilkinson was the Iron Master of Shropshire, which sounds like a walk-on part in the Lord of the Rings trilogy. But in 1774, it turns out, Wilkinson had a serious problem and the Industrial Revolution almost didn't happen.

There are history buffs in every country, the slightly off types who dress up in period costumes and reenact battles. In England, they even reenact the bureaucracy. I posted a request for information on Wilkinson at the U.K.-based Ordnance Society Web site, and dozens sent me e-mails with everything I needed to know about the Iron Master.

Back in 1774, the real Board of Ordnance had placed a huge order for cannons from Wilkinson—fifty-six 32-pdrs, or pounders, nine 24-pdrs and one hundred and two 9-pdrs. Old King George III was trying to put down those pesky Indian-costume-wearing, Boston-Hahbah-tea-dumping, tax-evading colonists in the New World. George Three Sticks also wanted to deal with the French once and for all.

With this huge order, what had been a quaint little ironworks had to change. Wilkinson desperately needed a source of power to operate his huge bellows. Lots of air was needed to get his sweet pit coal hot enough to smelt iron ore to pour into cannon casts.

The king didn't like to be kept waiting—hangings were a problem for entrepreneurs back then. (And you think you have problems.)

I need to go back a bit.

Back in 1720, the weather got better in Britain. No reason. *The Farmer's Almanac* predicted it. Crop yields went up, people were better fed and healthy. Perversely, a surplus of agriculture meant prices dropped, and many farmers had to find something else to do.

Fortunately, there was a small but growing industry making iron. Until the 1700s, metals like tin and copper and brass were in use, but you couldn't make machines out of them; they were too malleable or easily broken and somewhat expensive. Machines were made out of the only durable material, wood. Of course, wood was only relatively durable; wheel or gears made out of wood wore out quickly.

Iron would work, but natural iron didn't exist; it was stuck in between bits and pieces of rock in iron ore. A rudimentary process known as smelting had been used since the second half of the 15th century to get the iron out of the ore. No rocket science here, you just heat up the ore until the iron melts and then pour it out. Of course, heating up iron ore until the iron melts requires a pretty hot oven. Charcoal, the same stuff you have trouble lighting at Sunday barbecues, was the fuel of choice for the furnace. Charcoal is nothing more than half-burnt wood. But as we all know, if you blow on lit charcoal, it glows and gives off heat, so the other element needed to create iron is bellows, like who you get stuck next to at dinner parties, a giant windbag.

Medieval grunts got tired really quickly cranking the bellows, so simple machines, like a water wheel, usually used to ground wheat, were adapted to crank the bellows. Early ironworks, as a consequence, were always next to rivers. This posed two problems: the iron ore came from mines far away, and after a day or two, the forest started disappearing around the mill and the wood needed for charcoal had to come from farther and farther away. It is unclear if ironworks sold their own stuff or if middlemen were involved—questioning has been going on for hundreds of years if he who smelt it . . . well, never mind.

And the so-called pig iron you would get out of a charcoal-fire smelter was terrible—it had the consistency of peanut brittle. Trees, like all organic materials, are high in sulfur content, which made charcoal-smelted iron weak and not terribly useful for much, especially cannons.

In 1710, foundry owner Abraham Darby invented a new smelting process using coke, or purified coal, instead of charcoal—less sulfur, better iron. Unfortunately, coal was far away from the river-residing ironworks, so roads were built, often out of logs, over which wagons rolled, bringing coke to the river works. But that lowered profits, so many ironworks moved to be near the coke fields.

Demand for iron ore and coke took off, and mining became a huge business. One minor problem though—mines were often below the water table and flooded all the time. This cut down on dust but drowned a lot of miners. Something was needed to get this water out of the mines or the iron business would rust before it even started.

Many had tried to harness the power of steam for hundreds of years. But just a few years earlier in 1706, a steam engine invented by Thomas Newcomen actually, kind of, sort of worked. It was a clanky contraption that theoretically could lift two tons of water up 165 feet. Sometimes it did, most times it didn't. But miners were desperate, and Newcomen engines were the only game in town for the next 60 years.

In 1763, a technician named James Watt was employed at Glasgow University. His task was to maintain—more like fix—a Newcomen steam engine that the university owned. It was, as techies like to say, a POS, a piece of shit. It was a terrible kludge, literally held together by wet rope. It broke all the time.

So like all good engineers, Watt took it apart to figure out how it worked. It was nothing more than a giant cylinder with a plug, or piston, inside of it.

A furnace boiled water and pumped steam into a cylinder. These were low-pressure steam engines, also called atmospheric engines. High-pressure engines kept blowing up, killing off everyone involved. Low-pressure workers were survivors.

Unlike your car engine, the steam in an atmospheric engine didn't push a piston in a cylinder. Instead, steam filled the cylinder, which was then doused with cold water to rapidly cool it. When the steam turned to water, it created a vacuum, hopefully a strong enough vacuum to suck the piston down. This action then raised a rod that lifted a plunger of sorts, which tried to suck water up out of the mine.

Ingenious for 1706, it huffed and puffed and barely had the power comparable to a horse or two. Since the engine broke down all the time, fixing it was a full employment act for technicians like James Watt. Plus, someone constantly had to seal the cylinder to make a strong vacuum and prevent steam from leaking out of the craggy-edged cylinder. Wet hemp, Jamaica's finest, was the sealant of the day.

The professor in charge of Watt at Glasgow University, Dr. Joseph Black, was teaching courses, theorizing about a concept known as latent heat, starting back in 1761. Another professor at U of G around the same time was Adam Smith (of the invisible hand). In fact, Smith and Black were good friends. Latent heat is the reason a watched pot never boils or why you put ice cubes in soda. Latent heat means you can add heat to a pot of water, but it won't boil and give off steam until the entire pot of water is at 212° Fahrenheit. And no matter how much heat is applied by the hot sun at a baseball game, all the ice has to melt before a soda increases in temperature, right before the kid behind you spills it on your shoes.

As a favor to Professor Black, Watt ran a series of experiments measuring temperature and pressure and proved a prevailing theory that steam contained "latent heat." In doing so, Watt figured he knew why Newcomen's steam engine was all wet. Watt theorized that the cylinder had to stay as hot as possible, boiling hot, so new steam added to it would stay steam and not condense too soon. To create the vacuum, Newcomen had been splashing cold water in and on the cylinder. On each stroke of the engine, lots of steam was needed just to reheat the cylinder, so the engine was running at 25% efficiency.

And then a lightbulb went off in Watt's brain: Watt added a simple improvement to the Newcomen design, creating a separate chamber outside of the cylinder. This "condenser" was kept underwater, as cool as possible, and the steam condensed into it while the cylinder stayed hot for the next cycle. The power of the engine doubled to 3 or 4 horsepower.

Between 1763 and 1767, Watt went into debt up to his eyeballs to perfect his new design. His engine leaked like Newcomen's because the cylinders were not "true" and the condenser was not efficient. Improvements were small.

In 1767, John Roebuck, the owner of a Scottish iron foundry and a part-time venture capitalist, assumed Watt's debts of 1,000 pounds and gave him fresh money to improve his design. In exchange, Roebuck received two-thirds ownership of any patents. Patents were an important part of English law to protect property owners, even if the property was just ideas.

In 1769, Watt was granted a patent for his steam engine design by Parliament, which had recently taken over the patent-issuing duty from the king. Parliament was run by property owners, who, not surprisingly, were all for upholding property rights.

Almost simultaneously in 1769, old John Roebuck went bust, collapsing under the burden of his own debt. His foundry lacked a good source of power, which is why he was so interested in Watt's inventions. Roebuck went bust because he couldn't turn a profit with horses running his shops.

Another manufacturer stepped in. Matthew Boulton was born into the stamping business (buttons and buckles—Puritans loved them). His dad acquired the Sarehole Mill in an area known as Hall Green, where they rolled their own sheet metal to be stamped. Later, J. R. R. Tolkien grew up next door, and the area provided the background for his Middle Earth. Perhaps Boulton's mill sparked Tolkien's distaste for the industrial age.

Boulton struck out on his own in 1762 as a manufacturer of luxury goods, a "piecer." He created the Soho Manufactory out of a water mill a couple of miles outside Birmingham. He was constantly on the lookout for ideas and processes that could improve his 1,000-employee, three-story shop.

Back in 1768, James Watt had stopped by to check out Boulton's manufactory. They discussed Watt's new engine, now up to 5 or so horsepower, as well as its potential uses in the factory and even in driving carriages. It was a fateful meeting, because a year later, Watt needed to raise some money fast to buy out the now-seared Roebuck.

When Watt came back begging, Boulton agreed to buy out Roebuck's two-thirds interest in the patent. More importantly, Boulton agreed to fund the continued research by Watt into making his external condenser steam engine work.

The Newcomen design was still selling, despite all its flaws, but the market wanted more powerful engines. Watt's biggest problem was getting materials and labor to construct his engine accurately. The cylinder was key, and its "trueness," how accurately round the cylinder was, directly affected its power. Watt was excited when he constructed a cylinder that was within $\frac{3}{8}$ of an inch, the thickness of your finger, of being a "true cylinder."

In 1775, he went to London, where he had a few, shall we say, influential friends introduce legislation in Parliament to extend Watt's patent, which was set to expire in 1783. The bill passed, and the newly formed Boulton & Watt Company owned the patent on atmospheric steam engines for 25 years, until 1800.

So now it's 1774, and the king desperately needed those Wilkinson cannons. Wilkinson got the order because he had a secret weapon for making cannons. The Iron Master had a nifty precision-boring tool—a monster lathe. This tool cut cannon barrels true, making highly effective cannons with ever-so-narrow windage. No smelt-it jokes, please—windage is the gap between a cannon's barrel and the cannon ball. The smaller the windage, the greater the distance the gunpowder's blast propels the cannonball, rather than leaking out past it.

Wilkinson never patented the tool, he just used it in his own shop, which like everyone else's, had recently moved from river's edge to the coalfields. High-grade coal or coke was plentiful up in the hills of Staffordshire and contained almost no sulfur, so the resulting iron was sturdier, but he lost his source of power, the river.

Wilkinson solved one problem but ended up with another. Coke burned hotter than charcoal. He needed to crank 15-foot-high bellows to blow enough air to heat up the coke to an intense enough heat. His boring tool also needed a source of power to turn. It required teams of horses, which were expensive to feed, let alone clean up after.

James Watt's steam engines were in the area, pumping water out of coal mines, and Wilkinson thought he could use one to crank his bellows instead of horses. So, Wilkinson tried one. Success?

Nope. Instant failure. There was barely any power from Watt's engine to pump the bellows. So Wilkinson took the steam engine apart and probably started laughing. Watt's cylinder was awful—as jagged as England's shoreline. Even wrapped with wet hemp, it leaked steam with every stroke, robbing the engine of most of its power.

While Watt was proud of his ⅜ of an inch from true cylinders, Wilkinson had his lathe and knew he could make Watt's cylinders truer. Wilkinson recast Watt's leaky cylinder using his top-secret precision boring tool and found it generated four to five times more power, enough to run his bellows. This meant 25- to 40-horsepower engines, up from 5 to 8. The difference for miners and millers was staggering.

Being a reasonable businessman, he told Boulton and Watt that he could improve their crappy little steam engine by a factor of five, in exchange for the exclusive rights to supply precision cylinders to B&W.

Deal.

As an investor, I was getting more and more intrigued by this little tale. It had market demand (flooded mines), technology (Watt's condenser and Wilkinson's precise cylinders), capital (Boulton's money), intellectual property rights (Parliament's patent) and a ready workforce (ex-farmers). I was ready to invest—all that was missing was a business model.

It was Matthew Boulton who came up with one. Boulton and Watt didn't actually sell steam engines. No one could afford one.

Most of the early customers were Cornish mines. Beyond Parliament-sponsored joint-stock companies, the stock market and banking were not quite developed, especially for risky businesses. Limited liability for corporations wouldn't be the law until 1860.

Miners lived day to day. They used a cost book system of accounting (I slept through accounting too). At the end of each quarter, all the partners in the mine would meet at the counting-house to go over the numbers and split any profits. These count dinners were giant drunk fests, each mine vying for the prize of offering the most potent punch. At the end of the night, the mine companies were drained of cash and the miners drained of brain cells.

So instead of selling steam engines, Boulton just traveled around to mines (and later mills and factories) and simply asked how many horses they owned. Boulton and Watt would then install a steam engine and charge one-third of the annual cost of each horse it replaced over the life of the patent, that is, until 1800. Back then, a horse cost about 15 pounds per year, and I have seen figures for the parts cost of their steam engine of 200–300 pounds to build a 4-hp engine. A 50-hp engine cost around 1,200 pounds.

Not having four eating and shitting horses around meant saving 60 pounds a year. Boulton and Watt would charge 20 pounds a year. If the 4-horsepower engine cost, say 200 pounds, B&W started turning a profit after ten years and they had a 25-year patent. But they could charge 250 pounds a year for a 50-horsepower engine and turn a profit in less than six years.

It was in their best interest to install more powerful engines—they just needed to find something beyond pumping out flooded mines to drive demand for horsepower. A barrier lowering the cost of power had just been busted down, but I didn't see the gusher.

Something sounded familiar. It was from my conversation with Mr. Zed. Cheap microprocessors and cheap memory made computers cheaper, and they sell by the boatload. I started to wonder whether this same scale is what drove jolly old England as well.

Would I have invested in Boulton & Watt? Not yet. It wasn't clearly a home run. What was I missing?

"Good morning, Andy. Is this too early?"

"OK, power got cheaper," I said, cutting to the chase the next time Zed called to check up on me.

"So?" Mr. Zed asked.

"So Watt's steam engine meant horsepower got cheaper for England than the rest of the world."

"And who used it?"

"Miners."

"So the British became the world's miners?"

"Well, no."

"What did they become?"

"Ironworkers?"

"Are you asking me or telling me?"

"Both?" This was not going well.

"Does Silicon Valley provide the greatest silicon to the world?"

"No."

"So, find out what sucked up that horsepower. Why did they need so much of it? Find the scale."

"But where?" I asked.

"Everywhere. Underwear." And then he hung up. I think he'd seen this movie before too.

## > > > *Object Lesson*

FREMONT, CALIFORNIA—JANUARY 1997

OK, enough of the history lesson—it's time to find some stocks that go up. Shouldn't be too hard—this is Silicon Valley, not Shropshire.

"What are we going to ask these guys?" I asked Fred. We were headed in to see one of the recent IPOs, Versant. We owned a little, and the stock was running.

"I want see who their big customers are and then check out management. Make sure the CEO is really in charge. The software business is treacherous," Fred answered.

"OK, I'll see if I can dig up a little more about their database. This whole bandwidth thing is going to take off, and they are only one of two companies that have this whole object thing nailed. The stock is right around $20."

"If it works, if they can keep making their numbers, it could double," Fred said.

"We need a few like this one."

We walked in and were greeted by a full conference room. We swapped cards with the CEO, CFO, head of global sales, VP of marketing, VP of engineering and the director of investor relations. I was wondering who was running the company. I noticed Fred looking at the door after we sat down.

I jumped right in. "Can you tell us who is buying your products?"

"Of course," the CEO jumped in. Good sign, take-charge guy. "As you know, we are the leader in object-oriented databases. The entire telecommunications business has standardized on objects to classify and maintain their network elements. This means that AT&T can click on a screen and dig down into their network and identify faulty circuits, and someday even provision services. It will change the business."

"Who are your largest customers?"

"Oh. MCI."

We then learned more than any living human would want to know about object-oriented databases, how they differ from Oracle databases, how Microsoft will eventually move to objects, how the Internet will eventually become one giant object repository.

"How long does it take you to close your books at the end of the quarter?" Fred asked.

"Just a couple of days. It is pretty straightforward."

"Do you have competition?"

"Well, there is that firm in Boston." We knew about ODI. We owned it too.

"Besides them?"

"No. Not really. Oracle can't do what we do," the CEO insisted.

"Why not?"

"Well, they can, but they won't."

"Why?"

"The market isn't big enough for them. It would impact their regular database customers." Not a good answer, but we let it slide.

We bought some more stock in the high teens and then watched it drop into the low teens in February and nibbled a bit more. We'd seen this before. With a recently public company, the trading is erratic. The stock made up about 1–2% of our portfolio, so it was important to us, but Fred and I agreed that we needed to live with this one a bit before we really bought it in size.

"Get conviction," Fred reminded me again and again.

It was tough to get much information. Calls to the CFO were worthless. He kept repeating that they were the leader in object-oriented databases, which were going to revolutionize the telecommunications business. I tried to get to some contacts of mine at

MCI to see which departments were buying from Versant, and why. Would they order more, make them a key part of their infrastructure? I couldn't find anyone to explain it to me.

The stock kept dropping, but at the end of February it was no more than $11. If ever there was a time to pounce. But conviction was absent. It just looked cheap versus the $20 it had been six weeks ago—not a reason to buy a stock.

What kept gnawing at Fred and me was that though Versant was the leader in object-oriented databases (or so we heard), that might be a booby prize. Being a leader in a small market doesn't mean much, and the company admitted it was a small market. Did they have something special, some secret sauce, to their software, something they could charge a premium for? Was there some instant cost savings at telcos, so customers would come back again and again and buy more OODB? Who knows, I couldn't figure it out, and no one seemed to have much of an opinion. The analysts for the investment banks that took Versant public had an opinion, but I reminded Fred of the line that every sell-side analyst had an opinion and an asshole, but I didn't want to hear either one.

The company was no help. The CFO said they were in their quiet period during the month of March, so he couldn't talk. Gee, thanks.

We figured we would wait until they reported the first quarter of 1997 earnings, the first real quarter after their IPO, to see if the business was real, and then load up beyond 2% of the portfolio.

We didn't have to wait that long. On March 31 it was $9. By April 3, it hit $4. When they finally reported earnings the next week, their conference call was a disaster. Turns out that MCI *was* a big customer, but not as big as they had hoped. MCI delayed a few orders, and that giant sucking sound was the vacuum of lost sales and ramping expenses. Even more disturbing was that a bunch of hedge fund guys we knew, guys that loved to short, were on the call, asking detailed questions about MCI. A string of nasty questions hammered the CEO and CFO for 45 minutes; these hedge fund guys are relentless.

Well, no reason to own this puppy. We waited a week or so for a dead-cat bounce and blew out our position at $5.

What was most disturbing is that for two months or more,

someone knew the company was going to miss their numbers and leaked it to these hedgies. The CEO or CFO? I doubt it. The venture capitalist on Versant's board of directors? The Versant salesman who covered MCI? His brother? The sales guy at competitor ODI? Who knows? But someone knew and made a killing. It was investing when you know something no one else knows.

Ouch, lesson learned. It just means we needed to find more things that others *can't* know, that second derivative stuff.

## > > > **Pressure Drop**

OK, maybe this homework was good for me. Mr. Zed got me thinking—would I have invested in the steam engine business? Maybe. The 25-year patent was nice, the business model fairly unique. But pumping water from mines? Where is the monster market in that?

By the time the Boulton & Watt patent expired in 1800, they had 500 steam engines up and pumping. England was on its way to being an empire. What I found the most interesting was the drop in the cost of power. Something besides iron and cannons were using this cheaper power. Everywhere, underwear?

Iron was nice, but clothes were a much bigger market in the late 18th century. Individuals did all the steps of making clothes at home: carding, spinning and weaving. Automation was never thought possible, but as soon as new human-run tools and machinery came about, the need for power intensified.

Looms have been around. American Indians had them, so did the Greeks and the Egyptians—everyone used looms to weave clothing. But while looms are very simple, they are extremely labor-intensive. This wasn't a grandma whistling away process—a weaver must pay careful attention. In 1733, John Kay patented a wonderful device called the flying shuttle, and loom productivity popped. So much so that in 1755, a mob broke into John Kay's house and destroyed one of his flying shuttle looms. While weaving got faster, making thread or yarn was still old-fashioned. Now weavers demanded more yarn of higher quality. Cheap cotton from the New World began to make inroads against itchy wool and even comfortable but expensive silk.

In 1764, James Hargreaves invented the Spinning Jenny, which wound strands of cotton into thread. Around the same time, Richard Arkwright invented and patented a device named the Spinning Frame to wind thread into bundles of yarn. Although the Spinning Frame was originally designed to be hand cranked, Arkwright ended up needing horses to operate it, and even they proved not to be powerful enough, so he moved the whole thing riverside, changing the machine's name to a Water Frame. Around 1785, Arkwright was visited by Boulton and became one of the early manufacturers to use Watt's engine. Make power cheap enough, and someone new will figure out how to use it.

The yarn from a Water Frame was thick, and the thread from the spinning jenny was coarse. Common folk wore clothes that were basically like burlap—what they wouldn't have done for smooth underwear. One can only imagine how itchy clothing was in 1775. Royalty still insisted on silk. Comfortable clothing was yet another thing that separated the rich from the poor.

An inventor named Samuel Crompton crossed the Jenny and the Water Frame and invented the Spinning Mule. Taken on its own, it was no big deal, but it was possibly the single most important invention after the Watt steam engine.

This machine didn't just spin or twist; its spindles moved back and forth up to 5 feet, stretching the yarn. This effectively stretched the yarn to "silky smoothness," and then quickly wrapped it onto a bobbin as it unstretched. Like Emeril Lagasse making angel hair pasta, the Spinning Mule worked the same way—stretch, wind, repeat often.

By 1790, 400 spindles hung off the Spinning Mule, and no man or mule or horse or even running water could keep up with the power needed to run one of these things.

Matthew Boulton, call your office! Lots of Boulton & Watt steam engines came to run these stubborn Spinning Mules. Another barrier broken—cheap and silky cotton thread and yarn. But they still had to be run through a hand-operated loom to create cloth.

In 1785, Edmund Cartwright sought to fix this problem. His first issue was waiting for Arkwright's patent on the Water Frame cotton-spinning machine to expire. Once it had expired, Cartwright figured correctly that cotton mills would be built by the dozens and spit out an abundance of thread and yarn. Cartwright thought for a moment about starting his own cotton mill, but his business instincts kicked in, and he moved up the value chain. He wanted to leverage the abundance of yarn, not help to create more. Instead of contributing to the falling price of yarn, he thought about what he could do with cheaper thread. Then he worked on the missing piece of the puzzle: a mechanical power loom.

Without even looking at a hand-operated loom, he built a fully mechanical one. It didn't work, but that didn't stop Cartwright from getting a patent in 1785 for his mechanical loom. He persisted in the shop, and eventually his loom fully emulated the hand and foot movements of weavers with hand-operated equipment.

Cartwright opened a weaving mill in 1787 in Doncaster, with workers simply feeding in or fixing broken thread. He tried to use a waterwheel to operate the mill, but it barely budged his machine. He quickly contacted Boulton and Watt and hooked up their steam engine. Cheap power helped create a new market that didn't exist previously.

My sense is that Cartwright built his power looms assuming he could get enough power applied to them—which of course was a huge mistake. He didn't worry about power until it was a problem and then lucked out that Boulton and Watt had already licked it. Boulton and Watt had brought down the cost of power, probably by a factor of 10, or about 5% per year. Lucky for him, and lucky for Boulton and Watt. Not much different from the first Lotus 1-2-3 spreadsheets operating at a crawl on the first IBM PCs, driving demand for faster and faster 286 and 386 microprocessors from Intel.

Cotton was hot. Operators of Spinning Frames and power looms were demanding more and more raw cotton from the New World. The hands that were missing were not weaving hands but hands to pick cotton. Unfortunately, Africans pressed into slavery met that demand, accelerating the Triangle Trade. Finished goods out of England were provided to slave traders on the coast of Africa. Slaves from what is now Ghana, among other locations, were transported to Jamaica to harvest sugar cane and to Georgia to pick cotton. This sugar and cotton and other raw materials were brought back to England to be turned into finished goods, and the triangle started all over again.

Seedless cotton was tough to find. It took one slave all day to remove sticky green seeds from one pound of cotton, a hidden but stubborn bottleneck to cheap clothing out of England.

A Yalie named Eli Whitney headed south, and in the winter of 1792, as every schoolkid now knows, Whitney invented the cotton gin. *Gin,* in case you were wondering (I was), is short for *engine,* good old Georgia talk.

Operating a hand crank, one person running Whitney's cotton gin could clean 50 pounds of cotton a day instead of just the one pound by hand. Now that machines had broken the barriers all along the cloth value chain, the clothing business took off. And demand for steam engines took off with it.

In 1792, when the gin was invented, no more than 150,000 pounds of American cotton made its way to England; eight years later it was 17 million pounds. By 1850, 700 million pounds of cotton were exported to England. To put this in perspective, in 2003, 5.6 billion pounds of cotton were exported from the U.S. That's a factor of 5,000 growth in the first 58 years. Then cotton grew by another factor of 8 over the next 153 years, or a puny compound annual growth rate of 0. 'insert about 100 zeros' 1%. Hmm, you've got to be early on these trends. That's where the money is.

With steam-powered mills and looms and a steady flow of clean cotton, England now had the economic engine it needed. Import raw materials like cotton, run them through industrial machinery run by steam-powered engines and export finished goods like yarn and cloth and textiles. That was and still is the definition of an industrial economy.

The key is that finished goods can be sold at prices so much cheaper than handmade goods. Back then, it changed the way the world dressed, with less itchy clothes at that. Even Don Valentine would have called that a monster market.

I suppose this is no different from the way the world was changed by electricity at the turn of the last century or by radio in the 1920s or television in the 1950s, or maybe automobiles or washing machines or refrigeration or air conditioning. Industry supplied the product more and more cheaply, and an entire consumer economy was built around these cheap, revolutionary products.

Heck, entire economies evolved to supply this stuff—Japan with consumer electronics and then cars, Taiwan or China with all sorts of manufacturing and assembly. These are all gussied-up remakes of the Industrial Revolution movie—like *King Kong,* or Hong Kong.

Industrialization was not some master plan to remove workers from their century-old tasks. Instead it was a complete reengineering of life based on the ability to provide daily staples at much lower costs. Getting everyone together in one steam engine–driven manufactory produced higher-quality and lower-cost textiles than anything that could be done at home by old spinsters.

As long as England could keep prices for their cloth going down, they would both create new markets *and* keep competition away. Growth created by *and* protected by its own declining price elasticity. Hmm. This is something I want to invest in.

# > > > ***Rocker v. Pittman Prizefight***

SAN FRANCISCO, CALIFORNIA—FEBRUARY 1997

"Any questions for Bob or me?" asked Richard Hanlon, the investor relations guy from America Online.

"Was MTV really your idea?" someone from the back corner of the room asked.

"In fact, I was CEO," answered Bob Pittman. I started to chuckle. I had already met several others who claimed to have founded MTV. My thought was interrupted when the guy sitting next to me let out a sigh so loud everybody in the room looked over.

Fresh from a gig fixing the Six Flags theme park and then milking Century 21 real estate brokers, wonder boy Robert Pittman had been hired by Steve Case to be the public face of America Online. This was one of his first appearances.

Pittman had just given a presentation in the Grand Ballroom at the Robertson Stephens Technology Conference. We were now sitting in a breakout session in a small room with a conference table for 20 and probably another 20 seats scattered around the room. The press was not allowed in, only investors, so all questions were fair game.

"How's flat-rate pricing going?" a woman across the table asked. Microsoft's new Microsoft Network charged $20 per month, and AOL had recently responded by going from per hour pricing to $20 per month flat rate.

"Pretty good." (The guy next to me let out a snort.) "Sure, there are some busy signals, but it is a sign that our customers really like the service."

"You're kidding, right?" I heard from my right. I looked down at the guy's nametag. It read "Dave Rocker, Rocker Partners." Ah, the famous short. This guy lived to find companies in trouble. His hedge fund would sniff out corporate malfeasance, short the stock and then yell at the top of their lungs for everyone to come look at these scumbags that were ruining this company. Then he sat back, hoping the stock would crater and make him millions. At least, that's the concept. Rocker's problem was that there had been a bull market since 1983 and not much had gone down. It was a tough market to be a short in.

"Look, busy signals are localized. I live in New York, and when I get a busy signal when I call to check my e-mail, I just look up a number in Denver or LA and call that one—I get right through," Pittman calmly explained.

"But doesn't that defeat the purpose of local dial-up?"

"It's just a short-term thing. Anyone else?"

"Is there any magazine that doesn't come with an AOL CD sewn in? I've got a growing collection of drink coasters at home." This one came from the analyst from Robertson.

"The hit rate on these marketing programs continues to exceed expectations," Pittman answered.

"So we can expect to see a large expense this quarter for these marketing programs," Rocker asked.

"Like all subscription services, we write off customer acquisition costs over the expected life of the subscriber."

"Which is?"

"I'm not sure. But it's in years."

"But your customers don't stay for years," Rocker screamed.

"They might." Pittman started scanning the room for someone else to ask a question. But the rest of us were having too much fun watching Rocker grill Pittman, so no one volunteered.

"As far as I can tell, you guys are bleeding cash. You throw money at CDs and haven't bothered to upgrade your network, which is why you have busy signals. If you accounted for the marketing like you're supposed to, you'd be reporting losses," Rocker said.

"We endorse current analyst expectations of a slight profit for the current quarter" is all Pittman could say.

"But those are your own numbers. You fed them the numbers, and now you're endorsing their expectations?"

"Analysts do their own independent work." I watched the analyst from Robertson look down and saw the blood rush from his face.

"Aren't you losing more subscribers than you are gaining?" Rocker went on.

"Our churn is within acceptable limits," Pittman replied.

"What does that even mean? C'mon. You guys are getting all sorts of cancellations, but I can't seem to find them in your filings. What are you doing, just waiting for a quarter with big sign-ups so you can bury the cancels?"

"Our accountants sign off on our reporting." Pittman was starting to sweat, and had an I-don't-need-this-shit look on his face. "Anyone else?"

"Yes. Is it true Tom Hanks is going to be the new voice for 'You've got mail'?" This came from behind me.

"Well, not exactly. He is slated to star in a movie of that name, with Meg Ryan. It will be out next year from Warner Brothers. We might have made it ourselves, but who wants to own a movie company?"

"How are you going to pay for upgrading your network?" Rocker was back.

"Excuse me?"

"When I look at your balance sheet, your cash is draining fast. And you probably have to spend a hundred mill upgrading your system to get rid of those busy signals or all those subs are going to jump to MSN."

"We think we have adequate facilities to finance—"

"No you don't. Your stock is sinking like the *Titanic,* and your credit lines look like they have already been tapped. Unless you pull a rabbit out of a hat, you can't afford to put much into your network. And my engineering friends tell me you have to revamp the whole damn thing to a packet-based architecture or you won't ever be able to handle more subscribers than you have now, no matter how many CDs pile up in people's homes."

Rocker was right. The stock was sinking fast. The fairy-tale story of amazing growth had hit an iceberg.

"We'll get there. I have the utmost confidence," Pittman said.

"Is that enough?" Rocker said.

"Well, I'd like to thank everyone for contributing to the breakout session," Richard Hanlon concluded as everyone laughed and filed out of the room.

Nick Moore found me as I was running to another meeting.

"I heard the America Offline meeting was pretty brutal. The stock is getting touched up," Nick said.

"Round one to Rocker," I said.

"Those guys are pretty crafty. Their accounting is better fiction than Hemingway, but they always seem to pull it off. I'm not sure what it will be this time, what rabbit they'll pull from a hat, but I'm not shorting it. Rocker is going to get killed."

"What makes you so sure?" I asked.

"AOL has more levers to pull than Rocker does. As long as they are growing, they can cook the books and hide the losses for years."

"You think it's one of these exponential markets?"

"What do you mean?" Nick asked.

"I don't know. I've been playing around with these second derivative markets—things that grow exponentially."

"Don't hurt yourself."

"No one thinks in second derivatives—you know, the growth of growth, breakout stuff. Like, well, like people have a hard time thinking in four dimensions."

"You mean the Age of Aquarius?"

"That's the Fifth Dimension."

"Oh. Well, let the sunshine in. Surrey down to a stoned soul picnic, man," Nick said as he walked off.

"Never mind."

The way I heard the story years later from a friend who worked in AOL's business development group is that Pittman went out on the prowl for cash. He was close to signing a sponsorship deal with MCI or Sprint for maybe $5 million over a couple of years, which would have been a good start. Then into his office walked Daniel Borislow, the CEO of Telesave, a small and, many would say, fleabag long distance company. Borislow dropped a check for $100 million onto Pittman's desk in exchange for access to AOL's eight million customers.

Now put yourself in Pittman's shoes. You just got the crap beat out of you by Rocker, your stock is cratering, your balance sheet is bone dry and, like manna from heaven, $100 million is handed to you. At that point, you would have done a deal with Tony Soprano for 100 large. And a deal he did, in effect relaunching AOL as a media company, selling access to their customers. A grand master plan by Pittman? I doubt it. I think he has Dave Rocker to thank for forcing his hand.

In an act that defies belief, Borislow and Telesave decided to write the $100 million off over 40 years as a marketing expense. The fact that 40 years is 30 years longer than AOL has been in business or 20 years longer than the PC has been around, or even a few years longer than microprocessors have been around didn't seem to bother anyone. Rocker's short got squeezed by two lemons.

On the announcement of the AOL-Telesave deal, both stocks jumped and went on a three-year wild ride—while Dave Rocker twisted in the wind.

I could care less about AOL—a service for teenage girls. But it was clear they were going to spend billions on building out their network, and I wanted to find every piece of intellectual property needed to upgrade it.

That's what Fred and I cared about—the underlying technology that becomes part of the infrastructure of a new trend. If the trend is big enough, it doesn't matter who actually wins—AOL or Microsoft or Verizon or IBM. If we could just find some protected piece of IP, some design, some code, something that everyone has to buy in size, we'd have a ten-bagger on our hands. I was naive. I didn't realize how big an if that really was.

## > > > ***Sinking Like a Red Brick***

LOS GATOS, CALIFORNIA—SPRING 1997

"Thanks for taking the time to meet with us." We trucked our way down to Los Gatos, on the fringes of Silicon Valley, to meet with Red Brick Systems. We owned some shares. Their stock was flying, going up a point or two a day, and we needed to figure out if we should be buying more. We wanted to meet the CEO, but we were met by the CFO. He was wearing the techie uniform: a denim shirt and khakis. I had on a tan shirt and jeans; the anti-uniform, I suppose.

"Not a problem. Let's go to my office." Fred and I followed the CFO through a maze of cubicles until we got to what looked like an executive section of real offices with windows along the edge of the building. "Here we are, c'mon in." The CFO proceeded to close the door behind us. I thought I saw Fred cringe.

"Sorry our CEO can't meet with you. I've got my fingers on the pulse around here, and I've got our head of sales stopping by in a little bit."

He proceeded to walk us through their prospects. Red Brick sells data-mining software that can find patterns in customers' databases. This means that a retailer can sift through their database of sales and note that lemonade sells well on sunny days, and, gee, maybe they should stock up and put it at the front of the store when it's sunny.

We got the standard PowerPoint presentation, which looked exactly like the one they used on their IPO road show, with maybe just the financial numbers updated. Pretty dull. Khakis walked us through a bunch of case studies—customers would put in Red Brick and save three times the price of the software within a year.

Fred asked a few questions about follow-on sales and how long it takes Red Brick to roll up their financials. I thought it was pretty neat technology but that its results were just common sense, not startling. Still, it was selling like hotcakes.

The head of sales came in.

"What is the sales cycle like? How long does it take to close a deal?" Fred asked.

"Oh, I can close them pretty quickly."

"But is there the usual pipeline and sales funnel and all that?"

"Yeah, of course, but when I find someone who is interested, I can come to terms pretty quickly and get the deal done," the sales guy said as he glanced over to the CFO, who nodded slightly. "So, I—uh, I mean the company—can make its quarters." He sounded like that hedge fund guy who talked about making his month.

We learned more than we ever wanted to know about data warehousing, data marts and online analytical processing, said our goodbyes and scrambled out to my car.

"Well, it's interesting, but I guess I still don't get why anyone actually buys this stuff. It all seems so obvious," I said.

"Do you have your phone?" Fred asked.

"Yeah, sure. Why?"

"Call someone, anyone, and get rid of all our Red Brick shares."

"Really?"

"This thing is going to blow up."

I made a few calls, and the first trader I reached got the order.

"I'm happy to dump this thing, but what did you see?"

"The first sign was that the CFO closed his door."

"I noticed you shudder."

"Happens every time. The CFO closes the door, and the stock blows up. I don't know if he doesn't want others to hear how the company is doing, or maybe he is lying to us and doesn't want his staff to know he is a liar, who knows, but the closed CFO door sign almost never fails."

"But there was something about that sales guy, right?"

"Yeah, that guy was creepy. I got the impression that he thought that he was running the company. There is this fine balance between a CEO, CFO and sales. The CFO's job is to make sure the sales are real, the terms are legitimate and that customers

become repeat customers. Especially in software, when you can sell whatever and however much you want."

"The customer still has to pay."

"Yeah, but it's all in the terms and follow-up sales. These software companies are lumpy—they have to keep selling and selling to the same customers. They can report a great quarter and then 'Oops, we didn't close enough new customers' the next and you've got a $5 stock on your hands."

"But it's the CFO's job to make sure the deals are real."

"Those two kept looking at each other like they had some deal to make the quarters."

"I saw that. Does that really mean anything?"

"Maybe not. But maybe it does. I don't want to stick around to find out. You don't have to own everything. This stock is already running—what is it $25 or $30? Maybe it keeps going up. So what. We'll find something else."

We sold our shares at $26 that day, and of course, the stock ran to the $40s. But goddamn if Fred didn't nail it. It took another quarter, but sure enough, Red Brick stock started trickling down until the last week of the quarter, when they announced they were going to miss their sales targets, and then the stock plopped to $5. I think IBM bought it out for not much more a year or so later. And I forever value the closed CFO door indicator!

## > > > Waterfalls

I've always been fascinated with rivers, especially waterfalls. There is nothing better than finding a clump of water at the top of the falls and keeping my eye fixated on it as it free-falls—one Mississippi, two Mississippi, three Mississippi—accelerating as it falls, faster and faster. Knowing it will crash into a giant fiery wreck (OK, wet wreck) on the rocks and debris at the bottom of the falls, I avert my eyes and quickly glance up and select another clump at the top to follow, again and again, mesmerized. It is as if I am free-falling with it, exhilarated.

Waterfalls are the sign of a young river, vibrant, moving fast, cutting through everything in its path, straight to its destination. On a rafting trip down the Colorado through the Grand Canyon, I hiked four hours uphill to see the shortest river in the world, Thunder River. It wasn't really a river, just a giant plug of water that came out of a giant hole in the side of a cliff, a massive waterfall that blasted out of the water table, probably snow melted from the Rockies a few minutes prior, cooling off hikers from the 110-degree heat. I could have stayed there all day—a strange sight, my head bobbing up and down, tracking the water's free fall—if not for another three-hour hike back to the raft.

Why am I telling you this cutesy, back-to-nature nonsense? Because those clumps of water? That's me. That's what it feels like to invest in these declining-price businesses. You're in free fall, hoping, begging, praying that those economists' elasticity, Mr. Zed's scale, kicks in before you crash on the rocks below. Falling, falling—like in Alfred Hitchcock's *Vertigo*. And you're falling faster and faster—gravity is second-derivative stuff. Don't be queasy. If you're afraid of free-falling, buy Wal-Mart. And good luck with that.

Me, I'm on the hunt for waterfalls—big-time trends—barriers broken by the intense pressure of change behind them, cutting through everything in their path, accelerating at will. And hopefully, I can jump off the investments before the trend crashes into a pile of debris. Sick, but that is what I chose to do.

Everything else to me is a meandering river. It's Geology 101—Rocks for Jocks. Young rivers have waterfalls that cut through rock like a hot knife through butter. Old rivers meander, meaning if they hit some resistance, a resilient embankment, they just head off in another direction, without the strength to cut their own way anymore.

In fact, most of these big trends leave a trail of meandering rivers in their wake. Wilkinson and Watt launched a cheap textile industry, and today textiles may be a trillion-dollar industry. It will swing up and swing down, depending on lots of factors—the cost of cotton, invention of manmade materials, fashion, computer-based pattern cutters. There is money to be made in textiles. Just not for me. Too dull. I'll let others play that game, while I hunt for the next second-derivative waterfall.

The problem is that meandering rivers don't scale. They are just lazy—old man river. They don't provide sustainable growth like a waterfall. If you invest right, they can provide a nice ride, but they just as soon will reverse course and meander back to where you started.

Half the battle is figuring out if something is as vibrant as a waterfall or just a false hope, a meandering river in wolf's clothing, if I may butcher some scrambled metaphors.

How do you know when technology reaches a point where it breaks through a barrier and cascades? Is it 18 months away or 18 years away? Will the company you invested in still be in business by the time the barrier breaks? It makes a difference—fortunes are made or lost depending on time frame.

The barriers in the Industrial Revolution took time to come down. The steam engine needed 25 years to help lower the cost of cloth. Steamships and propellers and turbines unfolded over the next 100 years. I'm patient, but not that patient.

I suppose the good news is that these waterfalls are all related, almost like dominoes; one helps knock down the next one. Technology builds on past success—the old "standing on the shoulders of giants" thing. Investing is inexact. You can't possibly get companies and timing right. But if you can find technology that scales and imagine the barriers that might burst, all you really need to do is be in the same neighborhood. But when it works, sit back, count slowly so you know when to jump off and enjoy the free fall!

## > > > Music Play

PALO ALTO, CALIFORNIA—SUMMER 1997

"I don't understand. Why is it so hard to buy this stock?" I asked

"You try to buy these small cap stocks—they trade by appointment," the trader from Robertson answered.

"But you barely got 1,500 shares done, I need 20, maybe 50 thou. Can we move the bid up?"

"It won't help. You'll just scare everyone off. They'll see the price head up, figure there is a big buyer, and they'll stop selling, waiting for it to go even higher. You gotta have a poker face and just scrape and claw at this thing."

"All right, I'll talk to you tomorrow and every goddamn day until we get some of this thing. Jeez," I complained.

We'd been running our fund for about nine months and had raised a bit more money. Our investing had had some successes and some blowups, but we kept looking for undiscovered gems in the Valley. We had tripped across this sleepy little company, Elantec. Hambrecht & Quist had taken them public a few years before—none other than the infamous Monster Market himself, Don Valentine of Sequoia, was the chairman of the board. But Elantec had missed their numbers a few times and was thrown onto the ever-growing scrap heap of failed companies.

Elantec made chips to regulate the power in PCs, a pretty dull business, but what opened our eyes was a chip that helped smooth phone lines so telcos could offer DSL broadband Internet service. These chips were starting to sell but not in big numbers. The company did $10 million a quarter in sales, and if you were kind and rounded up the stock to $4 per share, it had a value of $40 million, or just barely one times its annual sales. That's as cheap as these things get, but if Elantec didn't start growing, it wouldn't be worth much more.

Fred and I went to visit the company a couple of times. Nothing exciting, it was tucked into the bowels of Silicon Valley on a street filled with nondescript one-story buildings and half-empty parking lots. There was a SpeeDee Oil Changer next door (maybe I could make these visits more efficient?). The CEO, David O'Brien, was a nice, aging man, a buddy of Don Valentine's we later found out, who was kind of parked there to babysit and perhaps turn the thing.

As a throwaway question at the end of our meeting, I asked, "So, besides power regulators for PCs and this DSL driver, what else you got?"

"Well, there is not much to them yet, but we do have these laser diode drivers."

Fred and I look at each other, and I can hear the silent sigh. Oh, laser diode drivers. Gee, that changes everything. You must sell two or three of those each quarter. Yippee.

This investment might have been a huge mistake. I'm thinking as loudly as I can so Fred can mind read, "Let's get the hell out of here!"

Fred ignored my mind-meld attempt. "What are they for?"

"If you try to write to an optical drive, you need a very powerful laser pulse, short, quick and bright. Our drivers enable that. They're tough to make. We have one, Toshiba's got one, but no one else does. And no one will buy Toshiba's because Toshiba makes optical drives too, so everyone is buying our chip." I've seen this before—the best way to lose customers is to compete with them.

"For what kind of product?"

"Oh, DVD read/write drives."

Now I sat up. "You mean DVD-R and DVD-R/W drives for video?" I asked.

"Yeah, PCs and consumer devices too. We can do CD drives, but I'm not sure why anyone would want those when DVD is on the way. It doesn't matter which one for us. DVD drives are pretty expensive, over a thousand bucks today, but they'll come down, and we ought to be able to sell lots of our diode drivers."

"When do you think it starts to ramp?" Fred asked.

"Oh, small quantities now, and then more and more each year."

That wasn't a particularly satisfying answer, but I supposed it would have to do. On the car ride back to the office, we decided we would keep buying the stock. It was $3—maybe it would go to $10.

It didn't matter when it worked, as long as it worked. We weren't trying to make our month, just make it big.

That seemed to be our model. We weren't looking for a stock to go up 30% or 50%, we were looking for big moves—3 times, 5 times, even 10 times, the elusive ten-bagger. Maybe there is some waterfall out there. You never know. In fact, the ones you think are going to be the huge home runs often end up as duds, and the companies with modest expectations all of a sudden go off on a tear. Elantec? Who knows? That DVD stuff is going to kick in someday, but my conviction was iffy. Still, a three-bagger is nothing to sneeze at.

Deciding to add more shares and actually buying the stock were two different things. These small companies *do* trade by appointment.

"Did you get anything done?" I again asked the trader at Robertson.

"Nothing done."

"Nothing? Again? My limit is $3¼, and this thing has been trading there all day. How come I'm not getting any?"

"Well, we gotta pay bills around here."

"What does that mean?" I asked.

"I gotta tack on an eighth."

"So?"

"So, I gotta buy it at $3⅛ to sell it to you for $3¼. And it's not trading there." Before decimalization, the only qualification to be a trader was to pass fifth-grade math to know how to deal with fractions.

"So you're telling me it's trading at a quarter, but I can't buy it there?"

"Nope."

"Well, let me know if you do accidentally buy us any."

I was annoyed. Even more so when I got out a calculator. Paying an eighth, or 12½ cents, on a $50 stock is one thing. But paying 12½ cents on a $3¼ stock is, let's see, 3.25 guzinta 12.5, carry the one, holy shit, almost 4%. These guys are almost as big a set of thieves as real estate brokers.

"The usual?" I asked the trader a week later.

"Good news today. I got a couple of thousand so far."

"Hey, that's great. Keep going."

"Yeah, I'm just buying it off the box."

"Oh, OK." I had no idea what she was talking about, but then again, I never understood traders, they had their own lingo, and for all my years on Wall Street, I just agreed like I understood, not wanting to seem the ignorant trading moron that unfortunately I was.

"Anything?"

"About six. Again, just buying it off the box."

"Cool."

"Yeah, I'll just mark it up an eighth off the box. You're OK with that, right?"

"Yeah, sure, as long as you keep buying stock. I need another fifty thou."

"I'll keep working it."

"By the way, what is the box you are talking about?"

"Instinet. You know that."

"Oh, yeah, sure, Instinet. I thought you might have been talking about some other box, of course, yeah, Instinet. Thanks. Keep going."

Note to self: I gotta get me one of those Instinet boxes.

• • •

We now owned 100,000 shares of Elantec. And we had a profit in it. Our cost was around \$3⅛, and the damn thing was trading close to \$3½. We did a little more work on these laser diode drivers, and sure enough, if you wanted to sell DVD read/write drives, you pretty much had to buy Elantec's laser diode driver. And they got a whopping \$2 for each one. Not much. But if they could sell a million of them in a year or two, it was something. I just saw an advertisement for an add-on DVD-R/W drive for \$800. It's starting. Someday, maybe they could even sell 5 million and contribute to growth. This puppy could run to \$10, well, if everything went right.

Meanwhile, I checked out Instinet. I mean, I knew about it; it was a stock matching service that lots of brokerage firms were using to trade. I put in a call to see if a small (but effective) hedge fund could get one of their boxes too. Some young sales guy called back and said they had just started a new program for small institutions and that we should talk. I didn't feel like an institution, but what the hell, I was heading to New York, so I set up a meeting with Instinet.

They were in the ugly Lipstick Building on Third Avenue, just down the block from the Citigroup whistle building.

"I buy a lot of small cap stocks, and I notice that my brokers are just buying them off a box. When I ask what box, they tell me Instinet. So, I'm here to get my own box."

"Well, let's see what we can do. We have a new program for small shops—we'll put the box in, it's PC based, and we'll run a private line to your office."

"Are there minimum amounts of trades I have to do?"

"Not really, but if you don't do much, we'll pull the wire and you can just send the PC back."

"Is there some monthly fee?"

"Oh, no, we just charge three cents a share."

"Really, I'm paying an eighth to trade right now. That's four times what you're charging. Heck, I sometimes get stiffed for a quarter. Three cents works for me."

"We like to see firms with \$100 million in assets." Gulp. We weren't even close.

"Oh, well, yeah, we will be there."

"Will be?"

"Oh, sure, we're out raising money and have commitments for a good chunk of that. I don't see that as a problem."

"OK, we need lots of paperwork, your partnership agreements and stuff. We can probably have you set up next week."

I guess "will be" worked. The next week, sure enough, FedEx delivered an IBM PC, fully loaded with Windows NT. Pac Bell showed up and installed a frame relay circuit to connect us back to Instinet in San Francisco. I took the equipment apart when Pac Bell left to see whose chips were in the network equipment. After half a day of figuring out what was basically a 1970s-era terminal-style user interface, I was trading away. I was buying Elantec "off the box." Sitting in a dumpy office over an arts store in Palo Alto, I can buy and sell stocks off a screen until I'm blue in the face and never talk to human beings again—the modern stock market.

# Part III

# Searching for Scale

# > > > B&W IPO

OK, back to my homework.

Boulton was attracted to Watt and his steam engine in 1769. He provided Watt with risk capital because he understood early on how the steam engine could change the manufacturing business. In exchange, he got two-thirds of the business, which, starting in 1775, reaped him 25 years of dividends.

Stock Markets 101 tells you that a stock is nothing more than the current value of all of those dividends. Boulton & Watt could have gone public, and the value of their stock would have been the sum of the next 25 years of dividend payments, adjusted for time and risk and competition. If B&W was a publicly traded stock, it would have done extremely well. B&W's dividends were quite valuable.

Boulton could have cashed out in year three, and many others could have owned his piece of the steam engine franchise. In fact, Watt might have been able to cut out Boulton altogether and just sell a piece of his business to the stock market, and use that capital to fund the business.

Would you have bought Boulton & Watt shares? In retrospect, sure, yeah, I'd have owned a million shares. But put yourself back in 1775. B&W had a clunky, smelly 4-rpm steam engine that pumped water out of mines. Who gives a rat's tail about that business? And worse, their customers couldn't even afford the damn thing. They more or less rented it, paying a third of what they saved on horses. But along came textiles, and B&W was beating consensus expectations, and Henry Blodget has a $400 price target.

The stock market function is an important one, a great mechanism to:

> Provide expansion capital for businesses,

> Agree on a price for a business and

> Transfer shares from owners to others who may have a completely different risk profile or time horizon.

You may own 10% of a socks factory but need to raise money for your cow farm. So, a stock market might provide liquidity, cash for your share of the business. In doing so, it is also a great nongovernmental mechanism for setting the prices of businesses. These markets ended up as a near-perfect way to allocate capital to businesses. A business that the market expected to have a bright future saw its price go up and therefore had to sell a smaller percentage to raise the same amount of money. In effect, the cost of capital went down. On the flip side, the market will starve bad businesses of capital to stop them from throwing good money after bad at dead-end operations. You'd be hard-pressed to find a politician who could perform the same function without blowing it.

But funding factories is a lot different from funding ideas and intellectual property. It couldn't be more different than day and night. Building factories and stocking them with machines requires huge outlays. Buying raw materials and paying for them well in advance of getting paid for finished goods requires big chunks of working capital. Building inventory, and lining up and paying transportation for the raw materials coming in and the finished goods going out, adds tremendously to costs. I get a headache even thinking about the logistics nightmare of a factory owner in 1820. Add to that insurance, if it is even available, and it is a wonder that factories made any money at all. But they did make money because they got to operate under the huge price umbrella of handmade goods. This means that handmade stuff was so damned expensive that even inefficient, soot-puffing factories and slow, expensive wagons and sailing-ship transportation could undercut cottage industries.

There was no vibrant stock market in 1775, for entrepreneurs anyway, but there is now. Bull or bear market, great and profitable ideas continue to get funded by Wall Street.

The biggest problem facing any new business, be it making

steam engines or static memory, iron foundries or semiconductor fabrication facilities (fabs), is finding capital to fund the business. Banks won't lend money to businesses they don't understand. Banks study the past financial history of a business to predict the future cash flow and the likelihood they will be paid back. New business? Forget it. Come back when it works.

Hey, that's where I come in. Pools of capital looking for high returns chase these businesses that banks pass on. I need to apply my IPO positioning filter. It can't be just a monster market—there needs to be an unfair advantage and a business model to leverage all this or the investment will inevitably collapse.

There must have been more than a steam engine and some textile mills to this story. Those Brits ran the table for 100 years. Something else was going on. Where was my partner Fred's hand waving "something else"?

Maybe I would have invested in the Boulton & Watt IPO, or maybe I would have waited until they screwed up, their stock hit $3 and then bought a couple of million shares. But there had to have been more great investments, more waterfalls related to the steam engine. Where were they? I have historic capital I'd like to test out and conceptually put to work. If I can find them, the plot to that Industrial Revolution will make more sense and I can better invest in the Silicon Valley sequel.

It took a while, but I found five more barriers that got busted during the Industrial Revolution, each time lowering the cost of clothing and other goods and providing more scale to the economic engine.

James Watt wasn't resting on his laurels. His steam engine patent was to expire in 1800, so he kept inventing. In 1782, he invented the double-acting, noncondensing engine. Instead of just using a vacuum to "pull" down the piston, the double-acting engine used steam to push the piston, first in one direction and then in the other. The steam is never condensed, it is just expelled after it is used to push the piston. This was the realization of a long-dreamed-of "Huygens engine," using force to move the piston, in this case expanding steam, but still low-pressure steam.

**River steamships:** Robert Fulton got his hands on one of the few B&W steam engines allowed outside of England and in 1807 built a 142-foot-long steamship, the *Clermont*, which soon made the 150-mile trip from New York City to Albany. Steamships, albeit with paddles and running on rivers or along coasts, were the first to lower the cost of transportation.

Investable? Maybe. Depends on how much the steam engines cost Fulton and how much he charged. From the sounds of this story, I'm doubling my position in Boulton & Watt—despite the U.K. patent expiring.

**Steam locomotives and railroads:** In 1815, George Stephenson was tasked with hauling coal out of open pits. Horses were too slow and coal was in huge demand to run steam engines. He built a steam locomotive, the *Blutcher,* which worked on tracks, instead of cogs and pinions and spikes. No one thought it could haul coal uphill without spikes, but it turns out that friction works.

In 1821, Parliament authorized a horse-drawn 12-mile rail line between the coalfields in Darlington to the river ports in Stockton. Edward Pearse, the major shareholder of the Stockton and Darlington Railway, met with George Stephenson, who told him to forget the horsies, his *Blutcher* locomotive could do the work of 50 horses. A quick showing of the *Blutcher* in action in Killingworth clinched the deal.

In 1826, a 36-mile Liverpool-Manchester railroad line was authorized to transport raw materials from ships to manufactories and finished goods back again. Stephenson and his son were asked to compete in a contest for the rights to design and operate the line. They won, and by 1835, they weren't carrying just materials—a half a million passengers were recorded.

Demand for railroads, for passengers and for industrial goods exploded. You could put in a 20-mile railroad for the equivalent of $650,000 and collect that much in fees every year, because it was cheaper than horses, a lot cheaper. Joint-stock companies became the rage, and the stock market was all too happy to step in and provide capital. Then more capital. And then too much capital.

By the 1840s, a railroad mania was raging, stocks selling on multiples of passenger miles, a precursor for multiples of page views that Yahoo stock would trade on 150 years later. An inventor named Charles Babbage complained that "the railroad mania withdrew from other pursuits the most intellectual and skilful draftsmen" and sought to invent a machine that might replace them, and make Yahoo possible. Charles Dickens marveled at railroad wealth. Investors made money, investors lost money, but in the best and worst of times, the railroads got built, and people and goods were shuffled about more and more cheaply. The Industrial Revolution hit its stride.

Railroad mania hit the U.S. after the Civil War. It gave the New York Stock Exchange something to trade besides government debt. Railroads helped create the pools of capital that funded innovation in the U.S. for the next century.

Man, I'd like to short horse stocks right here. Railroads look interesting, especially since they need some government mandate for the right of way between two destinations. Put up $650 grand to make that much in fees each year—no wonder there was a railroad mania. Gotta make sure to jump off this one when ticket and hauling prices start to crack.

**Ocean steamships and propellers:** The next barrier was a steam-powered Atlantic crossing. There was only one problem—how to carry enough coal to keep the steam engine cranking for that long trip. A self-proclaimed expert on the subject, Reverend Dionysius Lardner, announced in 1837 that the longest theoretical distance a steamship that carried its own coal could travel was 2,500 miles. He probably just made up the number.

An American named Junius Smith figured he knew math better than the great reverend. The volume of a ship, and therefore how much fuel it could carry, goes up by the cube of the ship's length. But the amount of fuel needed is in proportion to the surface area of the bottom of the ship, which has to be moved through the water, not its volume. The surface area only goes up by the square of its length. If you could build a long enough ship, you could go wherever you wanted.

A British engineer named I. M. Brunel also figured the rev was blowing hot air and started building a 236-foot steamship named the *Great Western.* Smith, meanwhile, retrofitted a coastal ship, the *Sirius,* and took off from England to New York. Brunel followed three days later, and a race was on, with Smith beating

Brunel by just eight hours. Steam lowered the cost of shipping goods across the Atlantic by allowing bigger ships and cutting the time and uncertainty of the crossing.

Both the *Great Western* and the *Sirius,* amazingly, were paddle ships. The next innovation was propellers. The steam engine could directly drive a shaft to which a propeller was attached. The screw propeller was more efficient than a paddle wheel because as moving water runs past the ship, the wake you might water ski on actually helps turn the screws, so once the ship is in motion, it takes less power to keep it in motion. In 1839, the *Archimedes,* a coastal ship with a propeller, was run at 10 knots and used half as much fuel as a paddle-wheel ship.

This is a tough one to gauge as an investable business. It's a big ocean, and there are no barriers to others building a ship that runs right next to yours. Heck, Smith and Brunel proved that on the first voyage. On the other hand, there was probably a huge business supplying parts to these companies. I would have looked long and hard at propellers: every ship needed one, and there must have been fifty years of innovations in size, efficiency and quality to invest in.

**Suez Canal:** The next barrier to be broken was the distance to India and the Far East. After 10 years of construction, the Suez Canal opened in 1869. Transportation costs dropped yet again, by a factor of three or more, and as importantly, distance and time became deterministic. The trip from Malaya to England to deliver tin took exactly three months, which was the same time it took for copper to arrive from Chile. This allowed commodity exchanges, like the London Metal Exchange, to create three-month-forward contracts. Contracts for the purchase or sale of a commodity three months into the future allowed buyers or shippers to hedge their business, lowering the cost of risk.

The canal itself is probably a sucker bet—no innovation, unstable politics—though it probably doubled or tripled the value of shipping companies *and* manufacturers who got the scale from lower time and costs for transport.

**Turbine:** In 1884, Charles Parsons came up with the final kicker to England's steam-driven Industrial Revolution, the turbine engine. The efficiency of steam power enabled massive cruise liners like the *Mauretania,* the *Lusitania* and of course, the *Titanic.* In 1906, the British launched the HMS *Dreadnought* warship. It was 526 feet long, and its four Parsons steam turbines provided almost 25,000 horsepower. That's a long way from Watt's four-horsepower contraption.

I'm all over the turbine investment—perhaps it can be used for manned flight. OK, I cheated on that one, but still, the turbine proved that you could invest in a cycle over a hundred years after it started as long as the fundamentals of the cycle still scale.

I suppose that tells me that it's never too late—as long as some new innovation can save costs and help the market scale.

## > > > It Works!

PALO ALTO, CALIFORNIA—MID-1997

Fortunately, they're not all dogs like Red Brick and Versant. Slowly but surely over our first year, things started working. We haven't raised much money, but our investments were starting to pay off. No home runs but lots of singles.

We were searching high and low for names we could own in a big way. The good and bad news was there were tons of companies out there to look at. We just had to be disciplined and find the ones that were underappreciated by investors. Sometimes they were private—we put money into private company Progressive Networks (soon to be renamed RealNetworks).

Sometimes we'd find public stocks that were already working, but we'd figure that some scale was going to kick in and their growth rate was going to tick up. If it did, the company and the stock would fly higher.

We bought a bunch of Network Appliance, famous for their networked attached storage. Companies putting up Web sites were buying these things by the dozen to sit next to their servers. Fred knew the CEO from an old investment and Mr. Monster Market Don Valentine was on the board. We bought it in the high \$20s, and it seemed to go up every day, punching into the low \$50s before long.

We owned some SDL, which made these small lasers that fiber optic guys might use. It bounced around but was mostly up. So was Zoran, which sold chips into DVD players.

Another name that worked was Pinnacle Systems. They made video editing systems, and every broadcaster was buying their stuff. We figured when these things got cheap enough, folks at home could start editing their record-only camcorder tapes, the ones gathering dust in the closet. We paid around $12, and the stock was pushing $30.

Golden touch? Not even close. But the names that worked made up for a lot of crap that we'd thought were high-road names—Larscom, Macromedia, Verity—that we were down in.

NetApp and Pinnacle both worked, but they weren't our kind of names. These "high road" names are dangerous because if they miss a quarter, the stock will immediately be taken out back and shot—the Street loves to wack 'em and stack 'em.

Fred and I much preferred the screwups—the low road—or the preglitched, as we liked to call them. Great technology, decent management, but some product transition or other factor causes the company to miss, and every investor pukes it out. No one has patience anymore. And we sit there with a catcher's mitt.

We found this cool compression software company named Stac. They won a lawsuit against Microsoft but missed every quarter and pissed most of the money away. What caught our eye was this little chip company inside it named Hifn doing hardware compression that seemed to be worth more than the whole company. Maybe they'd split it off. The stock ticked up by eighths and quarters day by day.

The strangest name we owned was General Magic. The company was the great scam IPO of 1995. Goldman Sachs took it public on the promise of electronic agents and bots for computers and phones that would scour networks for just the information you need—yeah, right. They raised $90 million, and maybe $60 million was left. The founders were long gone, and some new dude from Novell was brought in to turn it around. He wasn't saying much, but we wrangled a meeting and got a glimpse of his plans for a service that used voice recognition to pull up information in real time. It seemed modestly interesting if they could get it to work.

The company had $2.50 per share in cash, and we bought a million shares for not much more than $1. Not overnight—it probably took three or four months to get all the shares through Goldman Sachs. I think we were buying the shares of Marc Porat, one of the founders. As other investors starting hearing about

General Magic's new service, the stock started trading close to $2, still less than the cash in the bank.

In our first 12 months, we managed to scrape up barely $20 million in capital—how lame. But thanks to NetApp and Pinnacle and General Magic, we turned it into $25 million, a 25% gain. Maybe this investment thing really is going to get off the ground.

## > > > IR Is Dead

"And then the Suez Canal and turbines drove transportation costs even lower and . . ." I was on my pre-7:00 a.m. phone call with Mr. Zed. I think I had this industrial stuff figured out.

"Very good. Now forget about all of that," Mr. Zed told me.

"Forget it? I just figured it out," I said.

"I think you figured out how it was, not how it will be. Do you agree?"

"I suppose . . ."

"Don't suppose. Are you going to invest in ships or railroads?"

"No, but—"

"How about electric utilities? Textile makers? Auto companies?"

"Well, no."

"The Industrial Revolution is dead."

"But there are lessons there."

"Of course, you didn't waste your time. But don't think like an industrialist. Silicon Valley isn't an industry, it's a giant design shop, as far as I can tell."

"That's true," I said.

"So, go figure that out. Your numbers for your first year are pretty good."

"Thanks, but—"

"But 25%? That's nothing. How is it that Silicon Valley can generate all that wealth but hardly even make anything themselves? Can we invest in that model or is that same little quirk? Teach me—I'm not sure myself."

All of the names that were working in our fund really didn't make anything themselves—they just designed stuff made elsewhere. NetApp took commodity disk drives made in Singapore and put a software wrapper around them—and made a fortune. Mr. Zed is right. I need to go back and do the same homework I did for the Industrial Revolution on this whole tech thing.

## > > > **Shrink, Integrate**

On October 4, 1957, the Russians launched Sputnik I, a 22-inch-diameter, 183-pound satellite that didn't do much but beep. Most people think the semiconductor industry is a result of the space race that Sputnik sparked. In 1958, the U.S. Air Force did use semiconductors in the design of Minuteman missiles, and the Pentagon and the soon-to-be-formed NASA were large buyers of semiconductors. The military driving semiconductors sounds plausible, much as Wilkinson's cannon backlog drove the need for the steam engine. Great story, but I'm not so sure. The computer industry was already taking off during the post–World War II economic boom. I suspect military and commercial uses drove the semiconductor industry in lockstep, until the microprocessor blew commercial uses wide open.

But as far as transistors were concerned in the 1950s, they were discrete devices, one device per package. At Texas Instruments, a scientist named Jack Kilby was given the task of packing a bunch of transistors together. In late 1958, Kilby put five transistors on a single half-inch-long piece of germanium. Hold the champagne, though—Kilby cheated. He used tiny wires to connect the five devices to one another. His integrated circuit looked like a petrified centipede. Still, it was the first integrated circuit, and for it, Kilby won the 2000 Nobel Prize in Physics. I met Kilby at a TI annual meeting in the 1980s. He was about six feet and had a giant head—kind of a cross between Lurch and Uncle Fester, until you realized his head housed the massive brain of a genius.

Meanwhile, farther west, after reading the January 1959 announcement by TI of their integrated circuit, Fairchild Semiconductor doubled their efforts to get more than one transistor on a device. Jean Hoerni, a Swiss physicist, came up with what is known as a planar process.

Hoerni used a process called optical lithography, which is similar to how photographs are made by light shining through negatives. He started with a piece of germanium or silicon. Then he sprayed over it a material called photoresist. If you shined a light on the photoresist, it hardened, and then you could use a special chemical to remove the photoresist that was not hit by light. So Hoerni created a mask, like a photo negative, with a bunch of openings where he wanted to diffuse in impurities, and then flipped on a light. Wherever the photoresist remained after the chemical bath, the impurities would not diffuse underneath.

When finished, he had his integrated transistors, as many as he could fit. I think Hoerni started with eight devices.

But Hoerni did no better than Kilby; he still needed wires to connect the devices. In early 1959, his colleague, Bob Noyce, came up with the solution. Noyce blew in some oxygen and grew an insulator, silicon dioxide, literally glass, over the top of the entire circuit. Then, again using a mask and photoresist, he cut holes in the glass where he needed to connect to the transistor nodes. Noyce then deposited molten aluminum over the top of the glass, which ran into the holes to make a connection, so you were left with flat wires connecting the transistors. Ingenious. And soon, the cost of transistors became the next barrier to fall. This planar process has been perfected many times but is still in use for the billion transistor devices of today.

This story got me thinking. Planar meant, for the first time and only in a tiny way, that design and manufacturing could be separated. Over time, these photo masks would become like software programs: you changed them to create new applications, but the underlying factory or machine would remain the same.

With eight transistors on an integrated circuit or chip, Fairchild could go out to IBM and others and charge a premium price, as the chip saved IBM space. Inevitably, customers would come back and say, "You know, I really could use 14 transistors on a chip, with these 5 connected to these 9 others."

Fairchild was more than happy to oblige, at a price. But the larger the chips got, the harder they were to make—random defects had a higher probability of ruining larger devices. So instead of making larger chips with more similar-size transistors, Fairchild worked on making the same-size chips with more of the smaller-size transistors. A chip of a given size cost the same no matter how many transistors it contained. The costs were photoresist and aluminum and some labor. Shrinking the transistors drove down the cost per transistor, just as an efficient steam engine drove down the cost per horsepower.

Bing, bang, boom—the learning curve is invented. Shrink, integrate, shrink, integrate. This learning curve is the scale, the elasticity of the computer business. This was a field of dreams on steroids: if you make it cheaper by half, they will not only come, they will use three times as many. This is the real waterfall of Silicon Valley. Ever cheaper computers come from ever cheaper chips.

So much so that in 1965, Digital Equipment began shipping their PDP-8 minicomputer with 4K of memory for $18,000. It didn't do much, yet. But who cares—it undercut IBM mainframe prices, and lots of techies at Bell Labs started buying PDP-8s just to play around with them.

At the same time, Gordon Moore, who ran research at Fairchild, had seen enough of the scale his company was enabling to be quoted in an *Electronics* magazine article in 1965, saying the number of transistors would double every year for the next 10 years. Moore would probably be the first to admit that it was not that bold a prediction—he had already seen it in action. In 1975, he adjusted what is now known as Moore's law to say that the number of transistors on a chip would double every two years. What he left unsaid is that costs per transistor drop 30% per year, a heck of a lot faster than the 5% a year that horsepower got cheaper in the 18th century. This movie is running six times faster!

## > > > ***Four-Door Office***

PALO ALTO, CALIFORNIA—SUMMER 1997

"I'm sick of these meetings. How many more of these today?" I asked.

"Three more this afternoon," Fred answered.

"We've already done three. Any of these later ones any good?"

"You don't know until you meet them."

He was right. You have to visit tons of companies, usually again and again, before you can invest in them. We were kissing a lot of frogs, although I preferred the "turning over a lot of rocks" analogy.

"They all sound good until we get back into the car and rip them to shreds."

"There are a thousand companies in the Valley and five thousand soap operas. We just need to find a couple that we can live with."

"It seems that all we do is hunt around for some big score," I complained.

"Others are hunting. What we are doing is laying traps," Fred corrected.

Fred and I don't spend much time in our office. Our car is our office. After a 6:00 a.m. start above the art supplies store, the typical day finds us buzzing down Alma Street from Palo Alto at 8:00 a.m. Alma turns into Central Expressway, a direct shot into the core of Silicon Valley. We've got four, five, six meetings set up with companies, public and private, to figure out what's going on, what's the latest and greatest and whose piece of paper should we buy and ride. We decided to invest 30% of our fund in private companies, venture investments, as part of our edge. So, a lot of the day was looking at start-ups as well.

"Oh, you Wall Street guys on the West Coast. You start early, but you're done by one and on the golf course by two," I would often hear. I wish. That might be true for traders, but we never seemed to stop. Even at the end of the day, this job never stopped. The stock market closed at 1:00 p.m. out here, but the job was 24/7—I was always trying to work out some puzzle in my mind.

Jack Nash had a roving eye, always watching a quote screen, looking for something tradeable. We have a roving office, and we're always on the lookout for something ownable. One-on-one meetings with management are key, they're just such a pain in the ass. But the first rule of investing is never to buy something because someone else tells you to. Of course, I spent 10 years of my life as a Wall Street analyst telling people they should buy stuff. God, I hope no one listened!

This ain't easy. Those soap operas all sound compelling. We really were at our best between meetings, questioning assumptions, recalling what competitors told us, finding white lies, bashing management, finding holes in the story. Holes aren't necessarily bad, as long as you know what they are ahead of time. New product introductions were always fun—customers stop buying old products waiting for the new ones to ship, the quarter is probably light, the stock's going to blow up and we can buy a million shares when everyone else is bailing. Those are the most fun, but rare.

More often, the investment thesis is subtle. A product lowers the cost of doing something, and *eventually,* customers will figure this out and buy the stuff in big volume, but they're not buying yet. You've got to have real conviction to step up and own this kind of company—you're staring over the edge of the waterfall, not sure when the growth is going to start. When you get one quarter after another of disappointments and a stock that is a dying quail, you start to question your own judgment. Sometimes the best thing to do is sell in disgust. And sometimes you should be backing up a truck and buying everything you can get your hands on.

It is always the wrong ones that blow up. Some of the favorite companies we owned—names like Worldtalk, Visigenic and one of our real favorites, Edify—turned out to be doggy stocks, howling in the night. It's not always the company's and management's fault. Markets change, competitors arise and technology adjusts. Not everything is destined to work.

We sold Worldtalk—it took me months to get out of that thing—and took a bath. Visigenic and Edify both got acquired by bigger companies, and we actually made money by buying more shares on the way down. More lucky than anything else. Another company saw a use for their technology and paid up for it, so we were made whole, but the opportunity cost killed us. The capital should have been invested elsewhere.

But you do have to rely on management. When you own a million shares of a company, you're stuck with it. You can't get out overnight, so you have to trust management to run a smooth ship, no surprises. This is easier said than done. We weren't the type of fund that lived and died by quarterly profit announcements by companies. We never bought a stock because we thought they'd beat estimates by a penny, although that is the only thing that plenty of other hedge funds did. Earnings were signposts along the way.

I could understand the technology of a company within a few minutes of hearing about it. I could tell you what their next two or three products would be and maybe even how they would price them. But I couldn't for the life of me tell whether the CEO was a bumbling moron or a management genius.

Fred, on the other hand, had the gift. He could spend a few minutes with a CEO and almost instantly know whether he was worthy of investing with. I asked Fred again and again how he did it, but he never gave me a satisfying answer. It was always something like:

"Running a company is like driving a tank down the street—except the tank has no windshield, just a rearview mirror, and there are five or six managers pushing pedals and pulling levers and turning dials and adjusting settings almost by trial and error, trying to drive as fast as they can and keep the tank going straight, and all of a sudden a giant tree drops into the middle of the street and the team has to somehow steer around it without spilling their coffee."

"And?" I ask.

"And I guess you have to make sure managers are up to that task."

## > > > Institute for Pry-Vat Investors

NEWPORT, RHODE ISLAND—FALL 1997

Enough of this living-in-the-past crap. It's been a year since we opened our fund. Despite decent performance numbers, up 25% in a year, we are still scratching and clawing, trying to raise money. I'm not sure why it's been so hard, but I'm getting tired of the fake smiles and, well, of being nice to people. I'm just not very good at it.

So, it's off to Newport, Rhode Island. I've always wanted to visit the Tennis Hall of Fame. OK, that's a lie. I didn't even know it existed until a week ago, when I was invited to make a pitch to some potential investors. I flew from Palm Springs to Boston, getting in after midnight, and then drove like a banshee to Newport. Raising money takes you from one pocket of conspicuous consumption to another, without your blinking an eye. The trip was uneventful beyond stopping to explain to the nice state trooper that I couldn't have been going 90, but that the sign said 95 South and I was indeed driving south of 95 miles per hour. I was in a hurry to be done with this stupid fund-raising.

My head hit the pillow at three, and the alarm went off at seven. I was an early speaker in the program and needed to caffeinate. The event was put on by the Institute for Private Investors, which, according to the bound guide, had 500 individuals representing 220 families, and provided "innovative educational and networking resources to families with substantial assets." Yes, I think we've hit paydirt.

I grabbed a large cup of coffee and a Danish dripping with white goo and sat at a table, going over my notes.

"Good morning."

"Good morning." I looked over and greeted a well-put-together 30-something-year-old in khakis and a blazer. (This is Newport, after all.)

"You one of the speakers?"

"Yup, I think I'm on pretty soon, just refining my talk."

"You that tech guy from Silicon Valley?"

"Yes, I suppose that's one way to look at it."

"Well, I look forward to your talk. I've been trying to get my family more involved in technology, but it's a hard sell."

"Well, it's a tough sector, but I think it is where all the growth comes from in the next decade. But it's volatile."

"Most people in the room will tell you it's way too risky."

"Can I ask you a question?" I asked.

"Sure."

"Who are all these people?"

"Some individuals but mostly family offices."

"What does that mean?" I asked.

"Well, there are so many children and grandchildren and cousins in wealthy families that usually some of the ones interested in finance form a family office and manage the family's wealth collectively. You know, allocate assets between fixed income and private equity, pick managers, that sort of stuff."

"But what kind of families?" I asked. Everybody looked pretty normal, not substantial.

"Big ones."

"Like what?"

"See those guys over there?"

"Sure," I answered, checking out three guys huddled at the next table, poring over documents.

"That's the Corning family."

"From Corning Glass."

"Oh, no, that's the Houghtons. They're sitting over there," he said, pointing to another table. "The Cornings are from the New York Central Railroad and Ludlum Steel fortune."

"Oh." I remembered that when I started on Wall Street, despite having worked five years at AT&T Bell Labs, my own substantial asset was an aging Mazda 626 with a yellow streak down the side from when I won a game of chicken with a New York taxi. Oh, yeah, I also had $937 in my checking account, but that was before stocking up on enough business suits to make it through a week.

"That man and woman over there are from a mining family, somewhere in Pennsylvania, I think."

"And you, if you don't mind me asking?"

"Supermarkets. That guy is from oil money. That guy's grandfather started some manufacturer, I'm thinking Morse Chain."

"Chain?"

"Chain."

"The chain gang? Someone's got to do it."

"Don't kid yourself. It used to be a great business. Every industrial motor was connected by chain. But now they are trying to diversify."

"Makes sense."

"It does, but it's tough. There probably isn't a person in this room worth less than 20 or 30 million bucks. The families are worth $50 million to a billion. It's not an easy problem. They can't invest in what got them here. Most of the industries they know best are now in Japan or Korea or Singapore. They already own all the real estate in Allegheny, Pennsylvania, or Horseheads, New York, so they come here and look for managers who can help."

"Help what?"

"The trick is to maintain the wealth and spit enough income to live off, and live well, I suppose. Oh, yeah. And never risk the nut."

"No risk?"

"Not no risk, just managed risk."

"Is there such a thing?"

"Probably not."

"But someone in each of these families was once an entrepreneur? They took risk."

"Sure, but that was then. Now risk is a naughty word."

• • •

So much for paydirt. I gave my presentation, and it actually went pretty well. I had only two slides that mattered. The first was taken from the top of a rickety old roller coaster about to head straight down, and you can't see where it ends up. The second was a list of the top market cap companies in technology—Microsoft, Intel, Cisco, Oracle, Dell, AOL, Compac—and how many billions they were worth.

My pitch was simple.

"Imagine it's 1982 and we are about to head into an era of massive wealth creation based on the proliferation of technology whose cost is dropping fast and ever higher-performing chips. If you knew then what you know now, how would you invest differently?

"Well, we are at the top of another rickety roller coaster, this one based on cheap bandwidth and ever-faster wires and fiber optics. It's going to be a wild ride, you can't see where it ends up, lots of people are going to toss their cookies, but lots of wealth is going to be created. So, how will you invest differently?"

It was as if I had the word *risk* tattooed to my forehead. I got a lot of nice comments after the talk but no real bites.

At the next break, I strolled around the room and slowly but surely met most of the attendees. Sure, I spent a lot of my life making fun of "members of the lucky sperm club," but I must admit, most of these folks were nicer and more down-to-earth than some of the blowhards I used to work with on Wall Street—the overeducated bankers and hormonally charged traders. These folks were born with money but didn't wear it on their sleeves. That is, until the Texan.

I sat down with my new friend, the supermarket heir, for the rest of the morning's presentations. Most were by money managers claiming to be able to beat the five-year Treasury by five basis points. Pretty dull, but lots of people were taking notes. "Don't risk the nut." I get it. And then the room started spinning.

"Gud mawnin'. Thank you to the Institute of Pry-Vat Investors for lettin' me talk. Many a you fine folk know me awready. I made a pile in the awl service biz-iness."

I leaned over to Mr. ShopRite and asked, "Awl service?"

"He's from Texas. That's *oil* service."

"Oh, got it."

"Well, I took a lot o' that dough off the table years ago and put it with some of dem Noo Yahk money folk. Sure 'nuff, dem folk know what they doin'. My family did A-OK despite all falling out of bed agin and agin."

I think he was talking about the oil slumps.

"I sold ma all cumpny a few years back and fig-erred it was time to do sumptin' else. So me and my daughter—stand up there, Agnes—we set up one of them family orifices. Hired a bunch of anal-ists to crunch sum numbers and all. Them folk cost a pretty penny, so I say to ma-self, let's open this thing up to other family orifices. Then anal-ists won't cost us so much."

"What the hell is he talking about?" I asked my tablemate, who ignored me, as he was busy taking notes.

"You see, I got me a slot on Tie-guh and Sew-Rose, and you ain't got one. Them funds are closed, the only way you gunna get your money in them is through me. So, c'mon down and sign up for my fund, and you too can get George Sew-Rose to manage your money."

"That's it? He's got a slot with Tiger Funds and Soros Management. C'mon. They're hot money funds, but so what?" I asked.

"Shh. I've been trying to get in those funds for years."

"And as far as Tie-guh, I know that Julie Robertsman for lot o' years, we pretty good friends. Now, that's a goddamn moneymaker."

"Isn't it Julian Robertson?" I asked.

"Forget it, he's rolling." I've heard that line somewhere before, I think after Bluto accused the Germans of bombing Pearl Harbor in *Animal House.*

"So talk to me affer-wards, and I'll git you into dem funds with ma slot. Thank ya very much."

And sure enough, a crowd grew around the Texan, clamoring for his precious slot in these two fast-money hedge funds. So much for worrying about risk. I guess Tiger and Soros aren't considered risky anymore.

I left Newport empty-handed. Well, not completely empty-handed—I had a ticket saying I owed $150 to the State of Rhode Island for taking too much risk on their highways.

> > > **Part IV**

# Intellectual Property

# > > > The Augmenter

I got back from Newport in a bad mood. I was frustrated that none of these families with substantial assets would invest with us. But worse than that, it might have been my last chance to get some money for the fund. All of a sudden, risk went out of favor.

Wall Street is buzzing because Thailand just blew up. I'm not sure what that even means, but Asian currencies are flying all over the place and mostly sinking like stones. Are Soros and Tiger causing this? Or are they getting killed? Who knows, who cares? All I know is that tech is seriously out of favor and we've given up all of our 25% gain by the time 1997 ends.

Damn—there is no use trying to raise money in a market like this.

The fraternal celluloid scene played out in my head.

"We've gotta do something."

"Absolutely."

"You know what we gotta do?"

My wife, Nancy, and I threw a party.

"Who is that guy?" one of my neighbors, Sharon, asked me.

"Who?" I asked.

"Is his name Doug?"

"Who?"

"That guy."

"Which guy?" I asked.

"That guy. Oh my god, it is. He invented everything."

"Who?" I asked again.

"The silver-haired guy. What is he doing at your party?"

"Oh, that guy. Yeah, Doug somebody. He lives next door.

Nancy invited him so he wouldn't complain about the noise from the party."

"That's not Doug somebody. That's Doug Engelbart. I studied all of his stuff. Augmentation and links and UI [User Interface]. He was in all of my books. That's really him, oh my god."

Sharon was starting to hyperventilate. I was considering getting a paper bag for her to breathe in, but if she passed out, perhaps she would stop ranting so much.

"All right, take it easy, calm down. I still don't see what all the fuss is about. He seems like a nice old man who lives next door," I said.

"No, you don't understand. He is the reason we are all here. He is the reason this Valley exists. He saw it all first. In the '60s."

"Was he hallucinating?"

"What do you mean?"

"Well, that VA hospital half a mile from here, at Willow and 101, is where Ken Kesey wrote *One Flew Over the Cuckoo's Nest.* Something may have spilled in the water."

"Not funny. Especially from you, Mr. Tech Investor."

"What do you mean?"

"Everything you use today on your PC, Doug Engelbart demo'ed 30 years ago."

"Like what?"

"Like the mouse."

"I thought that was Steve Jobs."

"Nope."

"OK, I was just kidding. Jobs stole it from Xerox PARC."

"Wrong again. It was Doug's."

"What else?"

"Hypertext."

"I thought that was that whacky Xanadu guy, Nelson something or other."

"Wrong again, sport Doug. Oh my god, here he comes!" Sharon exclaimed.

"I just wanted to thank you for inviting me. I'm Doug Engelbart."

"Well, you are more than welcome. I've wanted to meet you

because we have four boys over here that create enough noise to simulate a small but effective nuclear device. You probably want to call the police, I know I do, to see if they can quiet my own kids down."

"Never hear a thing. I love kids."

"Surely, you . . ." I said.

"You have a nice group of friends here."

"Thanks, Doug. I've heard a lot of stories about you."

"Well, they're probably not true."

"They're true," Sharon gurgled.

"Have you met Sharon?"

"No, hi, I'm Doug Engelbart."

"You . . . you . . . you . . . I know . . . I'm . . . Hi." Sharon was goo-goo–eyed.

"Doug, she claims to know your work, studied your work."

"Well, how nice to know my work. I've been in a few textbooks."

"Yaba . . ." Sharon was trying to say something profound, maybe she even was.

"I think Sharon needs some more wine. Doug, let me get you some too. Anyway, thanks for coming. Enjoy the party."

Now I was curious. It was time to find out more about my neighbor, who somehow must have gone deaf over the years, if he can't hear my kids screaming. A quick Web search the next day for Doug Engelbart pulled up a bunch of news stories. There was a picture of him getting some sort of medal from Bill Clinton. Hey, that's pretty cool. It was for scientific achievement or some such thing. I scanned the article, and it wasn't until the last paragraph that I read that Doug Engelbart invented the mouse. So, it really wasn't Steve Jobs.

Almost every other article described a meeting of the American Federation of Information Processing Societies' Fall Joint Computer Conference held in San Francisco. Sounded like a real rip-roaring conference. I'm sorry I missed it. Except it was held on December 5, 1968.

At the time, Frisco was tripping at Haight and Ashbury, free love, cheap dope, flower children, hippies, war protesters, Jimi Hendrix at the Fillmore. Maybe I would have liked to have been there, but then again, I was only 10 years old. My parents were a little strict about these things. But while the city was getting everything they wanted at Alice's or anyone else's restaurant, Doug was cooped up inside the Convention Center with information processors, giving demos. But while all those hippies burned out and faded away, except for all those never-say-die Dead Heads, Doug laid out the next 30 years of computing. No, take that back. He didn't just lay out the next 30 years, he gave real demonstrations of what it would look like.

Doug led a group of researchers at the Stanford Research Institute and had been working since 1962 on a topic they called "Augmented Human Intellect." Doug got a slot at the AFIPS conference to present his group's findings. Ho hum, a real snoozer, right?

But his team had put together a huge surprise. They had microwave links on the roof and phone lines hooked up to connect the Convention Center to their labs in Menlo Park. What Doug showed off was a system called NLS or oN Line System. On a computer screen with both graphics and text were multiple windows, a text editor with cut and paste, and an outline processor. A wooden-looking mouse controlled an on-screen pointer as a cursor. Multiple users could connect remotely. There was hypertext to be able to "link" to information anywhere on the computer or network. If you were stuck, a help system would provide assistance based on the context of what you were looking for. The 1,000-plus attendees were stunned. This was 1968. Water-cooled mainframes in air-conditioned rooms were run by the gods of corporate computing. Doug described a system that he used in his own office every day.

Engelbart's augmentation ideas took another 15 years to be implemented for the mass market, but he was the first to break the technology into horizontal layers.

Over time, several different companies could take a chip, program it with an operating system, add applications, user interfaces, networking and databases, and create a system that could, well, augment humans. It was the augmentation part that *is* the value of computers. Ask anyone who worked shuffling certificates or sorting airline tickets.

At the time, computing power cost a fortune. Cost was the main barrier and would remain the barrier for nearly 20 years. But when elasticity kicked in, computers became cheaper than rooms of humans. Augmenting often meant replacing, or helping those who remained.

With Engelbart's map, an entire industry came along and created highly profitable intellectual property. Bill Gates and Steve Jobs and Michael Dell and Mitch Kapor—these guys are heroes too, but perhaps they are just implementers of someone else's vision. More power and riches to them, of course, but Doug Engelbart laid out the future of the personal computer, and now it's history. I was intrigued.

I marched over to Doug's house a few weeks later to talk about a broken fence, but I was really intent on discovering his secret to scale.

"So, Doug, I study technology and markets, and I look for these hypergrowth stories. But you saw all this in the '60s. I've seen you quoted using the term 'scale,' " I said, forgetting to mention the fence.

"I did some research in the '50s and figured out there was a superscaling effect," Doug said matter-of-factly.

"But what do you mean by scale? What did you see back then?"

"Two things. I did a scaling study in the '50s that convinced me that components would keep getting cheaper and there was going to be all the bandwidth you could ever use—" Doug answered.

"That was before the integrated circuit," I interrupted.

"So that every knowledge worker was going to be equipped." Doug Engelbart rightly ignored me and kept talking. "The other scale was human scale—"

"You mean, computers easy to use," I interrupted again.

"Well, that's part of it. Yes, certainly there is scale from getting people to use complex systems, from hiding the complexity from them, so the hurdle is lowered."

"That's the human scale."

"No, the bigger thing I saw was that knowledge scales." He put his hands out palms down and interlocked his fingers and then raised his hands up.

"You mean from ease of use."

"I have a hard time explaining it. It's been hard for 30 years. But the combined knowledge of the human race scales, and if computers can augment people, then that scale is enabled."

"I'm not sure I follow."

"I'm sorry, I don't explain it well. I suppose the only thing I can think of is the alphabet. It's a hurdle, but once you get over it, you can keep adding people to it, and knowledge and the usefulness of knowledge scales, with almost no bounds."

"OK, thanks. Now, about that fence . . ." I was going to have to think about that one. There was no stock I could go out and buy tomorrow morning on that insight, but somehow I think Doug described not only the scale I was hunting for, but scale that was going to last for a very long time.

Maybe the alphabet analogy is a good one, but after thinking about it, I think Doug Engelbart is a modern King James. I know that sounds odd, but so does scaling human knowledge. Think about it—the King James Bible took religion out of the hands of the high priests and put it into the hands of the people. An entire generation became literate just to be able to read the King James version of the Bible. These same people went on to work in manufactories of the Industrial Revolution, where literacy came in handy to speed up training of workers.

Doug Engelbart's augmentation effort took computers out of the hands of the high priests of the corporate information technology centers. Some call it democratization, but I like to look at it as a literacy move. Since 1969, an entire generation has become computer literate, which eases training for jobs in a knowledge and intellectual property economy. King Doug indeed.

Computers were not just for boring accounting functions (the Cornish mines could have used one). They really could augment the human race and increase efficiency and productivity by replacing costly repetitive human functions. That was real scale, like steam engines scaling labor. Bing-bing-bing. On December 5, 1968, the world changed. Of course, you couldn't invest quite yet. A few more things needed to be invented, like microprocessors.

## > > > Get Busicom

In 1968, there were already 30,000 computers in the world, each with about a megabit of ferrite core memory per computer. Core memory was a tiny electromagnet, a diode wrapped in wire and sold for about 20 cents per bit. It was a big business.

That spelled opportunity. With six transistors, you can create a flip-flop, a memory device that let's you set it to a 1 or a 0, and it stays that way until someone comes along and changes it. At 1958 prices of $100 per transistor, a bit of memory cost a heck of a lot more than the 20 cents per bit of ferrite cores. But Moore's Law just requires a little time and a little patience and cost becomes no object. It would take until 1974 before semiconductor memory would cross the price per bit of ferrite cores and send them to the trash heap of history.

Gordon Moore saw this coming. So did Robert Noyce. In 1968, they left Fairchild and started a company of their own to make these semiconductor memories, Intel, which stood for Integrated Electronics. They actually had to buy the name from a motel chain. Hotel, motel, intel, I don't even want to know! Venture capitalist Art Rock and friends ponied up $2.5 million in two days. Moore and Noyce quickly brought over a young Hungarian from Fairchild, a chemical engineer named Andy Grove.

Intel was getting pretty good at integrating those transistor sisters into chips and not just memory. In 1970, a Japanese calculator company named Busicom showed up and asked Intel to create 12 custom-integrated circuits for a newfangled calculator. Intel assigned engineer Ted Hoff to the task but told him that there was no way Intel could afford the design of 12 chips. Hoff figured he would spend his life designing these one-offs for every Tom, Dick and Harry-san that came along. So he suggested a special-purpose processor, or microprocessor, that he could tweak or reprogram for the next customer. Management liked the idea, mainly because Busicom was willing to pay for the project without asking for ownership of the processor. Dumb move by Busicom!

Hoff and Intel, in effect, busted the computer world wide open. Sure, all they had done was create a computer on a chip—hey, Intel was a chip company, what did you expect them to do? But it was a programmable chip, meaning someone else could add value to the chip just by twiddling with some bits, by changing the list of instructions this computer on a chip executes. By programming it. Little Billy Gates would figure this out by the end of the decade. But this is the first major step in creating a horizontal business, where different companies could be mutually incented to create intellectual property that they could prosper with, *together.* The chip was worthless without being programmed. The program was just fuzzy 1's and 0's without the chip to execute it. Like cotton without a textile mill.

Not quite two years after Doug Engelbart laid out the road map without a master plan for the computer industry, the gears were already spinning. The semiconductor industry, as nascent as it was, subtly went from selling piece parts or basic building blocks to selling designs, real intellectual property. As usual, no one knew it at the time, but this was just what was needed for an intellectual property economy to emerge.

The most obvious metaphor and parallel between the Industrial Revolution and the digital revolution are the steam engine and the microprocessor. Both are worthless as stand-alones, but when attached to some process, each lowered the process's cost and increased its performance. Steam engines were attached to bellows in iron foundries and to spinning frames and looms in textile mills, replacing horses and water. Eventually, machines and factories were designed knowing that steam engines would power them, as they did the spinning mule.

Microprocessors initially "attached" to calculators but eventually new products, like personal computers, were designed with the microprocessor as its core.

Both steam engines and microprocessors never stopped improving. Watt added sun and planet gearing and double-action pistons. Intel and others continued to integrate more memory and the ability to handle bigger numbers into microprocessors.

Hoff, working with a guy named Federico Faggin, used 2,300 of those integrated transistors to come up with the 4004 microprocessor, which used 4-bit-wide data paths and executed a whopping 60,000 operations per second.

The folks at IBM, if they even bothered studying the 4004, would have surely laughed. IBM was charging millions for 32-bit computers with millions of bits of memory. But what Hoff and Faggin implemented was a computer architecture that was manufactured using a technology that got cheaper by 30% every year. It could eventually intersect the cost and performance of those big honker IBM machines. Not could, would.

Intel never rested. In November 1972, they came out with the 8008, with 3,300 transistors. It used an 8-bit data path instead of 4 to handle larger numbers, but still was mainly a chip for calculators. About the same time, Texas Instruments was creating their own microprocessors for their proprietary line of calculators. They decided not to sell processors on the open market so no one could undercut them on calculators.

In April 1974, Intel came out with the 8080, with 4,500 transistors that could do 200,000 operations per second. Match that with 1K or 4K memory chips and you've got yourself a real computer. OK, it may have been a chintzy little do-nothing machine, but it was a computer. Altair and Imsai were two early, and too early, hobbyist computer companies that used the 8080 and some memory that was filled via switches on the outside of a box. Results of programs were written to little lights above the switches. If you could afford one, you added a "TV typewriter" and it was a real personal computer. To harness this device, Bill Gates and Paul Allen wrote some code so users could write programs using the very simple BASIC computer language for this machine.

But competition for Intel came fast and furious. RCA was making an 1801 microprocessor that the automobile industry was using for engine control. As a kid in high school, around 1974, I used to sneak into an RCA facility and steal these 1801s and other chips in an attempt to make a home computer. I got a few lights to flash, but no computer! Mostek had the 6502, Motorola the 6800. Zilog mimicked the 8080 with their Z80, using the same instruction set inside the microprocessor and adding a few extensions of their own.

With the help of two much smarter high school friends, Dave Bell and Greg Efland, I actually built a Z80 home computer, complete with 64 1K memory chips, a graphics interface to a TV (my dad converted the TV set so I wouldn't electrocute myself) and a Panasonic cassette recorder to store programs. We stole a copy of the Gates BASIC interpreter and were on our way. Of course, we spent most of the time writing computer games, but what do you expect from a bunch of high school kids. I wrote the world's greatest clone of the arcade game Dominoes (honk if you remember it). We thought of starting a company but noticed ads for computer boards from a company named Apple in computer magazines and decided, or our parents did, that college might be a better use of our time.

I met Ted Hoff in the late 1980s. He told me that whenever he took his TV in to be repaired, they would always tell him there was a problem with this microprocessor thingie in the set and then ask him why he was laughing. OK, these guys do have a strange sense of humor.

In the 1970s, Motorola was making TVs. (Quasar, dum-dum-dum, by Motorola.) Intel watched other companies do well with the integrated electronics provided by them. Why shouldn't they slap a battery or a power supply and a little plastic around their parts to make even more money?

Digital watches were hot in the early 1970s. Intel bought a company named Microma in 1973. Their watches with cool red seven-segment LED displays were selling for over $100. But as volume increased, Intel was able to make the integrated circuits inside the watches much more cheaply. Even though they were driving costs down the learning curve, no one quite understood the impact of lower costs on the end markets. As cheaper models were introduced, Microma was stuck with an inventory of expensive watches that wouldn't sell. As others sold the necessary chips to new watchmakers, the market was flooded with cheap, under $20 watches. Intel quietly sold Microma in 1978, swearing never to forget this valuable lesson. Texas Instruments had the same problem, taking a bath in an early version of personal computers and again and again in calculators. They should have just sold the chips that went into calculators to everyone, instead of the calculators themselves.

I once asked Gordon Moore about the whole Microma experience. He quickly pulled up his sleeve and pointed to a Microma watch on his wrist and told me he wore it often to remind himself to never be that stupid again. Intel's lesson: make the intellectual property, not the end product.

The cool thing about a computer on a chip is you can start a computer company without knowing much about computers. Steve Jobs and Steve Wozniak created Apple Computer without knowing that much. Wozniak had to write some software to get data on and off a floppy disk drive, which no one else had, and their Apple I became a hit. IBM knew lots about how to milk big bucks out of big computers, but nothing about microprocessors. So a stealth group in Florida contracted out the work, creating a Frankenstein-like IBM PC in 1981, using an Intel microprocessor, Microsoft software and a Western Digital disk controller. Design and manufacture were now separated in the computer business too.

## > > > Publishing Chips in Taiwan

SAN JOSE, CALIFORNIA—SPRING 1989

"You what?" I asked incredulously.

"We don't have a fab," Bernie Vonderschmitt told me again. No other CEO of a chip company had ever uttered those words to me before.

"I guess I don't understand that."

"What's not to understand? We don't have a wafer fab or any factory. We don't need one. We don't want one."

"Can you do that?" I was still confused.

"We're doing it."

"But Jerry Sanders says 'real men have fabs.' " Sanders was the flamboyant silver-haired CEO of chip maker Advanced Micro Devices. He had hired Ray Charles to play at the company Christmas party in 1984, right before a nasty two-year recession hit the industry. Credibility was not Sanders's middle name. He spent billions on wafer fabs and was questioning anyone else's manhood who couldn't similarly spend billions.

"Yeah, we may not be real men, but we'll be rich men. Jerry will figure this out someday. He's a little slow on the uptake. Plus, AMD owns a piece of us."

"But every other successful chip company in the Valley owns a fab."

"Good for them, but now they are drowning with them. They have to keep feeding the beast."

Bernie was right about that. A fab cost $100 million minimum and lasted maybe three years if you were lucky, before you had to build another more state-of-the-art one. It's what kept investment bankers in business, funding all that spending.

"A couple of years back," Bernie continued, "we took on venture capital and had a tough choice to make. We knew we had a unique and patented chip design, our field-programmable gate arrays. But we had a lot of work to do before we could get them to market. This meant a lot of designers and a lot of programmers."

"OK, everyone has this problem."

"More so with us. We sell an architecture and have to keep it current."

"So, either you keep your design current or your fab current?"

"Right. I could have gone back to other venture capitalists and raised the $100 million I needed to build a fab, but they would have owned the company, not me and my team. So we looked around to see if anyone had a fab they weren't using completely and maybe wanted to rent us some space."

"Did you find one around here?"

"No, we found TSMC instead."

"Who?"

"The Taiwan Semiconductor Manufacturing Company. All they do is run a fab and sell finished wafers to us at a fixed price. We can put anything we want on those wafers, same price. So we crank out more designs, and these guys will manufacture them all."

"This is a big change."

"It's really no different than the publishing business. You don't have to own a printing press to write a book or publish it. Someone else prints the pages and binds them into a book at a fixed price, no matter what the book is about."

"Can you make the same margins as Cypress or LSI Logic? They own their own fabs, so they must have some advantage."

"Actually, they make 45% gross margins in a good year, and we'll make 55% in a bad year." Gross margins were the percentage of profits after expensing just the materials used, not the research and development or sales costs. This was new—same business, no factory, but higher margins? Xilinx could afford to spend more on their designs than manufacturing. If this works, this thing is going to be a home run.

"No fabs is a pretty bold step. Will investors let you do this?"

"That's why we picked Morgan Stanley to take us public, Andy. You've got your work cut out for you."

"Oh, great. We are supposed to just show up and collect our fees on IPOs."

"Not this time. This won't be easy. Now get to work."

It turned out to be easier than I thought. Investors on the road show needed a little coaching on what it was like to be a "fab-less" chip company, that it wasn't an oxymoron. What put everyone over the top were the company's profit margins, that "55% in a bad year" thing. Investors "get" profits—it is their common language.

My problem was in believing that someone would just make chips for Xilinx or any of the other fab-less chip companies that quickly followed. My annual December trip to the Far East was coming up, so I scheduled a side trip to Taipei. It was a bit more than a day trip to Kansas City.

TSMC was located in Hsinchu City, a bumpy hour-plus cab ride from Taipei. I had never been to Taiwan before, but I had a whopping 18 hours to figure out how this fab-less stuff worked—no time to see the sights. Hsinchu City looked a lot like Parsippany, New Jersey: a bunch of industrial parks, a couple of malls and one medium-size hotel. What was hard to figure out was that the place was teeming with activity, entrepreneurs run wild. I checked into the hotel and dumped my bags in the room. Before heading out, I rummaged through the nightstand until I found the phone book. My friend, Hank Zona, used to nod his head in someone's direction and whisper, "That guy has more chins than a Chinese phone book." I never knew what that meant, but now I do—14 pages' worth.

The address was simply Science-based Industrial Park. The taxi driver never heard of TSMC. This was 1991. By 2001, he probably worked for TSMC. I was met in the lobby by Dr. Morris Chang.

"OK, let's go then. You'll need a bunny suit."

I had been on enough tours to know the routine. I put the white booties over my shoes and slid on pants, a jacket and a surgical cap to tuck all my hair into. I was spared a mask over my face. We stepped through the blowers, and blasts of air came from the floor and side and sucked every tiny particle off us into filters in the ceiling. Marilyn Monroe would have enjoyed this room.

"This is Fab 1. The building used to be a textile factory. About a thousand sewing machines tucked side to side in here. I think you Americans called them sweatshops."

"What happened to them?" I asked.

"They moved to Malaysia a few years ago. Labor is a lot cheaper there. This is a Class 10 fab, no more than 10 particulates per square foot. Each little particle kills chips, since they are larger than the wires being written onto the chip. In this fab, we can do 10,000 six-inch wafer starts a week, for now. We'll double that soon and have already broken ground on Fab 2 and are spec'ing out Fab 3," Dr. Chang boasted.

"Wow, that makes you a medium-size player in Silicon Valley," I told him.

"We'll do more wafer starts than the entire Silicon Valley before long." His boasting quickly turned into bragging. I wonder if he knew Jerry Sanders.

"How do you pull this off?"

"It's real simple. We sell wafers at a fixed price, around 800 bucks. You put what you want on the wafers. We don't care. Sell them for what you want. We make money at 800 bucks."

"How much?"

"If we run this fab close to capacity, we can make $250, maybe $280."

"So, around 30% gross margins."

"Thirty-five percent on a good day. We don't change our process. It is more or less the same for everybody. Our yields are very high."

"But even the worst companies in the Valley make 40% or 45% gross margins."

"Yeah, but they waste all that money on their fabs. We worry about that stuff for them. I have process engineers, not design engineers. If the other companies focus on design, they can make 50–60% margins. Why wouldn't they use us?"

Why indeed.

"And you can survive on 35% margins?"

"We do enough volume, we can survive on a lot less. We don't pay $100,000 a year to PhDs. We also don't have to pay that much to technicians. But it's all relative. Our job applicants stretch around the block because we pay more than toy companies."

We left the fab, stripped off the bunny suits and headed to a conference room.

"Any questions?" Dr. Chang asked.

"Well, we are starting to see more fab-less chip companies in the Valley, and I want to figure out if they are for real or just some passing fad."

"Fad? Hardly. It's the future. You guys shouldn't make stuff. Let us. Go tell your companies we are here."

"But aren't the Japanese renting out their spare fab capacity?"

Chang started laughing hysterically. "That's funny."

"What is funny?"

"Mr. Kessler, have you ever negotiated with the Japanese?"

"No, can't say I have."

"Well, here is how it goes. You fly in, and they meet you for dinner. Sushi, shabu-shabu, whatever that silly stuff is they eat. Then you go to a geisha bar and drink lots of American whiskey. The next day, they are bright-eyed and your head hurts. Then they take you on hours and hours of tours of their facilities. Then you get put in a conference room with some smiling low-level drones, and they just nod as you talk. You ask them for some specifics on price, and they look at one another, shake their heads and do that sucking sound. I can't stand that sucking sound, lots of air rushing past their teeth. It is like, what do you Americans say, fingernails on a chalkboard."

I was starting to enjoy this.

"Then it's back to your hotel and you meet them for another dinner and more Asahi Super Dry and more geisha bars and two fingers of Jack Daniel's. The next day, you come in and ask for someone in charge instead of those smilers. You've got a flight at seven and need to check out and get your bags. You figured some deal would be wrapped up by now. They say, 'So solly, plesident of division vely busy, no can meet till rater.' Some more air sucking and you are ready to hit someone. Finally, some gray-haired guy comes in with contracts, saying, 'You sign here.' You can't figure out what the hell the contracts say, the numbers don't add up, but you were told by your boss not to come home without a contract. Another night of ugly geishas and Wild Turkey would kill you, so you sign, what the hell, it's not your money."

"Someone must be patient enough to get decent contracts," I said. I didn't want to interrupt, this guy was on a roll.

"Maybe, but remember, those Japanese companies like Toshiba and Hitachi and Matsushita make chips too. They are your competitors. Why use them? The day demand picks up, you'll sit around waiting for your wafers to show up while they are shipping their own chips like mad."

"What about the Koreans?" I asked.

"They are just little Japan. There are four big companies there, and they do what their banks tell them to do. Plus, we outnetwork them. Taiwan sends lots of engineering students to U.S. schools, and they stay there and work in Silicon Valley. There are few Koreans at U.S. engineering schools. Korean-Americans, yes, that's different. No natives. So when someone wants to do business, we know who to deal with."

"And Singapore? They have Chartered Semiconductor, which I think does the same thing as you."

"They are OK, we compete. But you can get caned for jaywalking there. I'd be careful even going to Singapore."

"But why would companies trust you with their precious designs?"

"That is our biggest hurdle. But we don't compete with them. The publishing model works. We are the book makers, they write the words."

Someone has been spreading around this metaphor, but it seems to work.

"Won't design companies pop up around here to take advantage of your fabs?"

"We hope so, but it will be slow. We still make a lot of clothes and toys and shoes. You know what is down the block? Animators. Actually, it is just a bunch of artists with ink and paint. They make, what is that show you have? Oh yes, *The Simpsons.*"

"Really?"

"Yes. I have watched this cartoon when I visit the U.S., and I often wonder if the animators who work here understand any of the jokes."

"D'oh," I said reflexively.

"Pardon?"

"Nothing. Many of those jokes get past me too," I had to admit.

"We have a long way to go before we move beyond manufacturing. Silicon Valley will be the center of innovation for many years because they know what the market wants. We know how to make it for them. Pretty good relationship."

And there it was—one of the top Taiwanese companies making chips for 35% profit margins "on a good day" for an American company that ships their designs over and sells the chips they get back for 55% profit margins "on a bad day." And I'll bet Fox Television makes more on one episode of *The Simpsons* than they pay Taiwanese artists to draw for them.

The stock market teaches you the hard way—it's all in the margin.

## > > > *Getting Paid for IP*

PALO ALTO, CALIFORNIA—EARLY 1998

Finding great long-term investments turned out to be tougher than just finding interesting pieces of intellectual property that scale. I had to find a bulletproof way for the intellectual property to be delivered too.

It couldn't be just the price customers would pay; that could be fleeting. Yahoo was getting $50 per thousand page views. TV and radio were lucky to get $1. I didn't think they were going to meet in the middle.

I sat through a meeting with a private company that does some incredibly esoteric software to decide which data get priority on corporate networks, which are a security risk and which Web sites should be banned (sweetandsaucypizzagirls.com was one example). They had a lot of interest in their policy software, but no one wanted to pay for it.

"Cisco offered $200,000 for it," the CEO of the software company told me.

"Per year? Per server?" I asked.

"Nope, just $200,000. They wanted to own it, source code and all. You can't get paid for software anymore."

"So what are you doing?"

"We just implemented the same code on a chip. Turns out Cisco will pay us $50 for each chip, so we are designed into one of their switches that ships 10,000 units a month."

"And how much do you make?" I asked.

"Well, it's our design, so we can charge what we want. Don't tell anyone, but they cost us $15 to make out of Taiwan. It makes a difference how you get paid."

• • •

How true. It was all about how you were getting paid. Drug companies sell little patent-protected pills that cost pennies for $10 a dose. Hollywood sells copyright-protected silvery DVD disks for $19.99 that cost a buck at most to manufacture.

But then again, music is copyright protected but fits in a five-megabyte file and can move across the Internet in a few seconds. The CD is broken. Same with a lot of software; it's tough to get paid for it.

It's not just intellectual property—it's how it's packaged and how it's protected.

## > > > *Nobodies in That Deal*

PALO ALTO, CALIFORNIA—EARLY 1998

I was warming up, taking a few shots and getting my creaky body stretched before the games started. For the last five years, I've been playing pickup basketball on weekends on a tennis court behind Jay Hoag's house in Palo Alto. Jay, an old friend who used to run money in New York, is one of the top fund managers in the area, investing in both public and private companies. In fact, Fred and I modeled our fund a little like Jay's, but different enough so that we really didn't compete and so I could continue to play basketball at his house.

A core group of successful venture capitalists and company execs showed up each week. A few were like me—white guys who can't jump. It was hard for me because we were still trying to get our fund to a level of respectability, and here was a group of hitters in the Valley. The usual question was, "So, how much money you got?" It wasn't so much asset envy as a desire to, well, to jump with the best of them.

Because of this, I tried to avoid business talk, but I would overhear a few juicy conversations. This morning, two VCs were talking about a company trying to raise money.

"Did you meet with those guys from Cybersource?" This piqued my interest because I happened to be a small investor in the company, which was really two companies, one that sold software online and another that did fraud detection for credit card transactions.

"Yeah, they came in yesterday. They've been making the rounds."

"What did you think?"

"I'm not sure."

"Me neither. My concern is that nobody's in the deal." This was a not-so-veiled reference that no big-name venture capital firm was an investor in the company. Without that Good Housekeeping Seal of Approval, it's tough for a new player to step up and put in money.

One of the VCs turned to me and asked, "Andy, aren't you in this deal?"

My face probably turned red, but I answered, "Yup, but I agree with you—nobody's in this deal."

"Sorry, no offense."

"None taken," I said.

"Well, in that case, I don't like to say nobody's in the deal. I prefer to say that there are a bunch of nobodies in the deal."

I should have been offended at that, but oddly I wasn't. This was white-guy trash talk—you gotta take it to be able to dish it out. Plus, we were struggling and not destined to be top-tier venture capitalists with an A-list of portfolio companies and fancy offices on Sand Hill Road. But you don't have to be a so-called player to make money in Silicon Valley, just smart enough to find a few good companies and avoid the fashionable ones. Like public investors, VCs are notorious momentum investors—each one often investing in two or three companies in the same market, hoping something works. This was a big reason for the boom-bust cycle in the valley: VCs fund 30 plus companies in each hot segment, and after a run-up and boom in taking companies public, a shakeout is almost inevitable.

"Hi, Andy. This is Dominic Orr. We met a couple of months ago at the networking dinner that PaineWebber held in Palo Alto."

"Oh, yes, hi, Dominic." I was racking my brains to remember him. I can barely remember what I had for breakfast. Gigabit Ethernet was the latest hot market for venture capitalists—another overdone market segment. I had been to lots of meetings and dinners with analysts and companies, but this one started coming back into focus. I had sat next to a guy who used to work at Hewlett-Packard and Bay Networks and now ran one of the gigabit companies. He spent most of the evening trying to convince me that his company, Alteon, which sold networking cards like everyone else, was not in the commodity business. The real money was to be made in switches that sit next to Web servers. This made sense, but so what? There were lots of switch companies too.

"What about Cisco?" I remember asking.

"Oh, they do routers, which is layer 2. Some guys like Extreme and Foundry, who were also at the dinner, do layer 3 switching; Alteon is doing layers 4 through 7."

I had nodded in understanding, but I really had no clue what he was talking about. I remembered from my days at Bell Labs about seven layers of communications but had long ago forgotten what they meant.

Dominic continued. "So, we are doing another round of financing, and I remembered you had a fund that did public and later-stage private and was wondering if you wanted to come take a look?"

I was flattered that he remembered me, but my bullshit detector immediately sprang into action. We had a small fund, were not huge players in the Valley, and so something must be wrong with this thing. Which isn't necessarily bad—I just needed to figure out what was wrong before investing.

The next morning, I read about layer 3 switching and layers 4–7 smart switching and then instantly filed that knowledge into a holding tank in my brain. Then Fred and I went down to South San Jose to meet Dominic and the rest of the management team. They left the door of the conference room open. We heard about the benefits of layer 4–7 switching, which had to do with controlling the flow of information between a local-area network and a wide-area network. I liked the space. As bandwidth grows, these are precisely the type of products that will scale.

Alteon had raised $40 million in their last round from some big-name venture capitalists. It was a bunch of somebodies. Alteon's business was growing, although it had leveled off. I still didn't understand why they needed us.

While they were talking, I cruised through their historic numbers and projections. It all seemed straightforward until I noticed a

$10 million increase in costs the last quarter that didn't quite fit with the other quarters.

"What happened last quarter?"

"With our revenues?" Dominic asked.

"No, with costs. There seems to be $10 million in additional costs last quarter."

"Oh, that was our chip screwup."

"Your what?"

"Well, we make custom chips. We embed our software into silicon so we can operate at high speeds and also to make our products unique and defensible. LSI Logic makes our parts—or they did. There was a screwup, and I'd rather not say whose fault it was—except to say it wasn't ours."

"Ten million dollars' worth?"

"Yeah, we had to have them throw wafer starts at the problem to get enough chips to keep our shipments flat while we design our next chip. You can see our sales go flat too," Dominic explained.

If Alteon was a public company, their stock would have gotten whacked, down to a point where we might have stepped up and bought it in size.

"So that's why you need to raise $10–15 million more?"

"That's it."

"And the problem is behind you?"

"Seems to be. We've already gotten the next iteration of our chips back and they work, so we should start scaling again next quarter."

Alteon had great investors, but nobody was willing to step up to fund the company. They needed an outsider to come in to validate their thinking, even if the outsider was a nobody like us. Plus, they had it right: a monster market, a competitive advantage by having their intelligence embedded in silicon and a business model that should work. They charged $5,000 for what looked like a couple hundred bucks of chips and plastic.

I looked at Fred, who gave an almost imperceptible nod with his head. We were thinking the same thing. We were in on this deal.

## > > > *It Works Again!*

PALO ALTO, CALIFORNIA—MID-1998

Holy shit! I can't even believe it. General Magic stock, the one we had been buying for $1 and $1.50 when they had $2.50 per share in the bank, has started running. They launched a trial of their voice recognition system, and investors were intrigued. The stock went from $2 to $3. But this is unbelievable—the unexpected happened. Microsoft, a company worth almost 10,000 times more than General Magic, stepped up and licensed their voice technology—and invested in the company. The stock just this minute doubled to $6.

Fred was on the road, but I got him on the phone and we agreed to start selling, a little at a time, but start selling. We really hadn't sold anything. Our portfolio was more of a Roach Motel—stocks came in and never left. This was exciting.

We had visited the company half a dozen times and could never get comfortable with the management team or how they were going to make money on this voice service. When you are buying $2.50 in cash for $1.25, you don't worry about these things. But now the stock was valued at two or three times the cash. So, sell we did—at $6, then at $7, then at $11, and we even got some off at close to $14. You can't sell a million shares overnight—a valuable lesson—but over several months, we eased out of General Magic until it was a distant memory.

Other things were working too. Real Networks was now public—selling for $30 versus the $6 we paid for it. And then there was Inktomi—god bless Inktomi.

Inktomi ran a cluster of servers that provided a search service for the people on the Web. They were a wholesaler in that they didn't run a search service themselves, they ran it for others. The only real customer they had was HotWired.com, not really awe-inspiring. Inktomi also sold caching systems. When you pulled up a Web page with, say, CNN's logo, a cache might store frequently requested items close to users. You didn't have to go all the way to a Web server in Atlanta to get the CNN logo, it might be in memory at your Internet provider. Inktomi caches sped up Web surfing and made it cheaper for Internet providers to run their service since they might use less telecom bandwidth.

Goldman Sachs was teed up to take Inktomi public but was worried that there was no name-search company using their service, let alone any interesting customers for their cache software. So Goldman told Inktomi to come back when they had some real customers, and the company ended up doing a private investment round. We took a look. It was very interesting except for that little "no real customer" thing. But Fred's nose twitched, and he said it felt a little like Cisco did way back when and, what the heck, maybe we should do it. We made tons of due diligence calls, and everything was great except they had no real customers—but we already knew that.

So in February we invested. In March, Yahoo signed up for their search service, giving Inktomi a percentage of the ad dollars they generated per search results page served. Ka-ching. In April, America Online started buying Inktomi cache software. Goldman came back, and by June, Inktomi was a public company—priced at $18 and ending its first day at $36. We had paid $6.

We still didn't have much capital—barely $45 million. But since we'd started less than two years earlier, we were up over 60%.

It's working again. Like I said—holy shit!

## >>> ***Heartbreak Hotel***

PALO ALTO, CALIFORNIA—SUMMER 1998

"How's my money?" It was Frank Bonsal, making his monthly call to harass us.

Frank was one of the trio that bolted from investment banking firm Alex Brown and started the venture capital firm New Enterprise Associates. He and Art Marks worked out of a townhouse in Baltimore with Dick Kramlich out in Silicon Valley. It didn't seem like Frank did much with NEA anymore, just cruised around putting his own money to work.

"Hey, Frank, how you doing?" I loved talking to Frank Bonsal. The guy was a living legend. It was said that Bonsal could throw his hat in the middle of a room and people would empty their pockets and throw all the money they had into the hat, such a great moneymaker he was. I just enjoyed his aw-shucks good old boy style that masked a brilliant man.

Plus, he was the reason Fred and I were together. When Fred was running tech portfolios at JP Morgan and I was a sell-side analyst, he was one of my favorite clients. In fact, Fred was everybody's favorite client. In the early '90s, Fred and I met and discussed the idea of running money together—until we realized how much we didn't know. I was restless in 1995 and had called Frank Bonsal to ask for advice about what I might do next. He said he had another guy calling him, also asking him what he should do next and that the two of us were complementary and ought to meet. Some guy named Fred Kittler.

"I'm OK, but what the *hail* have you boys been up to, don't see too much good coming from you folks."

"Frank, the markets have been a little rough, but we just keep loading up on the names we have conviction in."

"That's it, boy."

"We look at a lot of private deals, but there is so much garbage, we are pretty picky."

"Well, I like some of the stuff you all are doing. Real and Inktomi are hot and I hear that Tut is a home run."

"We're pretty happy, but it's getting crowded out here. Lots of money is flowing into the Valley."

"Don't I know it. Just stick to your guns. Find those things that are growing like a weed. It ain't easy, but when you find it, you can't miss." Frank Bonsal knew what he was talking about. He'd been involved in home run after home run, always seeming to be early in companies that had big, almost never-ending growth cycles. "Not this horse crap of a quick flash in the pan. Find those big-ass trends you can ride like a bull rider."

"We like growth."

"Now, Andy, I don't mean just growth. I mean the stuff that you just plant the seed and it grows like a sum-bitch. You know what I'm talkin' about?"

"I think so."

"Look, you guys are doin' a great job. I like your style. You guys think a little different, a little ahead of the rest of the clowns out there. You'll find what you're lookin' for."

"We turn over a lot of rocks."

"Thatta boy. Listen, you like that multimedia stuff, right?"

"I guess."

"Good. Now, listen. A friend of mine in LA has got this interesting little company in the music business. It's hard to describe. You've got to see it for yourself." I thought I heard a little snicker—it was hard to tell when Frank turned serious.

"What's the name of the company?"

"Shotz or Snotz or Shnotz, something like that. I'll have the CEO call you. He's out there now in the Bay Area."

"Happy to see him for you, Frank."

"Nah, this is for you. Call me when you're done. See ya."

• • •

I made plans to meet with Danny, the CEO of Hotz, at the San Francisco Airport Marriott the next morning. I learned over time that when Frank said jump, you jumped. Plus I was open to see anything interesting, especially in the music business. Real Networks had a huge business shipping software for PCs that allowed music to be streamed over the Internet. Even search company Inktomi was cashing in; their top searches were people looking for songs and artists. There were a lot of oddball ways to invest, I thought to myself as I rode the elevator at the Marriott.

I knocked on the door of room 1211. When I saw the person who answered the door, I immediately checked my itinerary to make sure I was in the right place.

"Room 1211?"

"Yup."

"You Danny?"

"Yup."

"OK, I'm in the right place."

It turns out that Danny was the ultimate "oddball way to invest." He was wearing a black leather jacket with tassles dangling from it. He filled all of the jacket and then some—it appeared that he liked to eat a few too many Cheez Doodles. His black leather pants were obscenely tight, so I had to divert my eyes, and I ended up staring a little too long at the snakeskin boots he had on.

I followed Danny as he waddled into his room.

"So, Frank Bonsal tells me you have some hot music technology."

"Yup, let me 'splain."

Danny started talking, and I had a hard time holding back one of those nasty belly laughs. His round face was framed by flowing puffs of kinky black hair, sticking out in all directions. He had on a white puffy shirt, with a wide collar sticking out over his leather jacket. The top several buttons were undone, but I couldn't look long enough to count since his chest hairs were intermingled with four or five necklaces dangling from his neck. I had to check, and sure enough, Danny was sporting not one but two pinky rings.

"You all know that music is nuttin' more than a bunch of bundled harmonics." Danny's voice was a deep baritone, almost booming, and filled the room.

And then it hit me: Frank Bonsal had set me up with a fucking Elvis impersonator CEO. And a dorky one at that.

"Everybudy enjoys music, but not so many kin play. It's tough to git the pitch and tempo right, let alone figur' out a piano keyboard. So we help 'em along."

"What do you mean?"

"Well, we break down music to its harmonic fundamentals and figure out a baseline Tact. Then you just play along on your PC keyboard, and we make sure it stays along on the pitch 'n' tempo of the Tact. Tough to do, but it sounds real good. Lemme show ya."

He proceeded to click on a few spots on his laptop screen. Music came out of the speakers; I think it was Cindy Lauper, although I am embarrassed to admit it.

"So you jist play along." Danny put his hands on the laptop keyboard as if he were sitting down at a baby grand piano and then started to "play." Computer-synthesized music came out of the speakers, on top of the Cindy Lauper song. He was playing right along.

But then he started singing, "Girls just want to have fu-u-un."

He stopped playing and, thankfully, stopped singing. "OK, now watch this. It don' matter how I play." He started banging the keyboard like a child, just smacking the keys randomly. The music coming out of the speakers still played along with the song.

"Lemme do sumptin harder." He clicked a couple of times, and the song "Achy Breaky Heart" started up. "Yup, Billy Ray Cyrus, uh-huh!"

He banged away at his laptop and started in again. He threw his head back and closed his eyes and belted out, "Don't tell my heart, my achy breaky heart . . ."

"OK, I think I get it."

"Thank you, thank you very much." Ah, finally, the signature Elvis impersonator lounge act line. "Now you try."

"That's OK, just walk me through the hardware and financials and I can—"

"No, you gotta give it a whirl. Pick a song."

"You got 'In-A-Gadda-Da-Vida' by Iron Butterfly?" I was hoping he wouldn't.

"Sure, jist a second. Here ya go."

I banged the keyboard a bit, and it sounded great. All of a sudden I was happy I had blown off those piano lessons as a kid and never practiced. I resisted the urge to belt out the chorus. I banged away, a rock star at 10:30 in the morning in an airport hotel room with Elvis's ghost. I couldn't tell if I was a sucker in a big, bad practical joke or being tested by Frank Bonsal on my ability to make venture investments. Maybe he was just trying to tell me that sometimes the stupidest ideas are worth listening to.

"OK, tell me about the hardware." It was time to wrap this nonsense up.

"Well, we made our own chip to both create Tacts as well as harmonize the keyboard tempos." Danny's Elvis accent disappeared as he talked about the hardware. I didn't dare interrupt him, lest he break out in song.

"Here is a photo of our chip, pretty small, doesn't cost us more than $5 in volume. TSMC in Taiwan makes it for us. Over here is the harmonizer, the pitch control, tempo stabilizer. Here is a DSP to do Fourier transforms. There's not much else to it."

"What is that section at the bottom corner, labeled 780?"

"Oh, that. Well, I grew up programming DEC machines, so when I needed something to control the whole process, I just sat down and threw in a VAX."

"An entire VAX?"

"Sure, it's no big deal, just a little 1 MIPS VAX 11/780."

"You're kidding. I bought one of those 15 plus years ago for close to a million bucks."

"Yeah, it's pretty amazing. It fit right there in the corner, cost me about an extra 25 cents in chip cost, well worth it. Every chip has some 1 MIPS controller on it these days. It was just easier for me to stick in a VAX than to buy someone else's."

I suppose I shouldn't have been shocked by all this. No, not the Elvis stuff, the fact that a VAX now cost 25 cents. I politely asked a few more questions about finances and his business model.

He hadn't gotten that far into it when he started asking me for advice. I told him that he was really onto something and should allow kids to download his "Tacts" for a couple of bucks just to get out of taking piano lessons and he could have a hit on his hands. I told him that I was 100% sure that Frank Bonsal was very interested in investing, he told me himself, and that there probably wasn't room for our fund because Frank Bonsal really, really wants to do the whole round himself, and I would just call Frank every day until he does invest, and with that I ran out of room 1211.

To this day, I'm still not sure whether Frank Bonsal was serious about this guy or he was just pulling my leg, really hard. I may have gotten Punk'd. But I learned something—I think. Thank you very muuuuch.

## > > > Homeless in Palo Alto

"This market is killing us," I complained to Fred. "We were on a roll, and now all those gains are evaporating."

Just like that, poof, our early success started unraveling. Again. Turns out the Asian currency problems that hit in the fall of 1997 never really went away. That slide of a rickety old roller coaster I showed at the Institute for Private Investors meeting was right in more ways than one.

"You just have to slog through these things. What matters is what you own coming out of these times, not what you own going in."

"I never had time to enjoy it when it worked," I said. "We've been down every goddamn day."

"Yup. It's that currency stuff in Asia again. Nothing we can do about it."

"Up in the morning, down in the afternoon," I noted.

"Don't worry about it."

"I think it's that homeless woman on the bench outside."

"What?" Fred asked.

"I swear, every morning that she's there, we have a down day," I said.

"C'mon."

"Really, check it out. She's like some demon. She's taken possession of our fund."

"Stranger things have happened," Fred said.

"She's got those bags filled with god knows what. Research from Merrill Lynch?"

"Probably." Fred was tuning me out.

"Perhaps we can take her to that Soylent Green factory I heard about in Burlingame," I suggested.

"That's heartless," Fred shot back.

"Shit, I'll do anything to get this thing working." I sulked.

"Only one thing works. Go back to finding some new names," Fred scolded me.

I was trying. Our office in Palo Alto is above an art supplies store. It is basically a dump, a one-room, 600-square-foot space with some cheap desks, blue Cat 5 cable running around for our Ethernet network and a fax machine that never stopped humming out research notes. You can see why we don't spend much time there. Every day at 10:30 in the morning, a putrid smell of burnt toast and kitty litter wafts in from an Italian restaurant next door. Suffice it to say, we never eat there.

And we consider ourselves lucky to have the place. Office space in Palo Alto is crazy. Rents are higher than on Park Avenue in New York City. It's ridiculous. We tried to find better space, but the market was tighter than the lid of a Mott's Apple Sauce jar. So we tough it out.

It's just the two of us. We had a secretary early on, but we had to let her go. She was too much work. It wasn't an ordinary business, so we couldn't just say, "File these correspondences." We didn't quite know what we were doing, so it was hard to have someone help you learn on the fly. We set up our own meetings, sent out our own quarterly letters to investors, got our own coffee and took out our own garbage. Voice mail and e-mail and mail merges are just easier to manage than people.

It was just me and Fred—Fred and me. The economics were 50-50. Everything was by consensus, which meant that we each had the power of veto. I was his boss and he was mine, and I told Fred that I have a history of hating my bosses. We signed each other's checks—when we had enough money after expenses to pay ourselves, that is. It took a while. We didn't take a salary for the first two years. Pretty scary.

Embarrassed by our dumpy office, we try to hold all of our meetings at coffee shops in town—Café Verona, where the name for the programming language Java came from, is just down the block. It's our conference room. We met with a company there yesterday—passing the bag lady sitting on a bench at the bus stop in front of our building.

Palo Alto is a strange town. Not much is over two stories tall, so it feels like a middle-American town: drugstore, stationery store, Chinese restaurant. Except there are subtle clues that something is different. Stanford University is next door. Sand Hill Road, home to almost every venture capital firm, is a few miles away. A typical walk down the block finds a beat-up old Volkswagen Beetle parked behind a brand-new Ferrari F355. Next to a frozen yogurt store is a bike shop with selections that start at $1,299. There is money infused in the sinews of Palo Alto, although the place is by no means glitzy.

Some prospective investors insist on seeing our space, and we begrudgingly have them come on up. The response is typical, a bout of laughter followed by the comment "You know, I really like that you guys are keeping expenses down and focusing on investing." Then, strangely, they come into the fund, in a small way anyway. Maybe we are an experiment, like we're some backwoods investors. Hey, whatever works.

"Fred, a few more downsticks and we're working for free," I warned.

"What do you mean?"

"Remember that high-watermark language we put in our fund agreement?"

"Sort of?"

"Well, we get 20% of the upside. But if we go down, we have to get back to the original amount before we can charge our 20% again."

"So?"

"So, if we go down 50%, we have to go up 100% to get over the high watermark before we get paid another penny."

"Well, let's not go down 50%."

Like it was that simple.

I just wish that bag lady would spread her bad mojo somewhere else—we're getting killed here.

# >>> Sharp Tooth

What is with these Asians? Twice now, they have whacked our fund. Just as things started rolling, some currency gyration would give risk a bad name and we'd be back to breakeven. This was starting to annoy me.

Long ago, I figured out that I would never invest in Asia. Once a year, I used to travel to the Far East as an analyst for Morgan Stanley. Like William Kaye in Hong Kong, I don't think the Asians ever made any money. I always figured that was their problem, but the world is interconnected, like dominoes, so in reality, it was my problem too.

OSAKA, JAPAN—DECEMBER 1991

I almost missed out on the most startling revelation of the secret to the Japanese supposed success. Across a small conference room in Osaka sat an overweight, middle-aged Japanese man, with a thinning mop of jet black hair. But his most distinguishing feature was one of his front teeth. It pointed straight at me, like a loaded gun. It was perfectly perpendicular to his face and jutted out from his gums instead of hanging down. And like Mona Lisa, it always stared directly at me. I snuck looks at it while sipping green tea, and all I could think about was how was he going to drink from his teacup without drooling it all over his shirt. I couldn't pay attention to much else but his bayonet tooth, but luckily some of his words stuck. He spoke with a huge smile, and without realizing it, explained why Japan was doomed.

• • •

Traveling at 250 miles per hour on the bullet train from Tokyo to Osaka, I wasn't sure whether to be scared shitless or impressed by Japanese efficiency. Instead I struck up a conversation with my colleague, Takatoshi Yamamoto. We had met at the main Japanese train station on a brisk evening in December 1991. I was always in Japan around Pearl Harbor Day, maybe because most Americans avoid it.

Like everyone else scurrying around the station, we loaded up on supplies. He bought what looked like a comic book to read and suggested we buy some food. He picked out two bento boxes from a vendor at Track 5 and then headed to a vending machine and asked if I wanted a can of Pocari Sweat (which turned out to be something like Gatorade). I wasn't drinking anyone's sweat, so I politely declined and scanned what else I could have. I settled for coffee in a can.

We were headed to Osaka to visit Sharp Electronics, and I was just trying to figure out how Japan works. Yamamoto-san was the electronics analyst for Morgan Stanley Tokyo, which made him the mirror image of me. We got along well. He set up several days of meetings for me with chip companies, consumer electronics companies and even Nintendo.

"So, tell me about Sharp," I said.

"Sharp is one of my favorite stocks. They are a big player in memories and also in liquid crystal displays. I set up meetings with the president of both of these divisions."

"Great, I look forward to meeting them." There was a glut of memory chips on the market, and everyone was bleeding red ink. I couldn't believe that anyone was making money at it, in Japan, Korea or the U.S.

Just the day before, we had gone to Toshiba in Tokyo and met the tall, handsome, gray-haired president of their memory division. I knew that both Texas Instruments and Micron were getting killed selling memory chips, and wondering how Toshiba was doing, I asked. A stern look crossed the president's face as he shot a why-did-you-bring-this-American-fool-into-my-presence look to Yamamoto-san.

"Mr. Kessler, you must understand that we are big players in memory, and we must meet our commitment to MITI [Ministry of

Industry and Technology] for production. It is in all of our long-term interests to sell memories." Yamamoto-san was nodding.

"Mr. Kessler," the man from Toshiba continued, "you must appreciate the power of the Japanese." The word "power" was thrust at me, almost spit as "p-HOW-er." Yamamoto-san smiled and mentioned there weren't any markets in which Japanese couldn't outdo American manufacturers. I got the point. But Japanese or not, this guy was also losing money hand over fist selling memory chips.

I was fascinated by LCDs, which Toshiba also made, but I didn't get to ask anyone about them, so I was looking forward to the meetings at Sharp.

Laptop sales were booming, and someday, computer monitors would be replaced by LCDs, once they got cheap enough. I had done some homework on how LCDs were made. Basically, you take giant pieces of glass, a couple of feet on a side, and then use the same techniques as in chip making: print and deposit the transistors to turn on and off pixels right on the glass. A light behind red-, green- and blue-tinted glass is either blocked or allowed through for each of the million pixels. But dust was a killer. With chips made on six-inch-diameter wafers, 80% or 90% of the chips worked, a very high yield as they say in the industry. Dust or other defects kill the others. With LCDs, dust could kill every display on the giant piece of glass. Yields were more like 5–10%. Tough to make money, which is why no American manufacturers even tried. Shareholders hate money-losing businesses.

The coffee in a can tasted like a used kitchen sponge, and I began jonesing for Yamamoto's can of Sweat. I learned that Sharp was originally a maker of mechanical pencils, hence the name. They ventured into other markets like TVs and VCRs just as those markets were booming in the U.S., Europe and Japan. Now they make everything from laptops to camcorders to cordless phones.

As the train pulled into Osaka, I got a sense of a city of farms and railroad lines interspersed with giant modern factories. It looked like a drab version of Atlanta.

Lots of sushi and Asahi Super Drys helped launch me into a fitful sleep.

In the morning, we took a taxi over to Sharp headquarters. The white-gloved taxi driver spoke fluent English. "You American? I get lots of Americans, I take them all over Osaka. Here are some of my American friends." He handed me a stack of business cards. I politely shuffled through them and noted with amazement that I knew a few names, including Scott Cook, the CEO of Intuit, who I had met with a few weeks earlier. Small world.

We entered the lobby, which was filled with visitors. I was handed a five-page application to fill out to enter the building, which required that I promise not to steal any of their secrets. I noted with suspicion that Yamamoto-san had a 3 × 5 card to fill out.

We walked for what seemed like half a mile to a conference room, passing giant rooms filled with huge tables and people sitting around them, yapping away to one another or on phones. The rooms were like Wall Street trading floors, but without screens.

"This is all marketing," I was told by our guide. I noted maybe one personal computer off to the side in these giant rooms.

We got to the end of the hike and entered a small conference room. They all look the same with furniture from the 1960s: a green couch on one side, two chairs on the other side and another facing the center. I sat in one of the chairs and got a quick "Tsk, tsk" from Yamamoto-san.

"Sorry, Japanese custom, you must sit with your back to the window, and the hosts will face you."

In walked two gentlemen. We shook hands and exchanged cards. I got good at the two-handed grab the card and stare at it a while with interest, which always pleased. But I passed on the bowing. One gentleman ran the memory chip division and the other the LCD division.

We started with memories, and it was clear after a few minutes of listening that they were losing tons of money, probably $100 million a year. But I already knew that. We moved on to LCDs, and that's when I almost stopped listening. Years and several children of mine later, I would sit through multiple screenings of the animation *The Land Before Time*. The baby *Tyrannosaurus rex* is named Sharp Tooth, and it would always make me chuckle.

In Osaka, my Sharp Tooth was one of the smartest, most articulate Japanese managers I had ever met. He walked me through their production plans, screens per glass substrate, costs, market prices, overhead, yields, fully loaded depreciation and anything else I asked for. It took me a while, but I figured out that he was dropping between $1.5 and $2 billion a year in operating losses.

Still shaken from the "p-HOW-er" meeting the day before at Toshiba, I was very nervous about how I asked questions. Plus, it was hard to look up from my paper. I chose my words carefully.

"So, this product line is in investment mode?" I asked.

"Yes, I see what you are asking. Of course it is in very big investment mode, but so too is it in investment mode for everybody else. No one is in profit-return mode, if you understand my choice of words."

I think he just admitted that he is losing lots of money as are all of his competitors.

"Either we do this important market, or it will be in Korea or worse, in Taiwan. It is our imperative to invest, as you say, in LCDs."

"And a billion-dollar annual investment is what it takes?" I asked.

"Well, Mr. Kessler, probably more like two."

"But isn't some return expected, from, you know, from the stock market?"

"That's not of issue. Someone else can figure that out. We as a corporation and a nation have priorities." He gave me a smile that I will not forget, for a lot of reasons.

Yamamoto-san and I were then escorted to a large but austere office and introduced to Haruo Tsuji, the president of Sharp.

"What do you think of my company?" Mr. Tsuji asked.

"It it's quite impressive," I stammered out. I thought I was going to be asking the questions. "You are clearly a leader in LCDs."

"Yes, this is our most important product strategy. Every American will soon carry a notebook computer with one of our color displays."

"It is an expensive strategy, yes?"

"Of course. But we have the resources and financial strategy to dominate."

"Can you elaborate?"

He must not have heard me. "Thank you for coming," he said as he handed me a small wrapped gift.

"A financial strategy?" I thought. "Aren't you supposed to just make money and eventually show a profit?"

We next got a tour of the company museum next to the lobby. On display were the first mechanical pencil, some old TVs and giant VCRs from the late '70s, and some new projection TVs. At the end of the tour, they had a 17-inch LCD TV playing video of some Japanese golfers and, I think, a Pocari Sweat commercial. It looked pretty good. I had never seen video on an LCD, but something was wrong. It was too slow between frames. It's hard to describe, but my eyes started to hurt because some of the previous images were still there as the video played—the golfer's club was still in midair as the ball was hit. Very weird.

Three women with clipboards accosted me as I was leaving.

"What do you think?"

"Very nice," I replied. "It's a beautiful museum."

"You like the TV?"

"Yes, the TVs were great. I think I have a Sharp TV at home," I lied as I tried to get away.

"And what about the last one?"

"The last what?"

"The last TV, that one." One woman pointed to the LCD TV.

"Very nice," I said.

They all scribbled something on their clipboards.

"You like?"

"Yes."

"No, no. What you like?"

"I liked the commercial."

"Good TV?"

I figured I would never get out of there at this pace. "Well, if you really want to know, the screen is a little small. I have a 27-inch TV at home."

I heard a few "tsk, tsk's" and more clipboard scribbling.

"And," I continued, "it's a little slow between frames, bad hysteresis, I think." I forgot what *hysteresis* meant, something from college physics about lags in fields. It sounded good, and I figured that would throw them for a while to get me out of there.

I got to the lobby, and we waited for a taxi back to the train station. I picked up an English version of Sharp Electronics' annual report and noted that the company was making money and had made increasing amounts of money for the last 10 years.

Our next stop was Nintendo. This meant a bullet train to god knows where and then a couple of slower trains to Kyoto.

Nintendo was in a white nondescript one-story building next to some railroad tracks. It could have easily been a warehouse on the South Side of Chicago. Management rarely met with investors, but we were able to meet with a few hardware designers in a conference room near the lobby.

Nintendo was fascinating. It was the most valuable company in Japan, maybe even the world. Why? Because it was the most profitable company in the world. They were selling tens of millions of Super NES platforms, which at $99 was probably at a loss. But they sold hundreds of millions of game cartridges at $40, which cost them $6. Nice business if you can get it, and they had twitchy fingers around the globe addicted. It struck me that this was the first Japanese company I had spoken to that actually sold software; the rest were just manufacturers with huge factories.

The hardware designers gave me a 12-page document with a big red symbol with Japanese kanji characters inside it stamped on the front page. I skimmed through it; it looked like the design and specifications of their next game platform. I got excited. Maybe this was some giant scoop, and I could go back to investors in the U.S. and point to some part or another in the next Nintendo game machine.

In the taxi back to the train station, I asked Yamamoto-san, "So, what does this mean?"

"The meeting?"

"No, this red symbol and Japanese words inside of it."

"Oh, that means 'top secret, do not distribute outside the company.' "

"Really. Wow. Can you help me translate the rest of the document?"

"I could, but it's not worth the bother."

"Why not? This is hot stuff," I screamed, barely able to bottle up my excitement.

"Kessler-san, do you really think they would just hand you secret documents? They have been trying to figure out for the last 18 months what their next platform will be and have been bouncing ideas off everybody. They just want feedback."

"Why give it to me?" I asked.

"Because maybe you can get it in the press in the U.S. and competitors will pick it apart, and then Nintendo learns valuable things. I would just throw it out if I were you. Not everything is what it seems in Japan."

I was learning that more each day.

We finally headed back to Tokyo and my flight to New York from Narita. I scanned the headlines of the only English-language paper I could get my hands on. One article that caught my eye, but just barely, was about the Japanese Fair Trade Commission, whatever the hell that was, signing a consent decree with Nomura Securities, Daiwa, Nikko and Yamaichi, who promised never to compensate their clients for stock market losses again.

"Again?" I thought. "Protection against stock market losses? Who gets that? What's this all about?"

The JFTC reminded these firms, the article continued, that if they were caught committing similar offenses again, it would lead to criminal charges.

I asked Yamamoto-san, who had once worked for Nomura Securities, what this was all about. He shrugged. The Nikkei had peaked at 40,000 a year before and was now 23,000. He said most people figured it was a wrist slap—a little housecleaning is good—and the Nikkei would be back.

A few years later, with the Nikkei at 15,000 and dropping, Yamamoto-san came to the Morgan Stanley offices in New York. He looked like he had been through a monsoon.

"You OK?"

"Things very tough."

"What do you mean?"

"Lots of money disappear. You remember our visit to Sharp?"

Who could forget? There were already a few sequels to the *Land Before Time* animation.

"Yeah, sure. How are they doing?" I asked.

"Big problems. They had $2 billion, about a third of their cash at a nonbank bank."

"A what?"

"Nonbank bank. It's really just an investment fund. They were speculating with Sharp's cash, in the stock market and in real estate. They used lots of debt."

"Go on."

"Well, with Nikkei down and real estate down, the nonbank bank failed. That $2 billion is gone."

It hit me right then and there. This is what Sharp Tooth was telling me, but I didn't know what he was saying. It seemed to me that not only did Sharp lose $2 billion, but they lost all their earnings. Nomura potentially rigging the Nikkei by paying clients back for losses meant every company could count on a rising stock market. Speculating was a one-way street, and paper profits could be washed through their income statement as earnings. No wonder Sharp was profitable.

LCDs were losing money, but the company was profitable because they were showing speculative stock market and real estate gains as if they were the company's profits from operations. But the profits were bogus, a sleight of hand. Sharp didn't make money at all. Ouch. If that's true, the entire Japanese electronics business was, well, a profitless pit. Turns out it was worse than that.

## > > > *The Yen-Scary Trade*

NEW YORK CITY—OCTOBER 1998

It takes what seems like 20 escalators to get to the ballroom and meeting rooms at the Grand Hyatt on 42nd Street—Goldman Sachs holds their annual Communicopia Conference here every year—an almost forced synergy of technology, media and telecom companies. It was a little awkward for me—I used to compete against these guys in my days at Morgan Stanley. But I had gotten sick of going to tech conferences only in San Francisco, so I decided to make the trip and get a little East Coast sensibility. I was in for a shock.

As I entered the waiting area outside the ballrooms a little after eight in the morning, I was met with a loud roar. There was a packed crowd around the Bloomberg terminals and lots of yelling and shouting and another set of people on the outside of the scrum, screaming into their cell phones. Michael Dell's keynote address at the conference could wait. This looked a lot more interesting.

I strolled over to the commotion. Some guy leaned over and said to me, "Serves them right."

"What's going on?" I asked.

"Oh, you haven't heard? The yen-carry just barfed," he told me.

I just nodded my head.

"The BOJ and the Fed just fucked Tiger," he added.

"Cool."

"Serves them right, man. It was too easy."

I looked around for Nick Moore to explain the "yen-scary trade," but I doubted he'd made the trip. This wasn't the first time I had walked into a room of investors and had no clue what was going on. But I was a quick student.

"Tiger's got to unwind $10 billion," another person told me as I strolled through the chaos.

"Jeez," I said.

"That yen-carry trade was for suckers anyway—it was always going to blow up someday," I overheard.

"Pretty obvious. Rates in Japan are what, 50 basis points? Five basis points? They're giving money away over there, begging people to borrow. So Julian Robertson took the bait," someone volunteered.

OK, it was starting to make sense. Julian Robertson runs Tiger Management, a hedge fund with something like $20 billion in assets. He was buddies with Barton Biggs at Morgan Stanley, so I had met him a few times. I even sat next to him at a black tie event for Bob Dole, where he flirted with a young analyst from London sitting on the other side of him and didn't say boo to me.

"Uh-huh," I said.

"Tiger borrowed yen up the wazoo at these cheap interest rates and just put it into U.S. Treasuries paying, what 6%, 8%, whatever," my new international currency expert friend continued.

"But doesn't the yen go up?" I asked.

"Sure, but as long as it goes up less than 6%, the yen-carry trade is free money. See, if the yen goes down, you have less to pay back. The only real risk is if the yen goes up by more than 6 or 8%, then you've got a broken arb."

"Is that what happened?" I asked.

"Yeah. Remember, the dollar has been going up versus the yen for the last three something years. With all the screwy stuff going on with Soros in Russia and Long Term Capital and god knows what they've been doing, the dollar has been getting hit."

Ah, Tie-guh and Sew-Rose getting beat up. The Texan from the Institute of Pry-Vat Investors meeting in Providence must be getting killed.

"I think the BOJ said enough is enough to the yen slide. It's up 8% just last night. Here, read this quote from Japan's finance minister: 'With regard to foreign exchange, we are of the view that the excessively undervalued yen will do no good, not only to the Japanese economy but to the world economy as a whole.' Shit, that's all it takes," he told me.

It was, what, six weeks since Russia went under. George Soros, who had already broken the Bank of England back in 1992, had been making noise in Russia. He started mouthing off on August 13, when everybody was on vacation. He was long and wrong on Russian debt and began calling for the devaluation of the ruble. It seemed to many to be a calculated gamble to get the International Monetary Fund to step in, pour money into Russia and bail out foreign investors like Soros. Robert Rubin, Clinton's treasury secretary, had done it before in Mexico back in 1995 with Brady bonds. Surely Russia was as important.

Apparently not. On August 17, Russia defaulted on its sovereign debt. Oops. Ten days later, Soros claimed to have dropped $2 billion. The dominoes kept falling.

"Ouch. But why do they care?" I wanted to know.

"Because they're trying to reflate Japan. If they lend billions to some hedge fund, it's money that's not going into the stumbling Japanese economy."

"Oh."

"Tiger has been living off this trade. It's probably 120% of their performance over the last few years. The rest of their investments suck donkey pucks."

I'm not sure what a donkey puck is, but I didn't know this guy until two minutes ago, so I let it slide.

"I heard he's got $10 billion to unwind," someone leaned into our conversation and stated.

"Really, good luck reversing that," my friend responded. "I'll bet the dollar gets hit big time. I wonder who else has this trade on. You don't want to be in the way of this freight train." And then he walked off.

I went to a bunch of interesting presentations that day. Almost everybody talked about building out broadband networks to deliver their programming or to sell stuff. This validated Fred's and my view that a huge spending cycle was taking place; I was just hoping for more details. But listening to Michael Eisner, the Disney CEO, explain his Internet plans was a lot like listening to me explaining my own plans to produce a blockbuster film: nice concept, short on details.

But the crowds were gone, the rooms mostly empty. Every time I went out into the hall I'd see folks from Goldman Sachs shaking their heads and talking in hushed tones.

I heard one of them say, "Shit, every goddamn hedge fund in New York had that yen-carry trade on. So much for doing any more trades with those guys for the rest of the year." Yeah, poor Goldman Sachs.

But I was confused. Here we were scrambling around looking under rocks for great long-term investments, and every other hedge fund, or so it seemed, was doing some funny hedge of cheap yen money and T-bills. That's investing?

The dollar quickly fell to 25-year lows against the yen as all these hedge funds unwound, selling dollars to buy yen to pay back their yen-carry loans. It was ugly out there. Some say Tiger lost close to $3 billion reversing their yen-carry trade.

## > > > I Want Out

PALO ALTO, CALIFORNIA—OCTOBER 1998

Despite all the scratching and clawing and begging over the last year and a half, we had a measly $43 million in capital at this point. But we were still feeling our way toward finding decent investments. It wasn't easy. We had found our groove during the year, or so we thought, until a loose White House intern and so-called geniuses running monster-size hedge funds back east made the waters treacherous. We had been up 80% for the year at one point last month, but with the market in panic mode, we were now breakeven for the year and sinking like a rock.

The dominoes landed with a thud in Greenwich, Connecticut. Soros, then Tiger, then the Nobel laureates at Long Term Capital went down ugly. The 100-year flood hit, and the hedge fund business was reeling. If you remember, Long Term Capital was a bunch of very bright guys, even a few Nobel Prize winners, who modeled everything and convinced themselves that they could find investments with guaranteed returns—sure things. So convinced of their perfection that they used their $2 billion in capital to borrow $125 billion in various securities. Then they added leverage to their leverage and controlled $1.2 trillion in various derivatives, each supposed to return tiny amounts. Those tiny amounts would look good as a return on their $2.2 billion. The joke was on them. When the dollar unexpectedly dropped, they were hosed.

Their stupidity messed up my world too. Maybe it was the best thing that happened to us. For one thing, we got that block of stock from the sweating guy at Ssangyong. Maybe that would turn into something interesting. That meeting was eye-opening. If the Koreans are dumping shares to pay back loans, who else is puking things up? Is this another time to be out there with a catcher's mitt?

In the middle of all this craziness, the phone rang.

"I want out." It was our most annoying investor—let me call him James Duck. He'd been in since day one, and we couldn't toss him out, although I often wanted to. He called every time the market dipped to complain about our performance, our methods and that the world was going to hell in a hedge basket.

I put my hand over the phone and yelled over to Fred. "Fred, it's James Duck. He wants out again. You deal with him, he's your friend."

"I can't talk to him again, you gotta talk to him."

"Start buying. When this guy always calls to redeem, it must be at bottom."

"What do you mean you want out?" I said to James Duck.

"This market makes me nervous. Something is wrong."

"It sounds to us like Long Term Capital was a bunch of over-educated dopes who used too much leverage."

"Yeah, but this market scares me."

"There's a flight to quality. Look at treasuries, that's where everyone is parking their capital." I tried to sound calming. It wasn't working.

"You guys, and my money, are going to get killed."

"We already have. It's not real. It's just the Street taking bids down."

"But you're going down."

"Maybe, but we've already lost all of this year's gains. We were up 80% through September, and now we're flat for the year. But if you look at trading volumes, there is not much there. Someone is selling, there are no buyers—so the Street is just moving their bid lower and lower, trying to steal the shares. It's not real selling. Risk just has a bad name for now."

"Get me out."

"I'd love to, but we do have a 30-day notice rule, and you'll have to wait until the end of the month, so you can't get out today anyway."

"I'll fax you a redemption request."

"Why don't you wait until the end of the month, because you'll have to wait until the end of next month to get out. Maybe we'll see a rally before then."

"So, there is no way that I can get out today?"

"Nope. We put in the 30-day notice to protect all the limited partners from these types of situations—excessive costs of rapid-fire selling—to handle redemptions. We're not a mutual fund. Plus, I think this Long Term Capital thing is almost over."

"You better be right. I hate losing money."

"Me too, but it's part of the game."

Luckily, it did blow over. Tiger got bailed out of the yen-carry. Soros licked his chops on the Russia default, and with the urging of the Feds, Wall Street stepped up and injected a billion plus into Long Term Capital to keep them from going belly-up and stinking up the market forever.

The risk of owning "risky" technology investments abated. Real buyers, like us, poured in. Those low bids started to lift ever so slowly.

## > > > God's on Our Side

Screw it. We decided to stop raising money. It was taking up too much of our time without much result. Fred and I figured that we'd get investors once we proved that our model really worked.

We had been banging our heads trying to find investors to come into our fund. My hoops friend, Jay Hoag, who had already gone through this fund-raising stuff a few times, told me "the second best answer you can get from a prospect is No." I now know what he means. Most people don't say yes or no, they say Maybe and then stop returning your phone calls.

We did get a few investors each month to come in, but they were usually not anyone that we had marketed to, but instead someone who had heard about us. In fact, once we stopped actively raising money, more money trickled in. We called it second-hand or word-of-mouth marketing. It was the strangest damn thing.

The Tiger/Soros/Long Term Capital disasters in the fall of 1998 ripped the market to shreds. Our fund was in the riskiest of risky investments, at least on the surface, and the flight from risk devastated our performance. So much for raising money anyway. At the beginning of 1998, I had made the executive decision to submit our performance numbers to a few hedge fund services like MAR/Hedge and TASS, which track returns. I figured that someone might find us when our numbers got respectable. Now I was submitting big red negative numbers each month. We were now officially *ugly.*

The day after Long Term Capital blew up in 1988, we were actually down for a brief moment from where we started back in the fall of 1996. How fucking depressing. You fall below the high watermark and you start working for free. I guess it was fun while it lasted. A grand but failed experiment. I could always go back to being an analyst—maybe Morgan Stanley would hire me back. Back on the American Airlines JFK-to-SFO and back shuttle.

But then a funny thing happened. The homeless woman disappeared from the bench outside our office. It took me a few days to notice, but sure enough, she was gone—vanished in a poof.

And just as mysteriously, the dark cloud over our fund started to lift. Our numbers went up almost every day during November and again in December 1998. It happened that fast. We went from down for the year to up 100% in two short months. The value of our investments literally doubled from that day when James Duck wanted out at the bottom.

The biggest gainers were a few of our private investments that had gone public earlier in the year, like Real Networks and Inktomi. But just about every public company we owned went up in value. Our biggest laggard was Elantec, which went from $3 to $4½. Hey, we'll take it.

It's a goddamn yo-yo. We were up 50% for the year in the summer, and then underwater by October, and now, in December, somehow we had doubled our investors' money for the year. I wouldn't have believed it unless I had seen it with my own eyes every day.

And prospective investors started calling.

"What's your cagger?" one guy asked.

"My what?"

"Your compound annual growth rate?"

"Oh, just a second, let me look it up."

"You don't know it?"

"Not really. Here it is. Uh, 45%."

"Wow, really? Annualized?" he asked.

"That's what the spreadsheet says."

"That puts you in the top decile."

"Great."

"You better be ready. Money is going to pour in."

"Yeah, right."

"What about venture—the private stuff? What's your IRR, your internal rate of return?"

"It's 37%, but only two of our private investments are public. Hmm, let's see, can this be right? Our IRR for Inktomi is 6,972%." It was a silly quirk in the formula—an investment that goes up in value in less than a year has this huge multiplier effect on IRR.

"Like I said, be ready," he warned me.

Another investor called and asked to go through the same numbers. Then he asked, "What percentage of your fund is short?"

"None," I answered. This was one stat I didn't have to look up. Shorting is selling a stock you don't own (you actually borrow shares) at a certain price, hoping the price falls so that you can buy back the shares cheaper and then return them.

"You guys don't short?" he asked almost incredulously.

"No. We never have."

"But why not?" he asked.

We had been asked this question a million times.

"Well, there is an unlimited potential for loss." This means that if the stock keeps going up, you have to buy it back at much higher prices. Imagine shorting Microsoft in 1986.

"Still . . ."

"And any gains are short-term gains taxed at twice the rate as long-term capital gains," I added.

"OK, fair enough, but—"

"And you can only make 100%."

"Excuse me?" he asked. It was a flippant answer but the only real one.

"Sure. We like to spend our time finding things that go up by 5 times or 10 times. If we spend our time finding shorts, the most you can make is 100% and only if the stock goes to zero." Plus, I didn't say, there was already a huge pack of hedgies, more like a pack of wolves, chasing down every potential short. We didn't add much value in finding losers—that's a "what others don't know" game.

"So you're not hedged?" he asked.

"We think our hedge is to avoid the losers," I said. This was sassy but true. It was that quaint thing of finding great long-term investments. In down markets, they're not going to do well, but in the long run, if we could find the waterfalls, the upside would be huge.

• • •

The floodgates did indeed open up. Our biggest catch was the Sloan Foundation, which had been considering investing since last October. Sloan is a billion-dollar foundation in New York started by Alfred P. Sloan, the guy credited with scaling General Motors in the '20s and '30s. Beyond the check they wrote, I thought it was poetic justice to manage Sloan's money, since Alfred was famous for his centralized policy controls of the industrial giant. Here we were in Silicon Valley, investing away in companies whose products were decentralized in an almost chaotic intellectual property market. Silicon Valley is not your father's General Motors.

We also got a chunk of money from a group that managed pension funds for clergy. I'm not kidding.

"Fred, that bag lady who ruined our numbers is never coming back."

"How do you know?"

"Because we have God on our side now."

"But you're not—" Fred said.

"Even better," I interrupted. "We've got all our angles covered. Nineteen ninety-nine should be a great year."

And just like that, we now had $100 million in assets. We were finally in business.

# Part V

# The Next Barrier

## >>> Fleece Bank Internet Conference 1999

SAN FRANCISCO, CALIFORNIA—FEBRUARY 1999

Yup, I figured out that prowling around Silicon Valley was the right thing to do. The Japanese didn't make much, if any, profit. Taiwan and Singapore and Malaysia were more than happy to manufacture stuff for very low margin. That meant Fred and I could concentrate on finding design companies around here. Little slivers of intellectual property would go a long way and perhaps become quite valuable. Plus, this whole Internet thing was taking off, which was going to require lots of equipment to build out. So it was back to conference mode to find some new names.

I was pulling up a few quotes between meetings when I heard a familiar voice behind me.

"You actually own Trouble-Click? And Sink-tomi? They might collect those receivables someday, I suppose."

I turned and watched some poor soul in an ill-fitting suit scurry away into the crowd.

"Some people will never learn," Nick Moore said, shaking his head.

"Having fun?" I asked.

"I always enjoy the Fleece Bank or is it the Robertson Fleece 'Em Conference? They have no quality control, so the companies they bring here are awful."

"The numbers are good."

"Your numbers would be good too if you stuffed your Asian distribution channel with more product than you could sell in fifty years."

"OK, good point."

"Management comes here and puts smiley faces on their sinking ships, and the stocks all pop on Monday and Tuesday, and I short 'em on Wednesday. It's almost a sure thing. It's Openwave today and Open-grave tomorrow."

"Nick, what about the Efficient Market theory?" which suggests that all news gets priced into stocks instantly.

Nick let out a laugh so loud, heads turned across the room.

"Yeah, right, efficient market, good one. If it were efficient, we'd all be out of a job, you idiot."

Another month, another conference, and another lesson in Cynics 101 from Nick. This time I was at the Robertson Stephens Fleet Bank Conference at the Palace Hotel just off Market Street. It was no better and no worse than the H&Q conference. Too many people chasing too few good companies.

"I remember the days when there were a dozen or so tech investors on the buy side. Now there must be thousands."

"All rookies. See that guy over there?"

"The peach-fuzz-faced kid? He looks like a junior in high school."

"Yeah, him. I have no idea who he is, but I'll guarantee that he is some portfolio manager's kid who used to upgrade the Windows software on their machines and now is in charge of finding hot technology companies."

"C'mon."

"Watch this." Nick walked up to Peach Fuzz and checked out his badge.

"Whitaker Investments? Hey, I know your dad."

"It's my uncle," Peach Fuzz corrected him.

"Oh, sorry. You guys still using Windows 95?"

"No, I did the upgrade to Windows 98."

"Oh, cool. What do you like here?"

"Well, you gotta own Uniphase. Dense Wave Division and all. Plus interactive stuff is hot. Liberate came out of Oracle and has that Sybase guy and Take Two Interactive. I think that dude is married to a Victoria's Secret model."

"It's Take Two's CEO's dad with the model. You think those stocks are going up?"

"I think each of them goes over $100, maybe $120."

"Not gonna happen," Nick said matter-of-factly.

"They'll get close."

"I guess you don't know the price-name rule."

"What do you mean?" Peach Fuzz looked nervous.

"I've been doing this for years. Never invest in a company with the target price for the stock in the name of the company."

"What? That doesn't make sense."

"Sure it does, you'll learn. Uni-phase, Liber-8, Take-2. Actually, I think it's more like Liber-Eighth. It's not so much that they are screaming at you what their stock is really worth. It's not necessarily cause-and-effect, but the reason to stay away is because it's bad enough losing money, you shouldn't also risk ending up talking to yourself afterward too. You know, 'Am I an idiot? It was right *in the goddamned name!*' "

Nick had everything figured out. I made a note to myself to avoid NetZero.

"I gotta go," I told him.

"I'll bet Uncle Witty owned Quarter-deck, Level 3, 4-Systems, and the worst of them all, 3-Con."

"Take it easy," I told Nick.

"Some people never learn."

"Did you hear about Micro-tragedy? Could see that blowup from miles away?" It was Nick Moore again for my afternoon dose of cynicism.

Microstrategy was one of those scary software blowups. They sold "business intelligence" software, one of those vague names only a McKinsey consultant could love, so companies could track business trends. The stock was hot, and growth was through the roof, until someone figured out that they were signing three-year contracts and reporting the revenues right away, a Bozo no-no of accounting. The stock imploded, the CEO not only fired but forced to renege on some huge charitable donations he'd made with Microstrategy shares.

"What's with these software companies?" I asked.

"Too lumpy . . . and too easy to fudge," Nick pointed out.

"So . . . it's the greatest intellectual property business. Software companies have rooms filled with programmers. Then they sell bits—little magnets pointed north or south—that cost nothing for a couple of hundred grand or a couple of mill," I said.

"Yeah, but it's the worst business for investors. Software companies never have any backlog. So smart customers just sit around and wait for the end of the quarter and insist on 90% off. A nervous CFO almost always coughs it up. The crooked CFOs just book revenue and figure out how to get cash later."

I went to a Cisco presentation but got bored after a few minutes; nothing new there. I poked my head into a few rooms with private companies talking, but I didn't hear anything interesting. Most of it scared me.

"What's with all these newfangled companies? It seems like venture capitalists find anyone that can generate revenue and package them as the Second Coming," I asked. I shouldn't have set Nick off.

"Oh, you mean like Ariba-derci. Some Einstein decided there was a hot business-to-business sector. Duh. Isn't that what businesses are supposed to do, sell to one another? There's nothing new there except some high-flying stocks. B2B2F, as in fail. Or A2AD2D."

I had to think about that last one for a while, but I finally got the ashes and dust.

"Aren't there some safer ways to play B2B?" I asked.

"Like consultants?" Nick asked, with a menacing tone. You could almost hear the bile build up inside him.

"I sat through Scient or was it Viant?" I said.

"Consultants suck. Why bother. They have none of the upside and all of the downside."

"What do you mean by that?"

"They're sweatshops, there's no leverage. They don't have anything to sell. They just rent people. If they want to grow 30%, they have to hire 30% more people. You already know what they are going to make—not much. So, there's no upside, and when the cycle turns, they're going down just as fast as everyone else.

"Isn't IBM's new strategy to become consultants?"

"I Believe in Miracles? Yeah, good luck with that."

"Nick, you've got to quit finding me. I'm trying to get some investing done. Learn something at this place."

"Not at this conference you won't," Nick said.

"Why not?" I asked.

"Well, you can probably better learn what to avoid, like Jim Clark companies."

"I've already heard your Regret-scape pitch," I told Nick.

"It started with Silly-gone Graphics. Did you sit through the Healtheon, I mean Health-Be-Gone, presentation?" Nick asked.

"I've got a one-on-one with their CEO. Long or something like that, I think."

"You mean a one-on-done. He won't be there Long. They are just buying revenue to show Wall Street. They'll no more solve the healthcare tech problem than Lose-ent will save regional Bells from extinction."

"Do you like anything?"

"Flea-bay is interesting. But they shouldn't even be here. They are a buyer of technology, they don't create any."

Another young, confused-looking guy came up and started asking Nick a question.

"Nick, the real leverage is in wireless. These guys own spectrum and can price it under the baby Bells. With no cost for spectrum, they just wipe up, right?"

"Like who?" Nick asked.

"Winstar, Teligent, guys like that. The satellite guys too."

"Good luck. Un-in-Teligent and Win-Scar are just financial shams. They put in these $5,000 radios that stop working in a rain storm. No corporate IT guy will touch them. And don't get me started on Iridiot—66 satellites crashing around. Get a life."

"Nick, why am I the only one that doesn't walk away from you in the middle of your tirades?"

"You should."

• • •

"Yeah, and ask them if the check has cleared yet to the CEO's wife for the lease on the corporate headquarters," Nick screamed at yet another poor schmuck who scrambled to get away as I walked up.

"Have you gone to any meetings at all?"

"Why bother? All the action is out here in the hall, the casual banter portion of the program."

But enough of that. I was on a mission. It was time for me to figure out how this communications business scales because something funky is going on.

I had pitched to our investors that this is what we would do. Find companies that scale with cheap bandwidth the same way PC and chip companies scaled with cheap transistors—that whole sitting-on-top-of-a-rickety-roller-coaster thing.

I still had a lot to learn. With the market starting to work, Mr. Zed didn't push quite as hard, but I thought I owed him and all our investors the effort.

I now had to push myself—not the easiest thing to do in a hot market.

# Do Stocks Talk?

Nick Moore makes me laugh, but buying stocks is anything but fun. The trick is always to figure out what everyone else knows. Are we just heading over the cliff or does everybody know all of this and the clump of water about to crash on the rocks below? My goal is to invest where others *can't* know, but you had to deal with stocks every day, and stocks did what they damn pleased. The last thing you wanted to do was ask them what they think. In all my years on Wall Street, I can't tell you how many people tell me that stocks and stock charts talk to them:

"Looks like smart money is buying this thing."

"This stock is telling me it's going higher."

"It's down. Something must be wrong with the quarter."

"The chart says screaming buy."

"This stock looks like a coiled spring."

I think stocks do talk, but they say only one thing: "I'm gonna getcha, sucka." Stocks want to hurt you, make you feel stupid—they trade to maximize pain. I learned a long time ago to listen but avoid being talked into anything. Stocks are a voting mechanism, pure and simple. They are a collective vote of expectations of each company's future fundamentals. If investors think business will improve, that earnings estimates will rise, then the stock is going up. If investors think the end is near, a company is about to roll over, a stock will go down. It doesn't mean that those fundamentals *ever happen*.

If you think Intel is going to have a great quarter because Dell says box sales are strong, and the stock is going up every day, well, what a surprise, everyone else in the world knows that Intel is going to have a great quarter too. Chances are when they report that good quarter, the stock is going to drop. Pain inflicted, because you were late to the party.

Expectations change every day. Someone sours on a story or thinks a new competitor will eat their lunch, and a stock goes down. Or someone is at a cocktail party over the weekend and Versant's salesman tells him that he is under quota, and on Monday the stock goes down. It is next to impossible to catch these moves, but they more often than not tell you absolutely nothing about the long-run fundamentals of a company. Some portfolio manager is sick of seeing a stock on his screen, blows it out, so it's down three bucks on no news. Happens all the time. It doesn't mean the quarter is bad.

The best investors don't get persuaded by stock blips or charts. It's about staying ahead of the curve—anticipating changes in sentiment. You've got to anticipate what newspaper headlines will say next.

## > > > *Packet Racket*

Many others have written about the history of the PC business. I'm more intrigued by the network effect, linking all these machines together. Steam engines made cheaper goods; steamships delivered those goods more cheaply. Both provided scale. Microprocessors make applications cheaper; communications deliver those applications more cheaply.

"Do you know the first packet sent?"

I looked over and noticed for the first time the man sitting next to me at the table. I started chuckling because he kind of looked like a cross between Soupy Sales and Eddie Munster. It was lunchtime at George Gilder's Telecosm conference, and we were waiting for the featured speaker, Gary Winnick of Global Crossing, to explain how he sends billions of packets per second under the Atlantic Ocean. George Gilder has hosted his Telecosm conference for years. Tech luminaries like Carver Mead, Bob Metcalfe and Paul Allen were regulars.

"I don't know what the first packet was," I confessed. My tablemate turned out to be Leonard Kleinrock, a UCLA professor, according to his name tag. It turned out that he had been at the creation.

Since the 1978 introduction of the Apple II computer, to the 1981 announcement of the IBM PC, the world has been flooded with smaller, cheaper and faster computers. More than 100 million new ones get sold every year. But today, these are no islands—the power of these computers is in their ability to communicate.

The telephone network, which is optimized for your talks with

Mom, was the medium for computer communications. No one thought this out; it just happened that phone lines were running everywhere, so as computers were placed in the same everywhere, they used the phone network to communicate.

The problem is that from the very beginning, the phone network cut corners.

Fortunately, the Cold War gave us packets.

"It was the fall of 1969," Leonard Kleinrock started. I think I was watching *The Munsters* back then. "We had the first IMP from BBN. I think it cost ARPA around $10,000. Which doesn't seem like much until you remember that a Volkswagen Beetle cost $2000."

"We?" I asked.

"Oh, sorry, UCLA."

"Was Lew Alcindor involved in all of this?"

"Who?"

"Never mind. Could you translate the acronyms?"

"So anyway, this Interface Message Processor was a modified Honeywell 516 minicomputer. I think Bolt, Beranek and Newman, which was just a small consulting company at the time, had just landed a $1 million contract from ARPA, you know, the Advanced Research Projects Agency."

"G-job?"

"Well, in this case, it was a real government job. NASA and ARPA were both formed after the Russkies put up Sputnik. ARPA was in the Department of Defense. They were worried that if a nuke went off, phone networks would go down and the president wouldn't be able to command and control. So they studied survivable systems. Larry Roberts at MIT proposed a collection of computers hooked together via packet switching."

"OK. But who invented packets?" I asked.

"Paul Baran at Rand in Santa Monica gets a lot of credit for packets."

I know about Rand. It is a Santa Monica, California, think tank spun out of Douglas Aircraft after World War II. It's still around.

"NORAD, you know, the North American Air Defense Command," Kleinrock continued, "shoehorned in that mountain in Cheyenne, was worried about getting cut off from Washington, so the Air Force commissioned a study on how to resolve the vulnerability of communications networks. Baran wrote a paper in 1964 called 'On Distributed Computing.' It's on the Web. You can find it."

"So that was the start of packet switching."

"Sort of. Baran describes standard message blocks and store and forward transmissions and hot potato routing. The next year, Donald Watts Davies, a British mathematician, was working on block-switch networks and came up with the name packets."

Of course, packets are what make the Internet work today. The best description I've read goes something like this: "Packet switching is the breaking down of data into datagrams or packets that are labeled to indicate the origin and the destination of the information and the forwarding of these packets from one computer to another computer until the information arrives at its final destination computer. This is crucial to the realization of a computer network. If packets are lost at any given point, the message can be resent by the originator."

"So how did you get involved?" I asked.

"Well, my thesis proposal at MIT back in 1961 was called 'Information Flow in Large Communication Nets.' So they got me involved," Eddie, I mean Leonard, answered.

"So, wait, 1961. It was you that invented packet switching."

"It was a lot of us."

"But what happened in 1969?"

"Oh, right. So we had the first IMP at UCLA. It could store and forward packets. Of course, a message processor is pretty worthless on its own. The second one was installed at the Stanford Research Institute."

"Doug Engelbart's group?"

"That's it. Did I tell you this story already?"

"Nope. Go on."

"With two, you can tango. These two machines talked via NCP, Network Control Protocol. We get AT&T to provide a 50 kilobit per second private line between LA and Menlo Park up north."

"Yeah."

"So we hook up the two IMPs, and ARPANET was born."

"But what was the first packet?" I asked.

"Oh, yeah. I called them up on a regular phone line and said, 'OK, we are about to send an *L,* let me know when you see it.'

"They told me, 'There it is, we got an *L,*' and I heard a lot of applause in the background.

"I got excited. 'OK, OK, just a second, hold on, we are going to send an *O.*'

"I hear screams from their end of the phone. 'Oh my god, we just got an *O,* keep going.'

"I tell them, 'Get ready, here comes a *G.* Let me know when you get it.'

"Then I hear them ask, 'Did you send it?'

" 'Yeah, we just sent the *G.* Did you get it?' I asked them.

" 'No, wait a second. What? Oh no. Uh, the Honeywell just crashed.'

" 'Hey, who cares, we did it, success. Get out the champagne!' "

"Wait a second," I asked. "There were two IMPs in the world, and you were sending a request to log in?"

"That's right."

"What was the password? Swordfish?" I asked.

"I don't remember."

"A system setup using an AT&T line is now killing the phone network?"

"That's right."

"And a system that was designed to help maintain command and control for the president is now obliterating command and control for everyone else?"

"That's right."

"Amazing."

One of the researchers at the Stanford site, Norm Abramson, was a surfer dude who spent a lot of time in Hawaii. The University of Hawaii had locations scattered across the islands and was trying to figure out how to hook up a data network among them. They couldn't afford to run cable undersea to connect their computers, and modems were too slow, so they hit on the idea of using radio signals to transmit data. The problem though was interference. Maui might transmit at the same time and step on the Big Island's signal. They could use packet networks, but that didn't solve the interference problem.

In 1970, Abramson devised a system for them that checked for errors in the packets received. If the packets had errors, the receiver wouldn't send an acknowledgment signal back. If the sender didn't receive an acknowledgment (hence a collision or errors occurred), it would wait a little bit, actually a random period of time, and then resend the packet. Simple yet effective, AlohaNet was the first local area network, even though that local area spread across hundreds of miles.

By 1971, there were 15 ARPANET nodes scattered across the U.S.: UCLA, Stanford Research Institute, UC Santa Barbara, University of Utah, BBN, MIT, Rand, SDC (which I think is the State Data Center, part of the Census Bureau), Harvard, MIT's Lincoln Lab, Stanford, University of Illinois in scenic Urbana-Champaign, Case Western Reserve, Carnegie Mellon and NASA/Ames. This was a very interesting mix of academics, think tanks, government and quasi-military organizations. BBN was the only corporation, but of course, was getting ARPA funding to run the network. Fourteen other sites were a lot to keep in touch with, so in 1971, Ray Tomlinson at BBN wrote a message reader and writer so that BBN could send and receive notes on the system. He used the at sign, @, to denote the destination and e-mail was born. In 1866, undersea telegraph messages cost $5 per word. In 1976, 110 years later, Jimmy Carter and Walter Mondale were reputed to have used e-mail every day, at $4 per message, to coordinate their campaign schedules. At millionths of a cent per message in 2004, billions of e-mail messages are sent on average every day! S-C-A-L-E.

Someone forgot to tell Gary Winnick of Global Crossing this story and remind him that when technology is involved, prices go down. He got caught trying to charge the equivalent of the 1866-era $5-per-word prices as his company crashed into the sea.

• • •

Meanwhile, the conference droned on.

"Here is a slide of the number of Internet servers since 1992. Note the aberration in 1999."

It was then that I started fidgeting. I've got to admit, I absolutely hate conferences. One brilliant person after another gets up and flips on their PowerPoint slide presentation, starts babbling about some unimportant fact after another, and I am halfway to la-la land well before they hit their exciting nonconclusion. While this is a better conference than most, techno-geeks ought to hire stand-ins to deliver their talks.

"And here is a slide of bandwidth deliverable by packetized LANs and WANs."

My eyelids got heavy, so I was barely able to make out the chart. Dating back to 1975, it had a straight line up and to the right, with labels that read:

> 1 megabit per second, 1975

> 10 megabits per second, 1983

> 100 megabits per second, 1991

> 1 gigabit per second, 1999

> 10 gigabits per second, 2007

> 100 gigabits per second, 2015

> 1 terabit per second, 2023

I've seen charts like this before, but they never cease to amaze me. Like clockwork, bandwidth goes up in 10× increments. It's almost as if you become desensitized to the pace of advance because it becomes expected. Bored to tears, I scanned the room for someone, anyone, to give the high sign to, to make a quick exit to coffee and jokes in the hall.

Nick Moore wasn't here, damn.

My eyes got stuck in the middle of the room. There was Bob Metcalfe staring at the slide, looking at the line going up and up and up. He was shaking his head with a look of both amazement and disbelief, and this was the guy that invented it.

After a dozen of those IMP nodes were up and running, it was time to start giving demos to people who mattered. One of the ARPANET researchers was in charge of giving a demonstration to some bigwigs from AT&T. Keep in mind that the phone network was engineered to fail for only two minutes every 40 years. That is one of those six nine's, or four to the right of the decimal point, or 99.9999% reliability. As the story goes, researcher Bob Metcalfe was in the middle of demonstrating the packet network when, like any good demo, it crashed. This put smiles on the faces of those 10 AT&T execu-humps, and they merrily skipped back to headquarters singing the stillbirth of packet switching. Of course, they were right for another 30 years, but packet switching would eventually be trouble for circuit-switched phone networks. Metcalfe got back at them.

With the success of its new packet network, ARPA became "D for Defense" DARPA, to remind everyone it was your defense dollars at work, keeping communications alive in the event of a nuclear war.

Bob Metcalfe moved from DARPA to the Xerox Palo Alto Research Center. He was playing around with a bunch of new Xerox Alto workstations, trying to devise a fast network both to hook them together, and more importantly, to connect them to laser printers that Xerox was hoping to sell in large numbers. This was around 1976, and Xerox PARC was still a playground for dreamy scientists. Conference rooms didn't have tables and chairs—they had beanbag chairs.

But Metcalfe was no dreamer. He had read a paper about surfer Norm Abramson's AlohaNet and liked the idea. But what works for radio signals across islands might not work for busy computers connected with cables. The problem was the random backoff, the random amount of time before you resend the packet. You could never get much throughput on a shared network if each machine just made up the amount of time to wait. So Metcalfe, working with David Boggs, came up with a new scheme. First, each computer would check the network first and "listen" for a carrier. In that case, it meant that someone else on the network was transmitting a packet. If the computer heard one, it would wait to transmit its own packet. Aloha didn't do this. In this new scheme, collisions only occurred when two computers "listened," heard silence and decided at the same time to transmit their packets. So throughput on the network went up. Second, the transmitter wouldn't wait a random amount of time if a carrier was heard or a collision occurred, but instead would check how much traffic was on the network. If there was only a little traffic, the transmitter would wait a random but short amount of time. If traffic was heavy, it would wait a random but longer amount of time to resend. Less waiting meant speeds increased.

Metcalfe actually built a network too. It could transmit 2.94 megabits per second over coax cable. The speed of the bus inside the Alto computer was 2.94 MHz. The two original workstations were nicknamed Michelson and Morley for two turn-of-the-20th-century scientists who refuted the theory that the universe was filled with mysterious ether. Metcalfe and Boggs published a paper in July 1976 in the *Communications of the Association of Computer Machinery* magazine, titled "Ethernet: Distributed Packet Switching for Local Computer Networks." The name *Ether* stuck, and local area networks were born.

Metcalfe is also known for another famous observation: the value of a network goes up by the square of the number of nodes attached to it. Actually, for those keeping track at home, it's $n \times (n - 1)$. A single node has no connections, two nodes have two connections, one in either direction, three nodes have six, etc. This turned into the scale of the Web when millions of nodes were connected, and Metcalfe's Law is what made Napster and peer-to-peer file sharing such huge waterfalls.

In fact, maybe Metcalfe's Law is the formula for Doug Engelbart's scaling of human knowledge, just as Watt's steam engine scaled human power.

And Xerox PARC? I've been there a few times. The first was in the early 1990s, when Xerox management was hoping to impress Wall Street with a modernization kick. Xerox could commercialize projects, blah, blah, blah. I asked about the beanbag chairs and got quickly sniffed at: "That was the old Xerox PARC." Now they were serious.

In 1999, I was asked to meet an entrepreneur at Xerox PARC who was trying to commercialize a virtual whiteboard collaborative thingy. I never could really understand its uses. On the way to his office, we walked past this huge room filled with goofy scientists sipping lattes, each resting comfortably in his or her own red, green or blue beanbag chair. It's good to know that some things never change.

Metcalfe helped local networks scale—and scale they did. Every department inside a company was able to share files and printers, replacing sneakernet. Dealing with the outside world was another story.

It was the personal computer boom of the 1980s that dragged LANs into the mainstream. But they were not all the same flavor. There was Ethernet, of course, but Novell had a networking standard in Netware, IBM had Token Ring, UNIX computers used uucp, etc. It was a mess.

Around 1980, Xerox PARC gave Stanford University a bunch of Alto workstations and some of their new Ethernet networking cards. Like any large university, Stanford had a huge collection of computers: mainframes, minicomputers and even some homegrown Motorola microprocessor-based machines built at Stanford by grad student Andy Bechtolsheim, who would later use them to found Sun Microsystems. Plus, all these computers were scattered among different schools doing research—the med school, the engineering department, the business school, etc.

Len Bosack and Sandy Lerner get credit for inventing routers and then founding Cisco to sell them. These routers were basically miniversions of the store-and-forward IMP that Kleinrock and others used for ARPANET, except companies and universities could use them to hook up all their scattered departments and LANs, even across the country.

Still, 80% plus of all network traffic was on these LANs. Sure, the Internet had existed since Kleinrock's L-O crash, but no one outside of academics used it much.

In the early 1990s, as these networks proliferated, another pressure point was building, another barrier to be broken, unleashing all those users to the outside world. This would turn out to be the big one to surf.

Let me take you back to a story near the beginning of all this.

## > > > Clark's Outpost

WOODSIDE, CALIFORNIA—SPRING 1994

"You're such an asshole. John Doerr doesn't know everything," Bob Harris launched almost immediately.

"Yeah, well, that's what I'm doing," Jim Clark said.

"Well, you're being stupid."

"Me stupid? You thought I was working on MOTIF."

"Motif, Mosaic, who gives a shit. We can help more than some know-nothing VC," Bob screamed.

"Shit," I whispered to my wife, Nancy. "I think we are a little late. About three highballs too late."

Late indeed.

I got to know Jim Clark back when he was chairman of the computer company Silicon Graphics and I was still with Morgan Stanley. Frank Quattrone introduced us at one of the many road show lunches. Silicon Graphics was an investment banker's dream, always raising money in the stock market to fund one project or another. Clark was the technical founder, and he always seemed to be restless. I was writing about some new uses of technology, and Clark was intrigued. Back in 1991, he was pitching a new concept known as the teleputer, a computer, to be made by Silicon Graphics naturally, that would be networked with every other computer in the world and provide information, entertainment and everything else people might want. Pretty cool for 1991.

But as smart as Clark was in technology, he was a business dope. In fact, when he started Silicon Graphics, he sold two-thirds of the company to venture capitalists Dick Kramlich of New Enterprise Associates and Glenn Mueller of Mayfield for $600,000. To add insult to injury, these two VCs stayed on Silicon Graphics' board of directors and turned down most of Clark's requests. He asked for funding for new projects, like the teleputer. But he also asked for rich option and pay packages, probably in an attempt to get his fair share to make up for his getting screwed in the seed round. The board fought him on virtually everything he proposed, which from what I could gather, pissed Jim Clark off to no end.

I started working with Bob Harris in 1991. I thought Bob was the best investment banker in Silicon Valley. The list of companies he had taken public was staggering, from Microsoft to Sun Microsystems, but the company he was closest to was Silicon Graphics. He was their go-to banker. The board called in Bob Harris and asked for his honest opinion, something in short supply from fee-hungry investment bankers. I would always find myself sitting in the passenger seat of Bob's green BMW 540, scooting around the Valley, looking for deals, and would get dragged into a few too many meetings at Silicon Graphics.

The last few meetings were the most fun. Clark was fed up. He wanted out. TimeWarner had picked up on his teleputer concept and wanted to roll it out in Orlando, Florida, as something called the Full Service Network. Clark desperately wanted to be involved, but others at SGI cut Clark out of all the discussions. The Full Service Network flopped miserably and probably would have with or without Clark involved. Clark's last straw was to hit the ejection button from Silicon Graphics.

Bob gave Clark advice every step of the way, probably jeopardizing his working relationship with the Silicon Graphics board.

So Bob Harris and Jim Clark went way back. Long enough for Harris to be able to call Clark an asshole in a public restaurant.

"Jim, this is my wife, Nancy," I said.

"Hi, Nancy, nice to meet you. Thank god you guys are here," Jim said as he rolled his eyes. "Let's eat."

"Nancy, this is Jim's wife, Nancy Rutter," I said.

"Hey, another Nancy. You guys showed up just in time, it was starting to get ugly," I said, trying to change the subject away from Harris yelling at Clark.

"Nancy Rutter works at *Forbes ASAP* with Rich Karlgaard. I think she even edited some of my columns over the years."

Rich Karlgaard, now the publisher of *Forbes* magazine, told me the story about a very pretty Nancy Rutter going to interview venture capitalist Dick Kramlich for *Upside* magazine. By chance, she met Jim Clark in the lobby, and a week later, after some follow-up, Nancy Rutter was seen driving around in a Mercedes 450 SL.

"Why is Bob yelling at Jim?" my wife asked.

"I don't know," I said.

"You stupid son of a bitch," Bob continued.

"He needs to be yelled at," Nancy Rutter explained.

"Were you guys just on your boat somewhere?" I asked, again trying to steer the conversation to calmer waters.

"We just got back from Fiji. Didn't Jim call you from there?" Nancy Rutter answered.

"He called me from the boat while I was at some conference, ship to shore or satellite phone, sounded great," I said.

"Me stupid?" Clark screamed back to Bob.

"Muzak. Munsters, what the hell," Bob mumbled.

I thought it was time for me to break it up. "So, Jim. I'm an Illinois alum, and Mosaic looks pretty cool as a front end to a lot of things. Tell me more about the deal, and I'll get the barking dog here to calm down for a few seconds."

"I've already put in a couple of million. The deal now is $5 million for 20%. I've got all sorts of people bugging me. Kramlich calls every day. Mueller whines on the phone not to be left behind," Clark said in a complaining tone.

"Well, we're interested. Our fund just did a first closing. By the way, we're still waiting for your money. But we are all set to invest," I said.

"I think I've decided John Doerr and Kleiner is going to do the whole investment themselves," Clark said matter-of-factly.

"John Doerr? Jesus Christ. He's not the only one that knows anything." Bob just wouldn't let up. And we hadn't even ordered our food yet. "You're going to need a lot of help. We know this space."

"Remember William Morris?" Harris asked. We had set Clark up with an entire department of William Morris Agency to look into where technology and entertainment crossed.

"That was OK."

"Andy and I had breakfast with Brandon Tartikoff and those William Morris guys. Tartikoff said he enjoyed meeting with you," Harris said without yelling.

"I suppose. John Doerr sort of insists on doing this one himself," Clark blurted out.

"What?" Bob screeched.

"Yeah, he wants the whole $5 mill and nobody else. He's pretty adamant," Clark said.

"I think there's lots of ways to go," I said, jumping in.

"What do you mean, Andy?" Jim asked as he turned his back on Bob.

"Clark's Outpost," I said.

"What the hell is that?"

"I've been doing a lot of work on how this whole interactive media is going to be paid for. Mass advertising is awful. TV charges a buck for 1,000 impressions. That won't work on PCs. Once you can measure response rates, that model will die."

"I just came back from New York. I met with a bunch of magazines and told them we'd like to charge them a nickel or a dime for each page that people on the Internet view with Mosaic," Clark said.

"The way to protect the software is to make it the front end to something else. I'd sell people stuff, that's what Clark's Outpost is," I offered.

"I don't get it."

"It's direct advertising. Junk mail guys pay $400 per thousand mailings, hoping to get a 2% hit rate. If they can clear $20 on what they are selling, they break even. Everything over 2%, and they wipe up."

"So?"

"So, just put your face on the main Mosaic page."

"And?"

"And you'll get 20% hit rates. Everyone will click on your face to head into Clark's Outpost. You can sell them anything you want. PCs, TVs, video games, even books, I suppose."

"Sounds messy. I like software."

"I like software too, the margins are great, but it's impossible to protect. Microsoft has a business because they tie Windows to real hardware. Tough to pull that off again. But you can leverage yours with that direct marketing model, and you'll own the Internet."

"And drop that Doerr guy," Harris slurred.

Kleiner Perkins did the Mosaic deal by themselves, shutting my ass out. Why am I telling you this sad story? Because Mosaic broke the 80-20 barrier.

Marc Andreessen was working at the National Center for Supercomputing Applications at the University of Illinois and was sick of typing in command line prompts to get what he wanted from the Internet. So he and a few other folks devised a browser—with pages of links to other pages. Actually, it was what Doug Engelbart had envisioned and even crudely demo'ed in 1968. Andreessen made it hum by allowing his browser to pull multiple packets at a time from the Internet rather than one at a time. The free code spread like crazy. Users were no longer stuck on the LAN—they could browse the outside world. Clark met with Andreessen and hired him and his buddies for a company they named Mosaic Communications.

It was soon renamed Netscape when the University of Illinois sued over the name. I found out later that indeed John Doerr didn't want anyone else involved. Hey, all's fair. They had deep pockets and could set the rules. Kramlich and Mueller continued to hound Clark to be let in the deal, especially as Netscape began to be touted as the next Microsoft.

Our little venture fund did close, without Clark's money, and we funded a bunch of companies that did well because Netscape browsers were spreading faster than wildfires in a Texas prairie.

A few months later, Glenn Mueller took his own life on his own boat while down in Mexico. Mueller was not only one of the top five most successful venture capitalists in Silicon Valley, his wife, Nancy Mueller, had a hugely successful catering business. These two were the toasts of the town. Why Glenn Mueller took his own life is still a mystery, although there were rumors running around that he had bouts of depression or other emotional problems. Who knows? But Jim Clark took it hard. He blamed himself for cutting Mueller out of the deal. Clark gave the eulogy at the memorial service for Mueller. Bob Harris was there and told me that Clark broke down crying several times.

Over the next year, things moved fast at Netscape. Jim Barksdale, a former FedEx and AT&T Wireless executive, was brought in as CEO. Clark was "elevated" to chairman and, I think, had very little to do with managing the company. But he did own a big chunk of it. The business model that evolved for Netscape had nothing to do with charging a nickel or a dime or even a penny for each page viewed. Instead, they just gave away the browser to anyone who could go to their Web site and download it. Millions did.

Then Barksdale went around to corporations and told them that they were using thousands of copies of Netscape's browser software and that it was free only for consumers, not corporate users, so please pay up. Quite ingenious.

Revenues grew, and Netscape sucked up every available programmer in the Valley to create new versions of the browser and server software to spit out the Web pages to millions of users.

On the day of Netscape's IPO in August 1985, the share price popped from $28 to $54 in the first few minutes of trading, valuing the company at $2 billion. I walked into Bob Harris's office.

"Did you see where it closed?" I asked.

"Yeah, don't remind me."

"What, that we were three highballs away from investing in Netscape?"

"Yeah, that. And Clark is going to be an even more insufferable prick."

"Gotta get over it, Bob," I said.

"No I don't."

• • •

Luckily, those Cisco routers were around. Not only did routers hook LANs to wide area networks, or WANs, that comprised the Internet, but Cisco routers actually became the backbone of the Internet. New companies like UUNET and America Online would use Cisco routers in the middle of their networks to move packets around, as well as at the edge of their networks to connect to banks of dial-up modems so users could call in and connect.

Marc Andreessen took advantage of these routers. For Cisco, the effect was magic. Browsers blew away the 80-20 rule. They probably flipped it to the 20-80 rule, meaning only 20% of networking was local and the rest had to go through a router to request information and packets from the Internet. Demand for routers exploded. A simple invention, a tiny packet reassembly program named a browser, caused demand to shift rapidly. Without the browser and router growing hand in hand, we'd all still be waiting for the post office to deliver information and orders for products—we might as well have stayed in the industrial age.

Intel and Microsoft, based on Doug Engelbart's blueprint, put the horizontal into the computer business—thin slices of intellectual property assembled into a final product. The division of labor happened almost immediately. It was cheaper to assemble chips in Malaysia than in Michigan. Cisco's routers and Netscape's browsers just rode on top of the computer industry's platform, and the communications business layered into thin slices similar to the computer business and created another giant waterfall.

Unfortunately for Netscape, Jim Barksdale made every mistake in the book. Microsoft eventually woke up and developed its own Internet Explorer browser, by licensing some of the original code from the University of Illinois. Barksdale's plan was to acquire his way to success. Many companies began writing add-in software that worked inside of Netscape's browser. Netscape encouraged this, and there might be five companies doing video plug-ins and six companies doing 3-D code and another four doing database stuff. But Barksdale would immediately turn around and buy one of these companies, in effect freezing out all of the others, who would go work with Microsoft.

I sat in on a presentation by Jim Barksdale at an investors conference soon after the IPO. He set out his master plan. "Look, our model is Cisco. They grow their product offerings via acquisitions. We have a platform that affords us the same model. I am going to do one acquisition a quarter, until I get good at it, and then I'm going to do an acquisition a month." You could see the investment bankers in the room break into huge smiles. Hello, fees!

Netscape's stock kept running and running.

I walked into Bob Harris's office.

"I read today that Jim Clark is now a billionaire," I told him.

"No he's not," Bob shot back.

"Yeah, the stock's $80 something, and with splits and all, he has 130 million shares."

"But he's not a billionaire."

"Do the math," I said.

"No, you're forgetting something important my friend. He's got to pay taxes."

"You gotta get over it."

"No I don't," Harris repeated.

But Barksdale's biggest mistake compares to the Germans invading Russia in World War II and opening a two-front war. IBM was a Netscape ally. IBM had recently completed the acquisition of Lotus, the spreadsheet company. Except Lotus didn't really make much from spreadsheets anymore; they had reinvented themselves as a groupware company, selling Lotus Notes to corporations to keep track of e-mail and documents and help workers collaborate. Because of this, IBM was very interested in Netscape's success, almost as the anti-Microsoft. IBM distributed Netscape Navigator on every IBM computer shipped, and resold Netscape server software, a big bonus for Netscape to be able to leverage IBM's huge distribution prowess. If Microsoft was busy with Netscape, then Microsoft wouldn't have as many resources to compete with Lotus.

So what did Barksdale do? He bought a small company in the

Valley named Collabra that made groupware software. In one fell swoop, Netscape was now competing with IBM. Within a month or so, IBM switched allegiance to Microsoft Internet Explorer, and it was the beginning of the end for Netscape. Revenues stopped growing at the huge, spectacular rates they once had. The stock collapsed to new lows. It wasn't until America Online stepped up and bought Netscape that their saga ended. Fortunately for Netscape shareholders, AOL stock kept climbing and climbing, much to the short Dave Rocker's chagrin, and Netscape eventually was worth $10 billion.

Jim Barksdale went on to set up a venture capital partnership, the Barksdale Group, to invest in start-ups. I've heard it nastily referred to as a not-for-profit organization.

Over the years, I would look at venture capital deals, some good, some bad, some great. The great ones were hard to get into, and I was often left out, stuck on the sidelines again. I would always say to the CEO (under my breath, of course), "Listen, asshole, I've been thrown out of much better deals than this."

## > > > Music Play It Again

PALO ALTO, CALIFORNIA—EARLY-1999

As routers scaled, the waterfall started, allowing Metcalfe's exponential value of the network—the n × (n – 1) formula—to kick in. Then all sorts of funny stuff started happening.

"Get anything?" I asked the Robertson trader.

"I just got most of Springsteen's early albums."

"What?"

"Oh, sorry, it's been slow, so I've been downloading music."

"Let me guess, you're using Napster?" I asked.

"Yup, just about everyone on the trading desk is. I think it's clogged most of our Internet lines."

"Yeah, I've been pretty busy around here doing the same thing."

"It's quite amazing. I can't do much with it besides listen to it on my PC. I gotta get me one of those CD writers."

"Well, what I meant before is, did you get us any Elantec today?"

"Oh, sorry, a little. I can't seem to buy it off the box—someone else is hitting all the bids—but I did find a few accounts that are selling, so you are complete on 10 and we are still working another 10. Same limit?"

"Great, thanks. Yeah, don't pay more than four and a half." I had already bought 20,000 on Instinet. We owned 200,000 shares and growing. The stock was moving and ticking up every day. Some days it would hit five, until I stopped buying and then it would settle back. I wasn't sure why it was going up. Unfortunately, it was probably us. These illiquid stocks are nasty that way: you buy it and you become the market. It's why so few funds do small cap.

Still, it had taken me four months of scraping to get this size. What a pain in the ass.

"Oh, shit," I screamed.

"What is it?" Fred asked.

"They just halted trading in Elantec, news pending."

"That's never good news," Fred said.

"Fucking assholes, what are they doing down there? It could be something good—Intel buying them?" I said hopefully.

"Keep dreaming."

I waited while Green Day downloaded on Napster, and within a few minutes the news hit the tape: Elantec was taking a charge to write down one of their fabs—yields had been low, the process didn't prove out and they were going to shutter it and write down all the work in progress.

"I'll see if I can get to the company. It doesn't sound serious. I suspect that they were carrying that fab for no good reason. It might be good news now that they are writing it down—expenses go down, margins go up," Fred said.

"I'm not so sure," I sighed. "The stock is down over a buck. It just punched through the wrong side of $3."

"I'd buy more," Fred said in a voice that was almost too calm.

"Really, they are hammering this thing."

"Yeah, just buy it."

I got to both Robertson and H&Q and put in orders for 50,000 shares with each of them and then started working the box, banging keys, hitting every bid I could find. I was the market. I ended up buying 50,000 on Instinet.

Within 30 minutes, we had bought 150,000 shares, which really pissed me off since it had taken me four or five months to buy our first 200,000 shares.

"Great," Fred said. "Unless you have any objections, let's keep going on this one."

"I'm in." I wasn't so sure. If this thing didn't work, we were stuck with all these crappy shares. It would take me a year of scratching and clawing in the other direction to get out of them.

It was like the old vaudeville gag—Niagara Falls, slowly I turned, inch by inch, step by step. Day by day, little by little, 1,000 shares here, 2,500 shares there, we built our stake. Over a few more months, we were getting close to half a million shares. This thing was becoming an important chunk of our portfolio. It better work.

The company had only a shade over 10 million shares, and we were butting up against the 5% limit. Well, it's not a limit—it's just that if you own more than 5% of a company, you have to file paperwork with the Securities and Exchange Commission, a 13-D filing that says you own more than 5%. The downside is that you end up tipping your hand to the market.

I was against owning so much, but mostly because it meant unnecessary paperwork. Plus if this dog didn't hunt, we had the public embarrassment of owning all those shares, instead of an anonymous bonehead investment.

We checked in with the company every month and were due to go back in for a visit. So we agreed we would visit the company to hear the latest, then decide if we wanted to keep buying. The DVD stuff was a year or maybe two away, but we just knew that was going to be a decent business. Meanwhile, those stupid DSL chips just had to start spitting some earnings to get the stock back up to $5. Why were Pac Bell and Verizon dragging their knuckles?

"How's business?"

"It's OK," David O'Brien told us.

"DSL moving?"

"A little. The telcos don't seem in any big hurry. Cable modems are doing better, but we don't sell into that market."

"And the optical stuff?"

"It's starting to move. We're not sure why. There seems to be some stocking going on in Japan and Taiwan, but we don't see the end demand. DVD-R/W drives are down to $500, so that's still a luxury, but we keep an eye on it."

"Any other fab blowups on the horizon, any other potential writedowns we should know about?" I bluntly asked.

"No, I think we're good on that," O'Brien answered.

"I hope so."

"Can I ask you guys a question?"

"Sure," Fred answered.

"Well, you seem to be the only investors coming down here. I assume you guys own the stock."

"We do, a good chunk," I answered.

"OK, just wanted to know. The board was getting nervous that we were wasting our time with you guys."

"It's not a waste of time. And do tell Don Valentine I said hello," I said.

"I will."

It's like watching paint dry, waiting for this thing to work.

"So what do you think?" Fred asked.

"We own a boatload. I'm still not convinced this thing is going to work. DSL is stillborn, the laser diode is years away, management is sleepy and Toshiba could blow them out of the water tomorrow morning. Having said all that, there is something to this thing. But it's your call. You seem to think these guys have something, I'm just not sure what."

"Let's keep buying it. Don't worry about the 13-D filing. Think of it as free advertising."

"Elantec on the tape," Fred yelled over. Fred doesn't yell much.

"What does it say?" I asked.

"A dime. H&Q had seven cents. I figured it would be eight. They beat the numbers, but let's see how. The conference call is in a few minutes."

Over the last few weeks, I had kept buying the stock. We were up to 700,000 shares, and the stock was going through $5½, so I started getting less aggressive. Still, the share count grew. We had 45 days to file the 13-D, but it looked like the company was helping us look good when we did file.

Napster was on the cover of most magazines. Despite almost every other venture capital firm turning them down because of potential legal liabilities, Hummer Winblad out in the East Bay had invested. I thought that was pretty stupid. They installed Hank

Berry, a lawyer I had known at Wilson Sonsini years ago, as CEO of Napster. That struck me as kind of funny—you invest and put a lawyer in as CEO, almost as if you were expecting trouble. Still, Napster had tens of millions of users who were downloading billions of free MP3 files onto their PCs. The thing was an amazing success, although they barely generated any revenue. But there was a frenzy on the Internet for free music.

I was half-listening to the Elantec conference call as I downloaded every Elvis Costello and Stevie Ray Vaughan album.

Over the speakerphone, I heard, "The attach rates seem to be moving up, which helps our optical segment. We think we can grow it double digit this year."

"Fred, what does that mean?"

"I'm not sure, but it sounds bullish. I'll ask on the Q&A. I'm glad we are almost done buying this thing. It could start moving."

"Ten dollars? Eleven dollars?" I kidded.

"I don't want to jinx it by saying it could go higher than $10.50."

"I'll write that down. Fred says $10.50 or higher, sometime before we have all our limited partners beg us for their money back."

The next morning, the stock popped a buck or so, but then settled back down. We kept buying it, in dribs and drabs. We never did get to one million shares, because sure enough, over the next few quarters, they kept beating the numbers and the stock went to $10.50 and higher and higher and kept going.

Napster helped millions join the Music Pirates "R" Us program. A firm named Roxio wrote a clever program to write MP3 files as analog songs onto a CD. Now you could steal music and then create your own party disks. There was a run on CD writable drives for PCs that cost around $150. And sure enough, just about every one of them contained a little $2 laser diode driver.

Soon, as these drives dropped below $100, Dell and Sony and everybody else offered PCs with CD-R drives as standard equipment. That was the attach rate that Elantec was talking about—what percent of PCs have CD-Rs as standard equipment. It went from 0% to 10% to 20% and then, six months later, hit 80%, meaning that 80 million out of the 100 million new PCs that shipped to customers had a stinky little $2 laser diode driver.

A huge barrier to digital music distribution had now burst, and there was a huge waterfall of demand. No one could quite figure out how to invest in a pure play on music piracy. Napster was an ugly failure: it really was a transfer of wealth from venture capitalists to lawyers. Meanwhile, no one else could figure out how to charge for MP3s when they were readily available for free. (Wasn't that the point?) Sure, Intel and Microsoft benefited and disk drive companies sold more gigabyte drives, but that isn't hypergrowth. AOL saw dial-up customers increase monthly, broadband connections grew and Internet backbones proliferated, almost all, one could argue, for the ability to steal music.

While Wall Street scrambled for pure play ideas, we had this little doggy company in the bowels of Silicon Valley barely keeping up with demand for laser diode drivers for CD burners. The waterfall didn't even come from the writable DVD drives we were willing to so patiently wait for.

When Elantec hit somewhere between $50 and $75, it got discovered. Momentum funds, mutual funds that wait until they find stocks that consistently go up, were on it like white on rice. The company kept beating their numbers every quarter, and some analysts got wise and started touting them as a pure MP3 play.

Despite thinking it would be tough to go above $10, at $100 we started trickling the stock out for sale. On Instinet, of course. We also started using another stock matching service, called the Island, which was Web based. You didn't need a private line to your office or a special box, just any old PC. I could trade from home at 6:30 a.m., or from a hotel room, or, shhh, off a laptop from a hot tub.

I sold every single share of Elantec through Instinet and the Island. In fact, I was now doing 90% of my trades through these matching systems (who needed Wall Street?). We did our last trade of Elantec shares somewhere over $200. If you buy a stock at $70 and it goes to $200, it's tough to sell, figuring it might go to $300. If you bought it at $3, it's a lot easier to sell.

I sometimes wish I were smart enough to have seen this one coming. We had it only about half right. It was an accidental waterfall, but as a 50-bagger, a huge waterfall nonetheless, which made up for lots of disasters. Why can't they all be like this?

Why not? Alteon lived on the edge of data networks and was selling their switches like hotcakes, a direct beneficiary of that 80-20 barrier coming down. It went public at $18 and ran to over $100. Crazy.

We had a chip company, MMC, that sold parts to Cisco and was running hot. Another little chip company, Exar, was running. Remember the company Cybersource, with "just a bunch of nobodies" as investors? They spun off a software retailer named Beyond.com. It didn't look like a great business, but after cutting a marketing and promotion deal with America Online, even it went public.

Less than a year after meeting with Mr. Shim of Ssangyong, CS First Boston (or Worst Boston, as Nick Moore would probably say) took our little chip company public at $18. The stock soon traded over $100. The Koreans had a little currency problem? To our benefit.

Our performance was almost unreal. We were up 32% in the first quarter of 1999 and then another 52% in the second quarter, and we were already up another 20% in the third quarter. When it rains it pours. We now had almost a billion dollars in assets. A long way from the $10 million we barely scraped together back in the fall of 1996.

The market was flying but I needed some grounding. How did all this really work? How did money flow around the world? Why was I so lucky as to pick off some hapless, sweating Korean who was stuck on the wrong end of a trade now worth 40 times what he sold it to me for? There is always something sane to craziness.

## > > > *You Turned Down What?*

PALO ALTO, CALIFORNIA—SUMMER 1999

"I can't believe we just turned down a billion dollars. It seems to be only a couple of months ago that we were begging people for a million bucks." I sighed.

At two breakfasts a week apart at Il Fornaio in Palo Alto, we had been offered, and turned down $500 million each, from two different Middle Eastern groups.

"It's probably the best investment decision we ever made," Fred calmly noted.

"Someone is going to take that billion. It's going to find its way into the Valley."

"Not through us."

"I know, I know. I didn't feel like having money from Bahrain and Saudi Arabia either."

"It's not that. The billion we have is already too much."

"I thought you can't be too rich or too thin."

"I suppose. But you can be too big in this business."

"But 1% a year on another billion is—"

"Forget that."

"What then?"

"When I was at JP Morgan, they burdened me with assets until I broke."

"What do you mean?"

"You start chasing lousy businesses just to put the money to work."

"How?" I asked.

"Because there are only so many good investments out there. Five- or ten-baggers are not supposed to be easy to find. This bubble we're in the middle of is silly. Everything is a five-bagger—the worse the company, the more it goes up."

"I agree that we're not in some new funky utopian era. This thing will shake out. But it's not like we're chasing Pet Food 'R' Us.com."

"It doesn't matter. Who do you think is buying all that fiber and switches, General Motors?"

"So we ought to be giving money back to our investors?"

"Maybe."

"But I kinda like it. It was so goddamn hard to raise. I can't bear the thought of just shipping it back out."

"I know. But I'll bet that no one is going to want it back."

"Which is probably why we should force it back—the perfect contrary indicator," I said, realizing that, as usual, Fred was right.

"We can still find some great stocks. We just need to be smaller before this all blows up. If not, we're going to have a lot of blood on our hands."

"So we need to start selling stuff so we have cash for redemptions?"

"Not overnight, but we should think about doing this over the next year or so. In the meantime, this market is still flying. It's probably not a bad discipline to put on ourselves," Fred said.

"Actually, this might be fun. There are a few investors I've always wanted to throw out of the fund. I'm going to start calling them and toss them out. Can I start with your friend James Duck?"

"Start with that guy in Laguna who calls once a week asking for stock tips—or anyone who bothers us. We can work our way to the whiny investors next."

"And what do we sell?"

"Probably 20% of everything," Fred figured.

"But there are some great names in there—they could go higher."

"Isn't that the point?"

"I suppose you're right. No better way to rip those babies from our tight clutches."

"I'll try to think of it some other way, but forced selling is probably the only thing that will really work in this crazy market."

In a bizarre way, we had a hedge on our hedge.

## > > > Hot IPO

PALO ALTO, CALIFORNIA—SUMMER 1999

"Should we push for shares in MP3.com?" I asked Fred.

"Don't bother. We're not going to get any. I'm not sure who gets shares in CS First Boston IPOs," Fred replied, shaking his head.

"The thing is going to be hot," I said.

"So what?"

"We are the perfect type of fund that should be getting shares. We might actually hold it for a while."

"Not this one," Fred said.

"I guess you're right. What was that CEO's name? The young kid with the bad turtleneck we saw up at that H&Q thing at Snowbird?"

"Michael something."

"Robertson. Michael Robertson. What was he, 27? At least he was honest. He said he bought the MP3.com domain, got Sequoia to fund him and then started meeting record companies. He said he didn't even know what A&R meant. What a dumbass. Even I know it's Artists and Reviews."

"It's Artists and Repertoire," Fred corrected.

"See?"

"Young guys don't bother me. His problem is that he's got no business model. If the only piece of intellectual property he has is the name MP3.com, he's toast."

"Isn't Sequoia involved? Another one of Don Valentine's monster markets, perhaps?" I asked.

"More like Frankenstein," Fred shot back

"The lawyers for the underwriters will be worth every penny to keep them out of trouble," I said.

"That's right. This is another one of those silly ideas like

GeoCities. Get individuals to put stuff on the Web and then sell them something. Except his competition is Napster, not EMI."

"I'll put in for our usual 50,000 share allocation," I said.

Fred started laughing. "We'll be lucky if we get 500 shares."

"So what. I want to beat up those clowns at CSFB and get them to appreciate that we are players here."

"Are we?"

"We've got, what, half a billion under management and rising every day." What a change from a year ago. New investors kept pouring in money, plus, the value of our stocks had doubled again by midyear. From being too hard, it was now almost too easy.

"That is amazing," Fred said, shaking his head in disbelief. "But it doesn't make us players, not in CSFB's eyes. We don't trade enough. I'll bet most $50 million hedge funds do more in commissions in a month than we do in a year."

"Still . . ."

"Still, what? We are working for our investors, not Wall Street."

"I know, but those bozos should be allocating more shares to funds like us—the elusive long-term investors. If it's just flippers that get shares, then when the company runs into trouble, no one is going to be around to put more money in to support the stock."

"We'll look at it in two years when the stock is $5, they fire the CEO and take the cash and do something more interesting."

"If they last that long."

I put in for 50,000 shares of MP3.com. The indicated range was $9–11, which I thought would value the company at $500 million, pretty steep for a company that really didn't do much of anything. But this sucker was going to trade up, just like every other IPO in 1999. We never got many shares on any deal. Not just from CSFB but from anyone else. A hundred shares here, 1,000 shares there, if we were lucky. Even if we were investors in the company already and management specifically asked that we get a decent allocation, it was always an uphill struggle.

Fred was right. We just didn't do enough in commissions to become a major account with Wall Street. Plus, I was trading more and more through the Instinet box. To increase my chances of getting more than 100 shares, I told CSFB that I would consider buying more shares in the open market, with a small caveat that only if it didn't trade over $20.

"I've got some bad news and some good news." It was Vince, our salesman from CSFB. Nice guy. Kept us up to date on CSFB deals. I told him to stop calling with their analyst recommendations; I knew how that sausage was made.

"This is 1999. There is no bad news," I replied.

"Well, it's not really bad news. We priced MP3.com last night."

"Let me guess—it's not $9–11 anymore." Hot deals always saw their price go up. "What, $15, $18. You guys are going to be piggy?"

"They priced it at $28," Vince told me.

I spit up the coffee I was drinking.

"Nice. That values it at what, $1 billion?"

"More like $1.5 billion, if you count options and the like."

"A bargain at twice the price."

"Well, the good news is your allocation is 10,000 shares."

"Really? You sure that's not a typo."

"I couldn't believe it myself. That's one of the biggest allocations of any of my clients for any of my deals. Thanks."

"Shouldn't I be thanking you?"

"Sure, but I get a selling concession on these IPOs." His commission wasn't chopped liver on these deals.

"Well, you're welcome and thanks."

"It's what, 9:45 in New York now. My guess is this won't start trading until 11:00 or 12:00 New York time, so hang on."

"Great, thanks." I hung up.

"Fred, I've got bad news and good news and, oh, forget it, we got 10,000 shares of this MP3.com dog and those bastards raised the price to $28."

"Get rid of it."

"My thoughts exactly."

I put the MPPP symbol on my screen and waited for it to start trading. My guess is that every Tom, Dick and Harriet were logging into their Schwab or E*Trade account and putting in a market order for 100 shares of MP3.com, thinking they would get it at $28.

Suckers. Market orders get filled wherever the trader wants to set the price. This thing was going higher—although I didn't know how much—until all those retail orders were filled.

"Hi, it's Vince."

"Yeah?"

"This thing is going to open north of $50. Probably in the next half hour."

"I said I would buy more in the open market if it was under $20."

"You should up the limit."

"What is that, a $3 billion market cap? They did $700 grand last quarter."

"They are growing."

"I'm not sure we are long-term investors on this one."

"Suit yourself."

"Any idea why we got such a good allocation?"

"Still checking."

"Find out. I'd like more on other deals."

"It's trading," Fred yelled over.

"Look at that thing go. The ducks are quacking."

"Get rid of it."

"Got it."

I logged into Instinet and put the entire 10,000 for sale. Within a few seconds, they were gone, eaten like fresh meat by a swarm of sharks. I didn't care what we got for the shares—the whole process was a joke. We ended up getting out in the $60s, meaning our investors made over $300,000 by holding the shares for less than a minute.

"Fred, can we annualize this return?"

"It's a bluebird. Forget about it," Fred replied.

"Let's see, 100% in one minute. How many minutes in a trading day—hmmm, this is something like several zillion compound annual growth rate. Of course, past returns are no indication of future performance."

"Let's find some real company to put the proceeds in. These IPOs are creepy."

"OK, back to work." I took MPPP off my screen forever.

"Well," Fred lobbed in, "we solved the mystery."

"What mystery?" I asked.

"While you were out to lunch, Vince called."

"Yeah?"

"Mr. A&R's company peaked at $105."

"Ugghh. We sold too soon," I screamed.

"At $105, MP3.com was worth $6.9 billion, which is more than most of the real record companies. Michael Robertson was worth $2.66 billion at the peak."

"That little putz?"

"Yup. But that's all in the past. The stock closed at $63."

"We're brilliant!"

"You wish. Now—did you have some op-ed in the *Journal* this week?"

"Yeah, there was a piece that ran on Monday, 'The Upside-Down World of High Tech.' "

"Well, the syndicate guy at CSFB seemed to like the piece. Vince claims that's the reason we got 10,000 shares."

"Really, that's the strangest thing I've ever heard."

"Never underestimate the bizarre, upside-down world of Wall Street."

"The *Journal* pays me $300 per piece," I said.

"Don't quit your day job," Fred insisted.

Good advice.

The markets were crazy. Valuing a piece of shit music company like MP3.com at $6 billion is stupid. Should we write our congressperson and complain? Hell, no. This was working too well.

Our fund rose 42% in the third quarter of 1999 and then an unbelievable 66% in the fourth. I was shipping money out to investors at the end of each month, whether they wanted it or not, but the damn thing kept going up.

## > > > Fleece-Boston Conference 2K

SAN FRANCISCO, CALIFORNIA—FEBRUARY 2000

"I don't get it. Same conference, same stupid companies—but now it's Fleet Boston Robertson Stephens. Is every bank going to merge?" I asked.

"You mean Fleece Boston? Banks have name envy. But remember, nothing can beat Citibank Travelers Salomon Smith Barney Harris Upham," Nick Moore told me. I think I would have stopped going to these stupid conferences years ago if Nick Moore wasn't there to teach me what was really going on.

"This place is crazy. It almost doesn't matter what companies say—their stock pops five points after their presentation. I've been blowing out of one of our names, Tut Systems . . ."

"Funky Tut."

"The CEO just spoke and the damn thing is up 12."

"Who are all these people? Where are the usual tech dudes? Nobody's here," Nick complained.

"You mean there is a bunch of nobodies here," I corrected.

"Well put." Hey, a compliment from Nick Moore—I may have finally made it.

I was about to admit that it wasn't really my line when Nick interrupted.

"You know why nobody we know is here? They all got way too rich to go to meetings themselves, and they send their PBAs."

"PBAs?" I asked.

"Pretty Blonde Assistants," Nick said.

"PBAs and MBAs. Let's go check out those two snot-faced B-schoolers at the Quotron," I said.

Nick casually strolled over with me at his heels.

"I'm telling you, it's going higher," MBA One said.

"You're probably right," MBA Two agreed.

"Infospace has it all—content, distribution, quality management, analyst support. It's a sure thing," MBA One confidently declared.

"There is no such thing as a sure thing," Nick interrupted.

"There is the movie, of course," I added. I had watched the movie *The Sure Thing* the night before on HBO.

"They just signed a wireless deal." MBA One foolishly tried to derail Nick.

"Yeah, John Cusack, going to California to bag Nicolette Sheridan," Nick launched. "I suppose there is a sure thing, but wasn't the moral of the movie that there is no sure thing? He settles for Daphne whoever, the chick on *Melrose Place*." Nick clearly didn't spend all his waking hours on stocks.

"The moral is that you should sing show tunes," I told him.

MBA One and MBA Two, each with overmoussed spiky hair, look confused. And a little scared, I might add.

"Show tunes?" MBA Two asked.

"You guys were in diapers in 1985. The best scene in the movie is where Daphne flashes another car after they moon her, except a cop sees this and pulls over the driver, who only wants to sing show tunes."

"You know who that was?"

"No."

"Tim Robbins."

"Oh, yeah. Anyway . . ." I notice that the MBA twins were long gone, but that didn't stop us.

"And do you know what the cop gave Tim Robbins a ticket for?"

"Hmmm." Nick thought hard.

" 'Driving without your load properly tied down,' " I answered my own question.

"Very good," Nick congratulated me on my grasp of useless trivia.

"I suppose that's how I feel running money. It's like driving without my load properly tied down. Everything is flopping around so fast, it's hard to tell what's going on. If it should go down, like Infospace, it goes up," I complained.

"These kids are playing video games with people's savings," Nick shot back. "Just remember, the only thing for sure is that there is no sure thing."

"That's for goddamn sure," I said.

I tried to find Fred and go to a few presentations with him, but I couldn't locate him. Finally I called his cell.

"Where are you?"

"On 101, heading home."

"What gives?"

"I thought I was going to throw up."

"You feeling OK?"

"Oh, I'm fine. It was that conference—it made me nauseous." These were strong words for Fred.

"In what way?"

"Something's wrong. It's not supposed to be like that. I've been going to these things for 20 years, and they are never a love fest like that."

"You mean Tut shouldn't be up 12 points? I think it hit $60."

"It probably shouldn't even be $12. Are we still selling it?"

"Yup, I'll get rid of the rest."

"We probably should dump everything," Fred thought out loud.

"Fred, we should go to 100% cash and head to the beach," I offered.

"You're probably right. Let's just keep throwing people out of the fund and sell enough to meet redemptions. This thing feels like the finale at a July Fourth fireworks at Shea Stadium. You'd hate to leave before it's really over, but we should beat the crowds to the parking lot."

"Let's get rid of everything that's not a core position," I suggested.

"Nothing is ever core. Remember, we only rent these stocks," Fred said.

We sold plenty to meet our forced redemptions, but we should have just dumped it all.

> > > **Part VI**

v

v

v

v

# Burst

## > > > Dip or Bubble?

PALO ALTO, CALIFORNIA—MARCH 2000

"It seems a little too easy," I said out loud, for no particularly good reason. I'm not sure why "easy" bothered me so much, especially after what we'd gone through to get here. But it did.

"What do you mean?" Fred asked.

"I don't know. NASDAQ started out the year at 4,000, and it just hit 5,000 for the second time in three weeks. And everybody celebrates. Maybe this whole redemption thing wasn't so smart."

"People who celebrate Dow 10,000 and NASDAQ 5,000 are the same ones who obsess over stock splits," Fred noted.

"Good point. Still . . ."

"Still what? Yahoo is $200. Amazon is $70 after splitting. AOL is buying TimeWarner. Pets.com actually has a bid," Fred said with his best dripping sarcastic tone. "It's crazy."

"Twilight Zone," I said.

We'd just seen the list from the folks that track hedge funds—our 377% gain in 1999 made us the fourth best hedge fund for the year. We are on our way to being up 40% for the first quarter of 2000, our sixth quarter of big gains in a row. It is just too bizarre to believe—dogs and cats living together. Not that I'm complaining. That's what we are supposed to do, but the old Wall Street adage, a guy named George Miller first said it, rattles in my head: "Don't mistake brains for a bull market."

"What is that scam B2B thing out of Pennsylvania?" Fred asked.

"Internet Capital Group? ICGE?"

"Yeah. Where is that?"

"One twenty, down from $150," I answered.

"Down? Wow, what a concept. Even great companies are out of whack—is Cisco still $150? I thought I just read a Morgan Stanley report saying it's cheap at 100 times earnings. We've been up six quarters in a row now. You're right—it is too easy."

"So?"

"So, who knows anymore? What's going out the door on March 31?" Fred asked.

"Something like $50 million."

"Good. Keep selling stuff. It almost doesn't matter what."

"It's a massacre. Wasn't NASDAQ just 5,000 a week or so ago. I think I blinked," I remarked.

"It's 3,300 and probably going lower."

"It's the day before tax day—maybe people are selling to pay their capital gains taxes for last year," I offered.

"Maybe. But those trades don't clear for a few days. This may be something else," Fred said coldly.

"Buyer exhaustion?"

"I wish. That's how all these bubbles end. We're getting beat up, but it looks like they're taking the Internet names out first."

"Out back to the woodshed, like Old Yeller."

"And that silly Pets.com sock puppet. Couldn't happen to a nicer group of names," Fred said, almost a little too gleefully.

"Maybe this is real. I haven't seen that bag lady return to the bench outside."

"She was the ghost of bear markets past."

"Here's another one for you, Fred. Your friends at Internet Capital Group?"

"Yeah?"

"Forty dollars. Wasn't it just a hundred and a half last time we checked?"

"Watch them all squirm," Fred said with a mock satanic laugh.

"You're having fun with this?"

"When we head up, I'm always gloomy, worrying if it is all going to roll over. When the market blows up, I get in a good mood. I probably personalize this contrarian stuff a bit too much."

"Fred, you almost barfed during the Robertson conference just last month. Let me know when the giddy wears off—it's a great indicator."

"I think we'll be OK. Dot-coms won't be buying much equipment anymore, but the telcos will."

Fred was right, but only for a while. Telcos did keep buying. The NASDAQ meltdown of March and April 2000 was followed by a buying binge for infrastructure stocks—companies that made network equipment, chips, software, anything related to broadband. WorldCom announced record capital spending (little did anyone realize it was CFO Scott Sullivan classifying every expense as capital spending so he could write it off over years rather than right away).

NASDAQ came back, led by Cisco and networkers. The 80-20 barrier that Netscape helped break created a monster waterfall. Our investment, Alteon, had switches that sat at the same edge of the network as Cisco, and they were booming. Their stock was flying—$100, $120, $140 and rising all summer. Then one day, we woke up to this news release: "Nortel Networks buys Web switch vendor Alteon for $7.8 billion."

"Wow, it doesn't get any better than this," I told Fred.

"What are they paying?" Fred asked.

"$7.8 billion. That's more than AOL paid for Netscape!" I exclaimed.

"No, how much per share?"

"It's gotta be $200 plus."

"Read on," Fred said.

"Deal to close Q4, blah, blah, blah, $144 per share. Hey, wait a second, that's about where it closed yesterday. No premium? They're stealing this company out from under us. What the—"

"It already was trading at a $7.8 billion valuation. Let's see, they did about $50 million last quarter."

"That's only 39 times."

"Fifty million dollars in sales. That's 39 times revenue. They did 16 cents per share in earnings last quarter . . ."

"Blowing away the three cents that the street predicted," I added.

"I'll do the math for you, Mr. Electrical Engineer. That's a P/E, price to earnings ratio, of 225."

"Are you trying to suggest we should be happy that Nortel is stealing Alteon?"

"Something like that."

"So much for the efficient market theory!" I sighed.

"Oh, it's efficient. The inputs are just flaky. Alteon has to make $10 a share in 2005 to justify $144. They might—but now it's Nortel's problem."

"Well, I didn't get into the hedge fund business to own a Canadian telephone switch company. Nothing personal against our frozen friends to the north, but we don't have much of a choice here," I said.

"Nope. Blow it out!"

I spent the month of August at the beach with my family, with a Blackberry pager in one hand and a cell phone in the other, hitting the bid for almost a million shares of Alteon. Some of our shares weren't registered yet, so we had to tender them and get Nortel shares. Yuck. We didn't hit Nortel's peak of $80 something, but our anti-Canadian bias was useful. We blew Nortel shares out at $75, $65, $60, $55 and $50 and then poof—we were done. The cash disappeared at the end of the month to whatever investors were summarily tossed out that month. We sold bits and pieces of everything else, but not enough—all would have been enough. But we had the luck of the Canucks. I have been nice to Canadians ever since.

Fred was right to be nauseous. If everyone knows, it's over. The clump of water was about to break up on the rocks, the second derivative had played out, enticing investors in with the seduction of faster and faster growth. Metcalfe's Law was no longer a secret; you could see it in subscriber growth and Internet usage and equipment sales and page views and everything. Fast growth became an input and an assumption to value schlock like MP3.com and plenty of other garbage too. This also meant great companies went up way too far as well.

It all peaked in September 2000. The fourth quarter of 2000 is when the market really gave up the ghost. It was like the crisis of 1998, but with real volume, real selling. We were down 50% in the quarter. Fortunately, we had been returning capital to investors every month, forcing us to sell, and we ended up down only 5% for the year. It's not a great consolation prize.

## > > > Morgan Stanley Tech Conference 2001

SCOTTSDALE, ARIZONA—JANUARY 2001

"Did you listen to Shamazon? It looked like Bezos wanted to strangle Mary Meeker for showing up late."

"Nick, how come I knew I would run into you here?" I said.

"I'm still waiting for an answer why they classify order fulfillment as a marketing expense."

"Because it would show they are shipping a $5 bill with every order they fill?" I asked.

"That too. They're hiding how bad their gross margins are. They'll survive, but a company with low margins just isn't worth my time."

"Do you like anything?"

"Oh, you mean like High Village? Candace Carpenter as CEO of the decade?"

"You must like something."

"Oh, you mean like the shop until *they* drop companies? Webscam? Free-toys? Price-slime.con? Bye-Buy.com? They're all negative gross margin free-tailers."

"OK, so the dot-com names are crazy. What about B2B, e-commerce stuff?"

"Oh, Amoeba/Ariba, Commerce None? Those are even worse. Or all those Sink-ubators like Internet Capital Group and Divine Interventures—give me a break."

"Networking maybe?"

"Floundry Networks, no thanks."

• • •

"It's really over, isn't it?" I said.

"See those guys over there?" Nick asked.

"You mean those guys with the Ashleigh Banfield glasses? Are those the Janus guys we always used to see?"

"Yup, just a new look. Until six months ago, those guys used to never break a sweat. Money flowed in like water, so they would just buy more of what they owned. Helped their performance numbers. What did they care? Gemstar—Gemscar. It was just their investors' money—they got paid either way. They rode 'em up and they're going to ride 'em down."

"You're fouler than usual," I said.

"Doesn't bother me, I'll take either side of this thing. I'm just not sure who the next sucker is to come in and buy this garbage. The Asians are broke, and the Europeans don't buy anything without a dividend, so it's just the dumb-ass American public pouring into the Januses of the world. I'll take the other side of that trade every day of the week."

"You don't think fundamentals will hold up?"

"Not a chance—it was all funny money. AOL buying Time-Warner is just a farce. Even if business stays good, paying 100 times earnings and 20 times sales means they have to stay great for five or more years. How many tech cycles do you remember that have lasted that long? Any?"

"Nope."

"The stock of the greatest company in the world is crap if every investor already thinks it is the greatest company in the world."

Yup, sometimes you gotta wait for the next waterfall.

## > > > Global Pitches

Diligently, month by month in 2001, I sold what I needed to meet the forced redemptions at the end of the month. The market was all over the place but mostly down, down, down. The selling was relentless, which made my job tougher. Still, we had a September deadline to get completely out on our five-year anniversary.

We still visited companies—that doesn't stop. And we still got pitched new ideas from entrepreneurs looking for venture funding. But it was sometime in 2001 that I started noticing a difference to these pitches. They weren't coming from Stanford MBAs or three guys in Sunnyvale with a brilliant idea.

I got pitched by a group visiting from Bangalore to expand call centers for U.S. companies. Or from another group in Bombay doing contract software development work for hire. A group of Israeli physicists had a new way of creating transistors that could change the entire semiconductor business. There were some software coders in Norway working on applications for cell phones. A group out of Russia had some really cool 3-D technology. Japanese videogame creators. Finnish packet handling. And on and on.

We weren't set up to do foreign investments, but they all sounded fascinating. Maybe they'd work, maybe not, but something was going on outside of the four walls of Silicon Valley.

# Part VII

# The Margin Surplus

## > > > What Is Wealth?

I suppose this is the point in the story where I walk away and question the meaning of life. Except I can't seem to walk away, and I've never been good at navel gazing. But something bizarre had just taken place and I must have learned something.

I mean that was without a doubt the strangest few years of my life. Boom-bust, boom-bust and then, oh yeah, the big whopper BOOM-BUST. Trillions gained in '99, kazillions lost again since then. What a way to live. But inside that yo-yo is a lesson somewhere. I kind of realized toward the end that although I'm in the business of running money—we had a billion dollars under management at our peak—I barely had time to think out the most important question: What is wealth?

Wealth is fleeting, I suppose, from the looks of the last year and a half, but there must be some absolutes. Industrialists generated wealth. But what about now—in a postindustrial world? The answer makes a difference in how to put money to work.

Those "families with substantial assets" had wealth, but it wasn't static. Every generation it shrank unless they chased returns. No rest for the weary. But they don't like risk. Well, too bad. I think what I learned is that wealth comes not just from taking risk but from constantly taking risks.

The four-door office isn't a metaphor, it's reality. You can be a long-term investor, but you constantly have to adjust your sights to the next big thing. We may be in the midst of a long cycle like the British 100-year industrial boom, but that doesn't mean you can buy and hold and be on the golf course by noon.

What startles me is that those who generate wealth in Silicon Valley run at 100 miles per hour. They don't own anything of value like a textile mill or an auto factory. They own a process, the ability to constantly update their products and take advantage of that waterfall, some massive price declines and then move on to the next product or process.

The world had changed. The mighty economies of Japan and Korea and Thailand are not taking over. Their output of cars and laptops and VCRs and DVD players and memory chips and computer monitors and sneakers is booming, but something's wrong. They have giant factories with lots of lower-wage workers who wind wire, screw screws, bolt bolts, wrap plastic and stick in power cords. But that's not what anyone pays for anymore. Their economies achieve full employment, sure, but these countries are not economic powerhouses. Not anymore.

We were investing in companies with no more than 50–100 workers, most of them highly paid programmers and engineers, whose occupational hazard is coming down off a caffeine buzz and an occasional late night Nerf gun injury. Yet even after the market bubble burst in 2000, these companies would still be worth more than Ssangyong, a company a hundred or a thousand times their size. The stock market values small businesses with high margins over big businesses with low margins. Is that good or bad? Should I even care?

Whenever I try to figure out why this is, I keep thinking back and visualizing Mr. Shim, a walking, talking and sweating metaphor for how to invest. Something like "We think, they sweat." The spoils go to those with high margins.

You can make intellectual property, but real soon it's worthless. You don't really own anything tangible, just the ability to move it along, kick the can down the road, as diplomats like to say.

Ask economists, and somewhere in their babble they will tell you that the role of an economy is to increase the standard of living of its participants. Did the boom-bust, boom-bust yo-yo I just lived through do that? I think so, but with lots of change. America doesn't make stuff anymore—we design it. The numbers are fishy, but even after the rocky start in the 1990s, I think this new think/sweat thing will create more wealth for more people, not just in the U.S. but around the world, than the Industrial Revolution ever did.

The model I keep focusing on has the U.S. designing chips and someone in Taiwan making them for cheap. That sounds like a plan, but somehow this means we run trade deficits. Just the word *deficit* sounds so awful—no one likes to be called deficient. What is the right model? Maybe we should just manufacture these chips and everything else in the U.S.? Aren't all jobs good for the economy and our standard of living?

# >>> Industrial Economists

When I was a kid, every morning as I walked out my front door, I subconsciously held my breath and then looked up to see if the fog was in. If not, I would take a deep breath and head off to the school bus. If the sky was overcast with low, overhanging clouds, I held my breath for as long as I could. The first breath was always a nasty one, a sharp, stinging reek that would permeate my sinuses and make me wish I were somewhere else. The town I lived in was in central New Jersey, a highly industrialized stretch connected to the outside world by the Raritan River, Interstate 287 and railroad tracks that crisscrossed the town. It wasn't as bad as Perth Amboy or Rahway, with their giant Esso oil refineries that still stink up the New Jersey Turnpike and give the state a bad name. Nor was it an armpit like Camden. But it still stank.

Upwind were a combination of Union Carbide, Johns Manville, Sherwin-Williams, Dow Chemical, Hoechst and Johnson & Johnson. No wonder it reeked; I lived in an industrial sewer. These companies became a murderers' row, mostly killing off their own workers. Our neighbor worked for Johns Manville, until asbestos litigation shuttered the local facilities and the company hightailed it to Denver. Union Carbide killed thousands in Bhopal, India, in 1984, but a similar accident probably could just have easily happened in my hometown.

Not that I had any clue. It actually was a nice place to live—suburbia filled almost entirely with middle-class families: lower, middle and upper middle class. There were jobs for everybody. The lower lived well; they all owned houses in decent neighborhoods. The upper, well, they moved uphill.

But as I look back, I realize that the '60s and '70s were not only the peak but the start of the petering out of industrial central New Jersey and industrial America.

Unfortunately, most active Wall Street economists were trained in the 1960s and '70s. Government statistics back then tracked an industrial economy. I long ago figured out that I couldn't make a dime listening to industrial economists.

Even if they are fresh PhD in economics grads, class of 2004, they are industrial economists. Intellectual property is a foreign idea to them. So is the stock market. It just doesn't fit into their thinking. The math is too hard. You can't model the stock market. So they ignore it or look at it as a casino rather than as an important source and destination of capital. They are stuck in the era of Wilkinson and Watt and Classical Gold Standards. They cloud our thinking.

But investors still listen to them and dissect industrial data. Hmmm. I smell opportunity.

My hometown is now a haven and a heaven for the biotech industry. Up and down Interstate 287 are two- and three-story office parks filled with firms playing around with DNA, creating pharmaceuticals to cure all the illnesses the Industrial Revolution heaped upon us. A mall and a minor league baseball stadium have replaced the Sherwin-Williams factory.

Is there a long-term trade here? Of course, lessons are all over the place if you just turn the world upside down. Perhaps the Dow is more important than GDP.

Will the dollar go down or go up? Do interest rates matter? Are deficits bad or good? Should I even give a shit about economics?

It matters, I suppose, but not to me. I just want to figure out where the big quantum leaps are. Give me a big enough sandbox to play in, and I'll find the part of it not being used as kitty litter.

## > > > Grand Unifying Theory

PALO ALTO, CALIFORNIA—SUMMER 2001

"We are going to send shares to your account and some cash too," I told Mr. Zed.

"I'd rather you keep going, but you were smart to send money back over the last couple of years. The selling was the right thing to do."

"It worked out that way." I still felt guilty telling the guy who put us in business that we were no longer going to work for him, although we did give him back six times his original investment.

"And I understand why you are closing up," Mr. Zed said.

"You do? Then maybe you can explain it to me."

"Because it worked. It was supposed to take ten years, and a bull market squeezed it into three. Now, who needs the hassle? You can sit back with a more relaxed pace and think even longer term. You'll be an even better investor," Mr. Zed said.

"I suppose." That was pretty good. I'm not sure that he was right, but maybe that is how I should look at it.

"But now you have to tell me how you are going to think over the next ten years."

"The only thing I really figured out is that the industrial era is over," I said.

"OK, I understand that. You have an intellectual property economy. I understand the splitting of intellectual property and manufacturing. That's fine. But I can't seem to follow the money trail. What happens to all those dollars that you Americans spend on fine German automobiles or Chinese toys or Japanese laptops? It must show up somewhere."

"I think I know, but it is hard to explain over the phone."

"It's not just explaining away things. It is time for your grand unifying theory. How does the world work? What makes the U.S. such an enviable place to invest? Tell me."

"Well . . ."

I was about to launch into it but got interrupted.

"Oh, don't tell me now. Write it down for me. Just start from the beginning and explain how this all works. If you can do that, you will have it."

While I was thinking about it, real life went on.

## > > > *Sweating at the NUMMI*

FREMONT, CALIFORNIA—SUMMER 2001

"Hey, Phil, you sure this is the right entrance?"

"No clue. This place is massive." Phil was one of those Little League dads you get to know when your kids are on the same team. He is a big, burly firefighter-looking guy with a great sense of humor. The two of us often bellied up to a fence at games and made fun of the other side's coaches, who all seemed to want to win more than their kids. Other than that, I didn't know Phil from Adam. He worked above his garage, but what he did is a mystery. Investor, inventor, consultant, coder, contractor, designer, trust fund baby?

"I parked about a mile away. I've never seen so many pickup trucks in one parking lot."

"The tour starts at three, so we'd better figure out which door, quick," I pleaded.

Phil opened one of the doors in front of us and almost got trampled as a mass of people flowed out. We tried another door and were ushered into a lobby and told to step aside, a shift change was taking place.

"You guys with the school?" some guy in a rent-a-cop uniform asked.

"Yes, Menlo Park."

"OK, the tour has started, but you haven't missed the tram. Walk this way."

I knew what was coming. I looked at Phil, who said, "If I could walk that way . . ."

Nyuk-nyuk. Maybe this won't be such a bad afternoon after all. It was the middle of the summer, and there were a few too many kids hanging around our house, so my wife had insisted I take our two older boys on the tour of NUMMI. Looks like Phil got stuck with the same task as well. It's the curse of us independent types with no staff meetings to attend; we get sucked into going to these stupid events.

I had a vague idea what NUMMI was, a big ugly car factory in the heart of Silicon Valley. I had driven by it a million times—it stood out like a historic landmark in a downtown of glistening progress. Actually, where we were in Fremont was on the seedy edge of the Valley. I remember this place used to be filled mostly with disk drive companies that had long ago scrammed to Singapore and elsewhere. But lots of software and chip companies filled in the space.

"OK, you're late, and we've started, but please grab a seat," said a spunky five-foot-tall woman who was equally as wide. "OK, where were we? Oh, yes. NUMMI stands for New United Motor Manufacturing, Inc. We are going to take a tram ride in a moment, but I want to walk you through what goes on here and why we do things differently."

Phil was rolling his eyes as we sat through a lecture on the plant. Our kids were making paper airplanes out of the handouts. We heard that the whole setup was one giant experiment. From what I could gather, General Motors had built this factory years ago and was losing its shirt keeping it open, shipping thousand-dollar bills out with every car it made. It tried to close down but couldn't. Smelled like the United Auto Workers union had a veto, but somehow our guide skipped the reason. In 1984, Toyota, looking for a U.S. presence, cut a deal with GM to co-own the factory, but only if it was operated under the rules of the Toyota Production System and their culture of a "teamwork-based working environment."

Phil leaned over and whispered, "Are we going to have to do calisthenics before the tour?"

Our guide had been promoted off the floor and was singing the benefits of TPS. "It used to be thought that the biggest problem for an assembly line was when the line came to a stop. It's a problem, to be sure, but in Detroit the culture was ingrained in workers' minds; 'Don't stop the line at all costs.' If you 'grabbed the cord,' as we call stopping the line, sirens and bells would go off until the line was restarted. If you grabbed the cord enough times, you were fired, so workers quit grabbing the cord. And if you don't stop the line, what do you get?"

"More ugly Buicks?" I shot at Phil.

"If you don't stop the line, you get defects. Detroit had a big problem with defective cars. Lots of lemons came off the line. For Toyota, this would be a big problem."

"Big ploblem," Phil corrected.

"So, when we are on the tram, you will occasionally hear music playing. Each area of the line has a different classical tune so that supervisors can figure out where the line is stopped and apply workers, if need be, to fix the problem quickly. It is the ancient Japanese principle of *jidoka,* which loosely translates as 'don't pass the trash.' Now pick up your safety glasses at the counter and grab a seat on the tram, which I will be driving."

My two boys and Phil's kid got the front seat in the first tramcar, and Phil and I sat behind them. There must have been 15 of these two-row tramcars.

"This looks like the zebra train at the San Francisco Zoo," Phil said.

"Or a bad Disney ride," I said to Phil. "And you ought to consider wearing safety glasses all the time—they make you look a lot smarter."

The tram wound its way through the factory. I have been on so many company tours, especially of chip fabs in the Valley, the closest to manufacturing it gets around here. This one was the strangest. It was as if the factory was built around the tour, the tramlines laid down before the assembly line.

The guide was especially cheery describing what appeared to be the dreariest jobs I have ever seen. One guy tightening nuts, another attaching a wire, another tightening a harness—each of them dripping sweat. The lighting was bad, the factory noisy, and the air had a gritty, metal-flake feel to it, yet almost every worker we passed looked up and smiled. But it was one of those caged tiger smiles, sort of an I-hate-this-job-and-have-to-put-up-with-gawking-tourists look. Actually, Phil is smarter than he looks. The tram was just like the zebra train at the zoo, but it was real life.

"Forty-seven truckloads of rolled steel are delivered daily on this side of the plant. We bend it, paint it, weld it and bolt it. Four- and 6-cylinder engines are shipped over from Japan, also daily, and dropped in over in this area."

"Is that Rachmaninoff?" Phil asked.

Over the speaker, our guide chirped, "Oh, goody, our first cord grabbing. That music you hear means there is a problem in chassis. And we are headed that way."

A bunch of guys were standing around looking perplexed at some badly bent metal protruding off what I think was the suspension. Guys in blue jumpsuits were pouring in from around the floor, all stopping to smile when they saw the tram tour.

"OK, let's move on," our guide said as I spotted someone with a crowbar straightening the metal out.

"NUMMI is the home to over 5,000 jobs and is a landmark partnership between not only GM and Toyota, but the United Auto Workers as well." I knew they'd play a part somehow. She continued, "The company's core values are based on five cornerstones: teamwork, equity, involvement, mutual trust and respect, and safety."

"And smiling when the tram goes by," Phil added.

"Phil, you think equity means stock options? The tour guide is bucking for some."

"I doubt it. To the Japanese, equity is corporatespeak for 'You are lucky to have a job.' "

I had a snippy comeback, but we were interrupted by a rather loud version of Beethoven or Bach. It was tough to make out with all the clanging.

"Cord grab. Way to go," the clearly overcaffeinated guide screamed into the mike. "We are entering robot land." A bunch of robots were swinging around and blasting giant welding arcs a few times a second onto the body of what I later learned was a Pontiac Vibe.

"It's more like Tomorrowland. I wonder if those guys get overtime," Phil asked, pointing to the robots.

The tram wound around. We got filled with more trivia.

"You know, we have produced five million cars and trucks here since 1984. We have over five million square feet of space on our

211-acre campus. We spend $2.6 billion in North America each and every year, over half of that in California on payroll and parts from over 1,700 suppliers employing 18,000 workers."

"Phil, did we pay for this tour?"

"I think we just did, listening to this propaganda"

"I don't know why they bother. I'll bet they are still losing $1,000 for every car made here," I said.

Phil just nodded, and then said, "I'm glad my parents paid for my college."

It really was Disneyland. And like Mr. Toad's Wild Ride with strains of Mozart in the distance, we hung a sharp left.

"We are heading into engine and body mounting, the real nuts and bolts of the factory."

"Badum, dum." Phil did a rim shot in the air.

"Only the most highly skilled workers ever make it into mounting and Final 1, our multitiered environment. It is right here that the chassis come up from the floor, engines are dropped in and then bodies attached, one per minute."

I thought I heard some rap music coming from near the robots, and a lot of cursing from men in blue suits and yellow hard hats. The guide looked a bit worried but found the distraction.

"Oh, look, there is Johnny Davis. Hi, Johnny, wave to the good folks."

A guy who looked just like Charles Barkley glistening with perspiration waved to the tram.

"Johnny has been at this factory for 24 years. He is on the seniority list for overtime and was one of our highest-paid employees at the factory last year. If you are lucky, with enough overtime your pay can break six figures. Most of the senior guys approaching their retirement pile on the overtime and make big pay days, like Johnny here.

"Lucky?" Phil asked. I was thinking the same thing.

"Any advice for the kids, Johnny?" asked the guide.

"Yeah, stay in school," Johnny belted out in a deep baritone. I think he meant it. I looked in the workers' eyes, and no one was really happy. They weren't part of the future, they were stuck in the past, in a cage. Their only way out was to spend more years in the cage, earning overtime pay. It was as if progress had regressed to 1975 when we stepped inside.

Outside these walls was a teeming Silicon Valley, all about invention and innovation and productivity and modernity. The best innovation they could come up with inside this Nixonian-era hell was cord-grabbing Bach instead of bells.

"Phil, this is quite fascinating."

"Yeah, I agree."

"I just don't want my kids to like it too much. This isn't what I want them to aspire to." It wasn't the intent of the school that set it up, but this tour was turning into a version of *Scared Straight!*, the TV special from the '70s where teenage kids spend a day in jail and the inmates scare the crap out of them to stay out of jail.

"Yeah, it's like a Dickensian time warp, and we're now in some Victorian era sweatshop with the ghost of Christmas past," Phil said.

Phil leaned up to my nine-year-old. "So, Kurt, do you want to work here someday?"

"Oh, jeez, Phil," I muttered.

"No, I plan on being a rock musician."

"Are you sure?" Phil asked. "This looks like pretty neat stuff."

"Yeah, I'm sure. I'll be touring the country with my rock band, like AC/DC. Either that or doing whatever job my dad does."

"A few more bad stock picks and your dad might replace that tour guide."

"All right, enough out of you, Phil," I interrupted.

I love driving cars, especially those with 12 cylinders and an exhaust note that could wake whole neighborhoods. But making cars, that's a whole 'nuther thing. On the way home, through the Valley and across the bay, over the hills and through the woods, we drove past buildings with names on top like Intel, Cisco, Hewlett-Packard, Applied Materials, Oracle, Sun and countless other public companies and startups. I was home again, the real Tomorrowland. Call it postindustrial or call it an intellectual economy, I don't care. Anything but grabbing cords.

## >>> People

It's funny, but when you sit in the middle of Silicon Valley, you tend to think only in bits and bytes, packets and protocols, metatags and megahertz. But when I look at the end markets, look for the waterfalls, it's always, always about people. Wall Street needs machines to sort certificates, and United Airlines needs them to sort tickets. You can do these tasks by hand, but eventually it is either impossible to do quickly or too damn expensive, so technology has to sweep in. Jobs are lost, those jobs sucked anyway. The jobs designing the systems and writing the code are a lot higher paying.

Boulton & Watt replaced horses, but the boom in horsepower replaced people doing piecework, knitting socks, running looms, that kind of stuff. Let alone harvesting corn. Is working at NUMMI much better?

It would take two centuries, but eventually the jobs running engine-powered machinery would no longer be the best at raising our standard of living. Maybe in Sri Lanka, where wages are 45 cents an hour, but not in the U.S.

If an economy is really about increasing the standard of living of its participants, then technology is the tool of that increase. That's why Fred and I live in our car and go to eight meetings a day. But it's a little more complicated. It's not just about technology—it's about people, but brains not brawn.

Spreadsheets beat a calculator and graph paper. Microsoft Word trounces Remington typewriters and carbon paper. Cell phones beat phone booths. Google Web searches beat trudging down to the library to look something up in the dated *Encyclopaedia Britannica*.

It's all about people—replacing them, supporting them, augmenting them, setting their minds free.

Doug Engelbart was right—technology is almost like the alphabet, a platform to build on. Boulton & Watt saved future generations from a life of misery of shoveling shit and spinning sticky cotton threads.

Now the misery is mental. Who wants to sort airline tickets, deliver telegrams, add columns of numbers, take polls? Automating these menial tasks allows designers and those architecting these tools to flourish in our economy. It is the natural next step.

The Internet is not impersonal. Quite the opposite.

EBay replaced newspaper classified ads by creating online auctions. EBay saves billions by having their own customers enforce honesty via a reputation feedback system. Google's search engine ranks results by how many people's sites provide links to other Web sites. Yahoo aggregates personal home pages and job résumés. Barry Diller's InterActive is a front end for buying airline tickets and matching people for dates. Amazon is the premier destination to buy books and many other products by having customers provide reviews and suggestions and lists of books they are interested in. Most of the power of Intel's processors goes toward the human interface of the graphics display. Most of Cisco's infrastructure is to handle e-mail and serving Web pages.

When I go through our portfolio, I see RealNetworks streaming audio and video to people and Inktomi providing search results. Alteon's switches are used to fight off denial of service attacks on Web sites so people can surf safely. And Elantec's laser diode drivers, while not something you ask for at Home Depot, enable millions to create their own music CDs.

People helping people (and helping create billions in wealth for those that create the tools to have people help people).

The open-source community tapped thousands of programmers to create a Linux operating system that is attacking Microsoft's Windows. The Apache Web server, as in "a patchy" open-source kludge, has been perfected over time by an army of contributors.

It's about expanding minds, not expanding muscles. That is the secret of creating intellectual property. It is also the secret to finding the profits. The cost of humans is a great umbrella. If it costs $10 to sort each one of millions of airline tickets and $2 to sort billions of bank checks by $10–20 per hour human beings, you can charge millions of dollars for equipment. It is easy to profit from automating these tasks. For a while anyway, and then you have to move on and automate other, more difficult human tasks to extract profits.

We pay $40 per month for cell phone service because of the cost of the alternative—staying home or using pay phones.

People costs drive demand. Intellectual property augments people, which lowers costs, which drives profits that create wealth, although not always in obvious ways. Napster begat Elantec, and Netscape begat Cisco.

Not every big market makes for great investments. I always go back to the way I positioned IPOs to figure this out. Monster markets are great, but they have to be coupled with an unfair competitive advantage and a business model to leverage that advantage. Is that too much to ask for? Anyone who bought MP3.com envisioned only the monster market (if that). Investing will never be that easy—it's all in the details of the business and what other investors think.

The U.S. is an intellectual property economy. Maybe parts of Europe and slices of Japan are as well. But it's a big world—six billion people and growing. Someone has to make stuff.

## > > > ***BASE Jumping***

PALO ALTO, CALIFORNIA—SUMMER 2001

"I do a lot of jumping."

"Out of planes?" I asked.

"I used to. Now it's just BASE stuff."

I was having gumbo at Nola's in Palo Alto with Mark Allen. He is a guy who has done just about everything in Silicon Valley. My friend, Alex Balkanski, who used to run the chip company C-Cube, insisted I meet him. I was still searching for an intellectual property model that worked so I could somehow follow the money.

"What do you mean, basic stuff?"

"No, not basic. B-A-S-E, BASE. Do you know what that is?"

"I guess not."

"Did you see Vin Diesel in *XXX*?"

"Sure, pretty wild flick."

"Remember the scene where they jump off the bridge?"

"Sure, right at the beginning."

"That's BASE—buildings, antennas, spans and earth. There are a bunch of folks that jump off these things. Me, I kinda prefer the last two, bridges and cliffs," Mark Allen told me.

"Sounds like a lot of crazy folks. And that's what you do now?"

"As much as I can. Most of it is illegal in the U.S., so I travel around the world looking for the best drops, just like when I was in the chip business."

"You use a bungee cord?"

"Heck no. Just parachutes. You hold them in your hand. Then when you jump, you do the one Mississippi, two Mississippi, three Mississippi and then let throw the chute. Sometimes, on big verticals, you can count to fourteen, but it's real easy to lose track of your count when the earth is coming up at 32 feet per second per second. It takes a lot of discipline to hold on. But it's major league exhilarating."

"I know the feeling."

"You jump?"

"Not literally, but I run a hedge fund."

"I don't understand."

"Me neither. But what you just described sounds familiar. It's often the same feeling. Things are whooshing by, and you never know if you are going to hit the ground with a thud or get taken safely upward in some uptrend. Plus, it takes a lot of discipline to hang in to something you have conviction in."

"So, you've worked in this business for a long time?" I asked.

"Yeah, Cypress for a long time, the C-Cube, then a bunch of startups. Now I'm mostly floating around, sometimes literally."

"Floating or falling? If I'm not mistaken, Cypress had factories, and C-Cube didn't. But more importantly, you worked for T. J. Rodgers and lived to talk about it?" I asked. T.J. was the notoriously high-strung CEO of Cypress Semiconductor who burned through managers, but for the most part, ran a very profitable and valuable company.

"Yeah, he's not so bad. You make your numbers, you do OK."

"So, after running all those fabs at Cypress, you were the chief operating officer of C-Cube, which didn't have any fabs. What the hell did you do?"

"I just ran someone else's fab, you know, the foundries. It was their workers, but I spent my time getting out what we needed from them. I looked at it like a rental."

"Before you go on, I have a great T.J. story. I once hosted T.J. at an investor dinner in New York. I got a call from the CFO, Ken Goldman—I think he is at Siebel now—worried that T.J. would be late for the investor meeting. 'Not a problem,' I told him. 'I'll just send a car service to JFK, and the driver will hold up a sign with his name on it at the gate and bring him straight to the dinner.'"

"Yeah?"

"About an hour later, Ken calls back and says, 'Can you make sure that the driver spells it R-O-D-G-E-R-S?' 'Uh, yeah, why is that?' I ask him. 'T.J. hates when it's spelled R-O-G-E-R-S. It drives him crazy. Please make sure it's spelled right.' "

"That sounds like T.J.," Mark said.

"I couldn't believe it. I mean here is the CFO of an NYSE-listed company, with a billion-dollar market capitalization, and he is calling me about the spelling of his CEO's name on a driver's cheap cardboard sign. Something funny is going on in that place. It must have been held together with stress."

"Pretty close."

"Of course, Morgan Stanley was the same type of stressful place, so I called the car service. I told them 'Hold up a sign that says Mr. Rogers. Spell it R-O-G-E-R-S, like the Neighborhood.' You gotta get your kicks when you can."

"Good for you." Mark laughed.

"So, how does it work? It confuses the hell out of me, and I'm having trouble following the money trail," I asked.

"Well, it sounds complex, but it really is kinda simple. Look, we ship out a design, the Taiwanese make it for us, we mark it up and sell it to Sony, and the profit sits in Barbados."

"OK, OK, go back and fill in some of the details," I said.

"You've been to Cube's buildings in Milpitas in Silicon Valley, right?"

"Yeah, sure."

"There are fabs up and down the street, but in our buildings, we didn't have all that much, just a bunch of cubicles and lots of PhDs handcuffed to them."

"Who do what?"

"They design. It's amazing what they come up with. Processors, video compression stuff, jitter removers—I can't even tell you everything that is inside those chips," Mark said.

"Or you'd have to kill me?"

"Well, that too. But this stuff is so complicated. Lots of hardware, microcode software, it's genius stuff."

"Is that why they call it intellectual property?" I asked.

"I suppose. Anyway, these guys design these chips. We simulate them to make sure they are exactly what we want, then we e-mail GDS-II files to Taiwan."

"GPS files?"

"Oh, sorry. No, GDS-II files. It's one of those industry standards, a 2-D graphics description so we can make masks."

"So, you spend millions of dollars on some design, and then just e-mail it out of the country?"

"That's it. To a mask shop in Hsinchu City."

"Yeah, I've been there."

"Not the most exciting place in the world. So, anyway, we pay $750K on a set of masks. Then TSMC—you know those guys, the foundry?"

"Yup."

"They take the masks, which are like photograph negatives but the lines are 0.18 microns wide, and they make our chips. I still have to watch over them, adjust some of the process steps."

"And you get chips?" I asked.

"Well, not exactly. We pay them $2,500 and get an eight-inch wafer. There are probably 2,000 die sites, or potential chips, on the wafer."

"So, they cost a buck and a quarter per chip?"

"I wish. We take the yield risk. You know, dust and some other defects on the wafer means that lots of the dies are bad. Probably 75% or more will work. But we don't know that yet. We first have to test the wafer."

"Where do you do that?" I asked.

"Lowest bidder. Sometimes we do it in Taiwan. But usually it's in Indonesia, Malaysia, places like that. The rest of the steps are labor intensive, so we do it in low-labor-cost countries. They beat each other up to get the business," Mark told me.

"All right. Hold on. I want to be like Woodward and Bernstein and follow the money."

"Shoot."

"So far, you have e-mailed a design. Any money for that?" I asked.

"Nope."

"Then you pay $2,500 per wafer, from Silicon Valley to Taiwan."

"And the $750K for the masks."

"Oh, right, what else."

"Well, we do a wafer test, which puts a black dot on the bad die sites. That costs $100 per wafer. Then we saw up the wafer—dicing, it's called—and keep the good die. That doesn't cost that much, but it is labor intensive, as I said."

"Then that's it?" I asked.

"No, then we package, bond and test the packaged chip again. It doesn't cost much, but you find bad parts, so the yield goes down and your ultimate cost per chip goes up."

"That's it."

"Almost. The working chips are sent to a warehouse in Hong Kong."

"So, if I track all the money in this example, it costs $2 per chip."

"Depending on yield, $2, maybe $2.50."

"Then you sell them."

"Yup, millions of them."

"To who."

"Oh, we were selling them to Sony and Panasonic and Sharp and guys like that for their DVD players. Toshiba did their own chips, I think. But our chip did everything. You needed our chip, a laser diode, a power supply and some buttons, and voilà."

"How much did you get?"

"At first, we could get $20."

"For a $2 chip."

"Sure. It wasn't just silicon, it was what was on it."

"That's amazing."

"Yeah, competition came in, and prices dropped to $10. So, we designed another, smaller chip that cost us $1, so we could sell it at $5. That's why you see DVD players for $99 at Costco."

"Still, you are marking your chip up five times."

"Yeah, it kinda sucks, it should be more."

"Then the money that Sony pays you goes back into the U.S., back to Silicon Valley."

"Not really."

"What do you mean, not really? I see the quarterly earnings announcements and the revenues from these chip sales."

"The money never comes back in," Mark Allen insisted.

"What?"

"It sits offshore."

"But it's your money."

"Of course, it's our money, but if we brought it back in, we'd pay Uncle Sam 35%, so we create an offshore subsidiary and leave it outside."

"Invested in what?"

"Oh, the money is invested in the U.S. T-bills, bonds, whatever."

"How is that possible?"

"That's what lawyers are for. We just set up a wholly owned subsidiary of our company in Barbados or one of those warm islands down there. The cash is all consolidated into the company, but the actual cash and investments reside outside the country."

"But your chip eventually comes into the U.S.?"

"Sure, but it's sitting inside a Panasonic DVD player."

This was the piece of the puzzle I was missing.

"But you sell other chips, to companies in the U.S.?"

"Sure, we ship them from that Hong Kong warehouse, back to one of the backrooms in Milpitas. Actually, ship them is probably a misnomer. These things are pretty small and light. We can FedEx 'em back here for almost nothing."

"Then you sell them to companies here, and the $10 you get for the chip stays in the U.S.?"

"We would usually value them at cost, so the $2 goes out to pay for the foundry and packaging and all that, but we import a finished chip. So, if you look at the trade stats, we caused a $2 import. Our competitors, say Toshiba, might sell the same chip into the U.S. at a $10 value, same chip basically, but they import a $10 chip. That way they sell it at no profit in the U.S. and don't pay taxes."

"But you exported the GDS-II file?" I wanted to make sure.

"Yeah, but that has no real value. It's just bits in an e-mail file—no one buys it."

"No export, but millions in imports?"

"I guess. We help the U.S. run these huge trade deficits, even though we make a ton of dough doing it. Kinda doesn't make sense, but it works."

It does make sense. We run trade deficits and probably will forever. Here was this high-margin company, marking up chips 400–500%, making massive profits, with a stock worth billions, multiples of their current revenues, but they cause these statistical problems. They cause trade deficits. Should we care? I'm no longer so sure.

I started thinking of that Panasonic DVD player. It's $99 at Wal-Mart, but I am almost positive that Panasonic doesn't make bubkes selling them. Consumer electronics is a notoriously low-margin business. Between the chips, the boards, the labor to assemble them and shipping costs, I'll bet they clear as profit less than $5 per DVD player, maybe only $1, maybe they even lose a couple of bucks.

Worse, instead of a $2 or $10 trade deficit for each DVD chip that might have been imported into the U.S., Panasonic was creating a $90 trade deficit for every DVD player. They put together DVD players for us for practically no profit, but we run huge deficits. That doesn't sound all that bad to me.

Yet Mark Allen was selling them a chip for $10 that might have cost him $2. Or a chip for $5 that cost him $1. And Panasonic wouldn't have a business if they didn't buy his chip. Man, this is a great scheme.

But $2 or $10 goes out of the country for each chip that is brought into the U.S. Or $90 in cash leaves the country to buy those no-profit DVD players. I haven't finished following the money trail.

"You ought to come jump with me sometime," Mark Allen offered.

"I think I do it just about every day, more like virtual BASE-ing."

"What do you mean?"

"Never mind, I think I get my kicks free-falling in other ways."

But I was starting to understand how this whole thing works. "We think, they sweat" is rude but right. They get employment to increase their standard of living. We get profits, which means higher-paying jobs, and drive our stock market to increase our standard of living. In doing so, they pile up dollars. So what?

But all the dollars come back in at some point. I've got to find them. If I can turn that model into a way to invest, then this boom-bust thing will have been worthwhile.

## > > > Wealth How?

Each time I look for parallels between England's empire and the wealth they created, I find only contradictions with today's America. In almost every case, the U.S. is the opposite of England. Rather than running trade surpluses made up by gold flowing in, as the British "enjoyed" until 1870, the U.S. is running trade deficits and current account deficits, meaning we import more than we export and borrow more than we lend.

It's pretty obvious that Americans, me at the top of the list, have an insatiable appetite for Beemers and Toshiba laptops and Panasonic DVD players, and we suck them into the country as fast as others can make them. Are we being gluttonous, or are we just owed these indulgences? Add the U.S. federal government budget deficits and the capital that comes in from overseas, and we owe huge amounts to Japan and China and Taiwan and Germany. It sounds terrible. You know, I haven't even met my grandchildren, and I feel guilty borrowing their future away from them.

It's harder to make an investment case for buying stocks in the U.S. Maybe I just enjoyed the final blow-off of great investing in the U.S. Damn, that was fun while it lasted. Now we are all turning Japanese or Chinese or Indian.

Conventional wisdom suggests that we are at the mercy of strangers to lend us money to fund these deficits and consumer binges. And every Chinaman is going to jump off his chair at the same time and cause earthquakes in California unless we pay them back what they are owed.

So a nasty paradox exists. How can the U.S. be so advanced and innovative yet run these deficits and crawl on our knees, hat in hand, begging to borrow our own money back to pay for these indulgences? I can't see investing in U.S. companies of any kind only to see us default on massive loans to Japanese or European central bankers.

By the way, I love paradoxes. They usually mean someone doesn't understand what's really going on and you can invest in things other people "can't know." I start salivating when I hear that word *paradox*.

But perhaps it's a paradox (gurgle) because I'm looking at it the wrong way, and hopefully, everyone else is too. Despite the protests of a few straggling unions over the last five years that the U.S. is no longer an industrial economy, it's an intellectual property economy. That boom thing was the warning shot.

Those analogies to jolly old England fail quickly. It's not about running trade deficits and current account deficits—those are just economic constructs. Government statistics measure absolute numbers, hard goods in and money flow out. The 10,000-pound gorilla in the room is the stock market. Economists miss the most important statistic, profitability. That's all the stock market cares about, yet economists are shockingly silent on this statistic. Are they just stupid? Nah, they've just never run money.

The margin or profit over cost of goods and services is probably the only true measure of trade. If you look at it upside down, maybe those Beemers and DVD players are our gold and just dessert.

Since the Industrial Revolution (it's dead, long live it, yada yada), a new twist has been added to the economic system. Since the birth of the personal computer, companies can focus on thin slices of intellectual property, which can have very high, I mean really high, margins. Go ask Bill Gates if you don't believe me.

Software, microprocessor architectures, semiconductors, network architectures, optical components, cell phone components and databases are all pieces of intellectual property that can be licensed to others to build end products.

This stuff is so important that, in fact, the U.S. is a huge exporter of these pieces of intellectual property, but good luck finding it in government stats—it's practically invisible. Often, an entire architecture of a billion-in-sales chip can be e-mailed to that

TSMC factory in Taiwan, without a cash register ringing or a Commerce Department employee around to measure the export. That chip and other intellectual property are then combined, using low-cost labor with other low-margin components, like a power supply and some plastic, and turned into a laptop or DVD player.

Hollywood does this same thing with movies—e-mailing or FedExing a master copy to make DVDs overseas.

The mouse maker Logitech (who should send a Rolls-Royce to pick up Doug Engelbart every day) sells a wireless mouse for $40. As you would expect, it is made in China. Except the *Wall Street Journal* did some digging and figured out that China gets about $3 for the work they do—the rest of the value are chips and design and components from the U.S.

Let's open up that Toshiba laptop. With a $300 Intel chip (which has at least $250 in profit for Intel) and a $50 Windows license ($49.95 margin to Microsoft), the laptop is then sold by Toshiba back into the U.S. for $1,000. Toshiba and every other supplier are lucky if they make $50 in profit, *combined,* on the deal.

So, while in this overly simplistic example, a $300 Intel microprocessor and a $50 Microsoft operating system are exported from the U.S., a $1,000 product is imported, for a net trade deficit of $650. Yet on a profit basis, the U.S. clears 300 bucks, and the rest of the world maybe 50. Which economic system would you invest in? Yeah, me too.

Still, the paradox lingers (appropriate salivating Pavlovian response). A thousand of our dollars flow out of the U.S. while only $350 flow back in, multiplied 50 million times for each PC and laptop sold in the U.S. Traditional economic theory suggests the dollar should fall in value until trade balances. But as Deep Throat once said and Mr. Zed paraphrased, "Follow the money." Where is it? Where'd it go?

Well, the $650 difference has gotta go somewhere. It is assumed that it all sits in a central bank in Japan or Korea and is loaned out to local businessmen. Of course, that's their problem. In the past, they rarely found a business or a building that they didn't want to fund. It is almost as if their banks' only function was to create nonperforming loans.

Fortunately, capital sloshes around the globe to seek its highest return. Over time, capital looks at the $300 in margin versus $50, and the decision is not a difficult one. Those same dollars that we ship out to pay for our laptops and DVD players and Mercedes S-class eventually come back home, into the U.S., where they are welcomed with open arms. It's not because we somehow insist on those dollars back or beg for those dollars back; they naturally return.

Most of those returning dollars buy U.S. Treasuries, which are backed by the tax payments from the high wages that high-margin businesses pay to programmers and engineers versus low-paid factory workers. So far, so good. Foreigners own something like 45% of all Treasuries, some as reserves for their central banks in lieu of gold.

Some of those dollars, which are more risk tolerant, buy corporate debt. But the real smart dollars are invested in the high-margin businesses directly. Those dollars can and do buy Intel stock or Microsoft stock. Directly and indirectly, those dollars invest in a high-margin economy.

In fact, when they don't, and invest at home, they almost always screw up. Not just the bank loan problems of Japan, but witness the Korean mess in 1998, which helped provide an introduction for me to Ssangyong.

The biggest problem with our trade deficits is that too many of our dollars get sold and converted into local currencies, like yen or baht or renminbi, creating overheated economies and overinvestment in the same old low-margin manufacturing companies.

They'll figure it out. In the old days of the gold standard, countries were supposed to ship gold out to cover trade deficits. But everybody cheated, and as economists called it, sanitized their gold by printing more local currencies.

As far as I can tell, U.S. dollars are the new gold.

The old industrial model says trade deficits lead to a lower dollar. But that makes those imported cars and laptops and textiles and everything else from overseas more expensive and therefore less competitive. What good is that? Oh yeah, to save those NUMMI jobs. Yuck.

The message is real simple: Don't convert our dollars into your currency, that's what drives the dollar down. Instead, you should be intervening in the foreign markets and buying dollars, buying Treasuries, buying our stocks, if for no other reason than that is where the return is. Plus, it keeps your currency lower and your goods more competitive.

Sanitize or dry your eyes.

The Japanese finally figured this out in 2003 and are on the road to an economic recovery. George Soros and packs of New York hedgies may even figure this out someday.

In other words, we send them dollars to pay for all that great consumer stuff, you know, those nice 50-inch TVs and Toyotas and all, but they need to, in one form or another, send back all those dollars! And the sooner they do, the better off they will be!

Still, there is another paradox (drool). With those currency flows, foreigners will eventually own the entire U.S., or hold us hostage by threatening not to loan us anymore, i.e., not send our dollars back.

But the stock market is not 1:1—it is not a zero sum game. So those deaf, dumb and blind economists can't find the capital flows. One million dollars invested in a stock can make the stock go up by $10 million or even $100 million in value on a slow afternoon.

Money flowing from overseas back into the U.S. stock market may not even cause a loss of ownership. Foreigners may always own 13% of U.S. stocks, as they do now, because they are not the only ones investing. U.S. investors are investing their excess income in the stock market. Stock options distribute equity to new workers. I assume that someone will wake up to this model and make Social Security an equity program as well. I'm supposed to be unemotional about this (I run a hedge fund, remember), but no one I know thinks they will ever see a penny from Social Security.

The paradox is resolved by putting the egg before the cart, er, chicken, where it belongs. We are not a bunch of gluttonous consumers who are mortgaging away our future by overindulging and running huge deficits in foreign goods. Instead, the U.S. turns out high-margin intellectual property that the rest of the world uses to build finished products for the American market and for their own market. The trade surpluses that foreign countries run are their way of paying the U.S. for this stuff. We may run trade deficits, but we have more margin than they do. (So there.)

In fact, we are running a surplus. Hmmm, let's say we are running a margin surplus. As Jon Lovitz would say, "Yeah, a margin surplus, that's the ticket."

The U.S. has high margins not because we are exploiting the poor and downtrodden. Our stuff serves some useful purpose that the market sets a high value on—sorting tickets, moving messages, making cheap phone calls, shrinking tumors, lowering cholesterol or making us laugh at the movies.

The excess dollars that flow out of the U.S. create jobs around the world. In fact, they probably are creating a middle class in countries that never had a middle class before. Making stuff for us is a great way to end poverty in China and a few dozen African countries. But those outward-bound dollars that confuse everyone as deficits are in reality capital that gets reinvested back into the U.S. stock market. The virtuous circle is that this lowers the cost of capital for these same high-margin companies. Five hundred million dollars in trade deficits might actually create several trillion dollars in stock market wealth. So what's wrong with trade deficits again?

And the great thing about foreigners owning U.S. Treasuries is that I don't have to. Why earn only 3% or 6% or wherever they head to, when I can make 20% or 40% or a factor of 10 over 5 years investing in high-margin companies?

One more paradox. Economists love to focus on things like capacity utilization and output gap. The closer we are to full utilization, the more likely stock-market-killing inflation kicks in. Again, this is industrial thinking. In an intellectual property economy, there are few limits. Another copy of Windows costs almost nothing. Another Viagra pill has almost zero marginal cost. Another *Lord of the Rings* DVD costs 50 cents. This is why companies love to sell their IP overseas; it is an untapped market.

Inflation happens when you run out of supply of lumber or ethylene or oil. IP comes from a bottomless well. You only run out of usefulness. There is an infinite supply of DOS operating systems too, but no one wants them.

There is also an infinite supply of intellectual property for those that don't want to pay—call it HIP, hot intellectual property. More of a "We think, they steal . . . no sweat."

It's a problem with no good solution. Pirates used to rule the high seas, pillaging early industrial trade until the British and American navies put a stop to it and new laws were put in place (and a few pirates walked the gangplank). I watched C-Cube make a fortune enabling video CD players that took advantage of pirated movies in China. And our fund did well with Elantec, which sold a $2 diode driver that was suddenly in huge demand after Napster turned moms and pops and kiddies into music pirates. You've got to invest around the problem, before and if property protection laws are ever fixed. Again, it's one of those unemotional things. I have a feeling once this margin surplus concept is understood and how important intellectual property is to American wealth, a few modern pirates will walk the virtual gangplank, and investing in intellectual property will be much more straightforward.

The more I think about it, the more I like this margin surplus thing. And now, all I have to do is get in the way of a couple of interesting and probably ever-changing companies with pieces of high-margin intellectual property and I will have discovered the fountain of wealth. Why didn't I figure this out years ago?

## > > > J-Curve

"You're wrong, really wrong," he told me. Ouch. That stings.

"But my point is that we are in a different world. All the existing rules are built around an industrial economy, and we are now in an intellectual property economy," I replied.

"Oh, so, you are trying to pitch me the 'it's different this time' nonsense?"

"No, it's not different this time. It's one of those 'I see, said the blind man, as he picked up an ax and saw.' "

"Huh?"

"You see, the dollar is the new gold, and we export IP and import finished goods, and the difference ends up in our stock market and—"

"You are forgetting the J-curve."

"The what?"

"Oh, you rookies always forget the important stuff. The J-curve just snapped you in the ass."

I received an invitation via e-mail to attend the Annual Monterey Conference on the future of the euro. Alan Greenspan was scheduled to speak. So were the heads of the IMF, World Bank and the central bank of most European countries. I'd never been to the Monterey conference on currencies, so I thought it might be a great place to test my theory out on those that did attend the conference. Plus Monterey is only 45 minutes from my home. I could drive there, blast the group with my knowledge and then scram for home, hit and run economics.

So I sent an e-mail to Jim D. with a proposal for a talk at the Monterey Conference, titled "The Margin Surplus: Why It's Imperative to Drive a Beemer, Tote a Toshiba Laptop and Watch a Big-Ass Sony TV." That ought to shake 'em up.

The premise was real simple, my rudely named "we think, they sweat." We export intellectual property from high-margin companies and on and on. The conclusion was simple—the dollar probably needs to go up, not down, to close the trade deficit, exactly the opposite of what economists think.

"First of all, it's the Monetary Conference, not the Monterey Conference. It's in Washington, D.C.," Jim D. said.

"Oh, momentary dyslexia, sorry."

"And you really need to read up on the J-curve."

"And you on the scale," I threw back at him.

"Huh?" he said. "Look, I generally agree with most of your points. However, you need to be careful with your point that the only way to lower trade deficits is to have the dollar go up."

"But it works," I insisted.

"Only for a little. The so-called J-curve accounts for the fact that the initial effect of an appreciation of the dollar is to decrease the trade deficit—because at the higher exchange rate, the value of sales to foreigners increases relative to the value of our imports."

"Sure, because . . ."

"But over time, because our goods are more expensive, foreign demand for U.S. goods will fall and the deficit will increase."

"That's the industrial model."

"That's how trade works and has for hundreds of years. The mirror image of all this, of course, will be a capital account surplus. Meaning foreigners have to invest in the U.S. in order to balance our trade deficits."

"But it's the other way around," I said. "We run a capital account surplus, not because we run trade deficits, but so we *can* run deficits."

"I guess you're just focusing on IP and the fact that there's no good substitute for Wintel."

"That's it. There is no substitute. Same for drugs and Hollywood movies. In fact, we run deficits, on paper anyway, because we *undervalue* our intellectual property."

"But the J-curve never fails."

"It works for commodities or textiles or anything where we

have to balance labor costs. But for intellectual property, the J-curve is bogus. But when there is no substitute for Windows or for a Pentium or Viagra, when the dollar goes up, Japanese need to cough up more yen, the Chinese a few more yuan, and guys named Dieter a few more euros."

"But we operate at the discretion of foreigners investing in the U.S.," Jim D. insisted.

"No, it's the opposite. They have no choice but to invest in the U.S. We've got the margin. We ship dollars to them to pay for the Beemers and DVD players. But since we have higher margins, smart capital, return-seeking capital, not only wants to but has to invest back in the U.S., chasing our margins. This gets balanced out by the dollar reaching such heights that we no longer run deficits, meaning the value of our IP going out equals the value of the goods coming back in."

"And the J-curve?"

"It's our margin surplus that makes this all work. Lose that, and the J-curve is back in effect, and we are all toast and back working in auto factories."

"See you in Monterey?" Jim D. asked.

"I thought the conference is in D.C.?" I asked.

"It is. But not with you. Thanks."

## > > > *Why It's Imperative to Drive a Beemer, Tote a Toshiba Laptop and Watch a Big-Ass Sony TV*

*Mr. Zed: My grand unifying theory of why the U.S. is still the best place to invest. Rejected in D.C., but here it is:*

*I just love American customs and tradition. My favorite? Well, years ago, I got stuck in Detroit Rock City, on the night before Halloween, so-called Devil's Night. The Motor City was glowing. Quite literally. It turns out that Detroit's quaint tradition revolves around arsonists who randomly select parked cars to burn. Well, not randomly, 99.9% of the time, it is a Toyota or a BMW or other foreign-made cars (any Yugos left?) that get torched. Xenophobia? Patriotism? Loud message to job-stealing foreigners? How about just amazingly backward? These industrial-age "hoodlums" ought to be lighting up a few Fords and GMC trucks if they want to create more local jobs.*

*You see, car manufacturing used to be a great business. In 1962, General Motors made just over half of all cars sold in the U.S. market and had profits of $1.5 billion, the equivalent of $9 billion today. Now they are struggling to sell one in four cars and work on wafer-thin margins. But if foreigners want to bend sheet metal and tighten bolts for less than $20 per hour and still make barely 1% of sales as profit, why should we stop them? Instead of providing cap-*

*ital to U.S. automakers, Wall Street, as it always does, focuses on businesses that make higher returns. It's creating its own world order.*

*History does rhyme. In the 20th century, the resource-rich U.S. took over leadership of the industrial era. But now it is grappling with a painful transition to an economic system based on intellectual property rather than factories. We are all used to an industrial America, the Dow Jones Industrial Average and all that. But now all of those great traditions sparked by Watt and Wilkinson are coming to an end.*

*There is a classic Wall Street adage that says, "Money sloshes around the globe, seeking its highest return." It's been sloshing away from Detroit for decades. But where is it sloshing to? That's where I want to be.*

*In the U.S. the Industrial Revolution is dead. Kiss it goodbye. Heating, stirring, mixing, stamping and bolting have all been played out. These are no longer things that make America great. Instead it's, uh, thinking. I know what you're thinking, "Why didn't I think of that?" It's what people who think they are smart call intellectual property. This IP is the Silicon Valley model.*

*But how did we get here? The biggest change since World War II is that design and manufacture are no longer linked. Computers and communications move designs around in nanoseconds, while industrial-era factories locate near cheap labor.*

*A computer on a chip, an operating system, a wireless packet switching network—these are all highly intelligent properties that come from mind instead of matter. But so is a Nike swoosh, an anti-intelligent Adam Sandler movie or* Baywatch *rerun, a pill to stop the runs from eating a Happy Meal, Vanilla Diet Coke and a venti double decaf blended caramel macchiato with a twist at Starbucks.*

*The 225-year-old Industrial Revolution never did burn out but merely faded away into a pit of profitlessness. On the flip side, intellectual property is highly profitable, which makes Wall Street squeal with delight. Money would flow uphill, if it had to, to fund these high-margin intellectual enterprises. Money sloshes to margin!*

*The stock market sorts all this stuff out. A stock is nothing more than the current value of a company's future profits. Capital sloshing around, seeking its highest return, naturally funds highly profitable companies.*

*General Motors' days were numbered when Wall Street figured out the company couldn't dominate as they did back in 1962. GM should have been creating subsidiaries in Japan rather than trying to keep Japanese imports out of the U.S. Wall Street probably would have provided them all the capital they wanted.*

*As the Pink Panther Inspector Clouseau said when told, "That's a priceless Steinway baby grand piano," right after he had smashed it with a knight's chalice stuck on his arm: "Nuut anymeure."*

*Give GM expansion capital? Not anymore. Over time, stock markets are all-knowing and very persuasive. It's the stock market that is leading the change to the intellectual property economy we are in today, by canceling the credit cards of companies that don't fit the model. You have to squint to see it happening now, but it will be more and more obvious every day.*

*The whole Industrial Revolution was based on a premise that if a company designed it, they had to make it to get paid. No more. What began as coal-powered, steam-belching, industrial-factory-based economy has morphed into a highly elastic, horizontally organized, globally distributed, sleek, efficient economic system that a government-knows-best Keynesian would require a cough-syrup–induced hallucination to dream up. Instead, it happened naturally, based on labor-saving technology and disparate worker costs. The strangely named Fabless Semiconductor Association, whose member companies strictly design chips and don't own factories, has over 400 members, adding more than 100 during the downturn of 2002 alone. These are the high-margin companies in Silicon Valley. Intellectual property now rules.*

*Everything you know about what makes the world work—sovereign nation states, balance of trade, gold standards, fiat money as well as car torching—is up for grabs.*

*Simply stated, the world economy now runs on U.S. intellectual property. Santa Clara and Redmond sell chips and software at disgustingly high profits to foreigners who turn them into personal computers at disgustingly low profits. It's a great trade. We can buy a PC for $799, and they (China, Malaysia, Thailand) employ their unwashed masses. Our masses are already washed, heck, coiffed. In the U.S., the typical autoworker makes over $70,000. At an average manufacturing salary in the U.S. of $20 an hour, we can't afford to bond integrated circuits, wind inductors for read-write disk drive heads or stuff circuit boards. That's buck-an-hour or buck-a-day work. Exploitive? If we weren't paying a buck an hour, many third-world workers would be shoveling shiitake in their gardens for a buck a month. In fact, our appetite for multi-gigahertz PCs to surf for cheap prices and Britney videos is what creates jobs and a rising a middle class in the rest of the world. And slowly but surely, that middle class will consume our intellectual wares, as they can afford it.*

*That's the thing about intellectual property. It usually has a huge up-front cost to create and almost zero marginal cost to sell. One more copy of Windows or one more arthritis pill costs practically nothing. The next one sold is pure profit. It's in the best interest of Microsoft and every high-margin company in the U.S. to have a growing middle class worldwide to buy more of their stuff. Memo to Karl Marx: You don't exploit for profit anymore. Instead, you expand and enhance. Quite a change.*

• • •

*Whole economies are based on a disengagement of design and manufacturing—of intellectual property and industry. And just in time, or progress in the U.S. would have come to a screeching halt, and you and I would be waiting in line to load our punch cards into IBM time-sharing computers.*

*The British milked a lead in steam engines into a hundred-year empire, imported raw materials, ran them though foul coal-burning, steam-engine–run manufactories and then exported value-added finished goods. Their profit was a huge markup above the cost of coal. Homespun textiles, metalworks and pottery made in the rest of the world were more expensive and of lower quality. It wasn't even fair. The British wiped up and built their empire.*

*Now it's the opposite, which is why the Industrial Revolution is finally dead. A very bright star in Sunnyvale, California, e-mails the design for her chip to Taiwan, where it is manufactured and then shipped to Shanghai to be assembled into a Toshiba laptop. They keep a few for themselves and sell the rest back to us for margins so low that we can't afford to do it ourselves. The U.S. exports high-margin intellectual property, which others add sweat to and sell back to us at tiny markups. It's one of those funny win-wins that drives economists crazy (crazier?).*

*You may ask, "Uh, someone said something about my needing to drive a Beemer?"*

*OK, OK. It takes lots of dollars to buy chips and software and Viagra and McNuggets and Jerry Lewis movies. No problem, we just have to buy something from other countries, to put dollars in their hands.*

*In the early 19th century, the British Empire was almost stillborn. In 1815, the long inflationary Napoleonic Wars ended, and sure enough, wheat prices collapsed. Farmers began turning in their pitchforks and moving to the cities in droves to work in manufactories. Steam engines were driving textile mills to allow the British to sell cheap and comfortable clothing to the world. In fact, one particular machine, Samuel Crompton's spinning mule, hooked up to a Boulton & Watt steam engine, would repeatedly stretch and wind cotton thread and yarn until it was as "smooth as silk," like Kessler Whiskey. No one making clothes at home anywhere could match these mills for either cost or quality in terms of smoothness.*

*But landowners who controlled Parliament, and these farmers, who didn't know their ashes from their bellows, passed the Corn Laws. These tariffs set minimum prices on agriculture and kept out cheap corn and grain from the Continent (read, France). Workers started starving because they were not making enough in the factory to pay for now expensive bread. But factory owners couldn't raise wages because they were having trouble selling their manufactured goods overseas. Why? Because the French and Germans were paying for these goods with their wheat and corn, and the British taxed them out of affordability. How stupid—this almost killed the British Empire in its infancy.*

*With any foresight, the landowners should have dumped their unprofitable farms and invested the proceeds in highly profitable joint stock companies making pottery, shirts and potbelly stoves. England should have gladly bought French wheat and Dutch flowers and German barley and hops so that consumers in these countries could have turned around with the money they received and bought British manufactured goods. There was no substitute. Once you go silky smooth, you never go back. The Corn Laws foolishly lasted until 1846.*

*So, go ahead, buy that Beemer so that Germans can afford to buy our software.*

*Wait a second, I hear you screaming, "The U.S. is running trade deficits as deep as the Mariana Trench, $500 billion a year or more." Relax—it's just money, and funny money at* *that. You see, using industrial-era measurement tools, "money out, goods in," the common perception is that consumers in the U.S. are running these massive trade deficits, mortgaging their future and putting the health and well-being of the U.S. in the hands of devious foreign strangers—to xenophobes, are there any other kind?*

*Which reminds me of a great story:*

*An economist and an investor are helplessly lost on a hike through the peaks and valleys of the Dow and NASDAQ mountain ranges, well, the Rockies. The investor sticks a wet finger in the air to find his direction via the prevailing wind. The economist is studying charts and numbers, GDP growth, trade stats, unemployment data, inflation, hours worked, productivity, meticulously compiled by the Commerce Department, the Bureau of Labor Statistics and Bureau of Economic Analysis. "OK, I've got this figured out," the economist yells. "You see that big mountain over there?"*

*"Yup," sighs the investor.*

*The economist proudly announces, "We're on top of that one."*

*According to government statistics, the U.S. has been running trade deficits, except for a couple of brief surpluses, since 1976. But that's like the government counting railroad ties to determine the strength of the U.S. economy—it's the wrong measure.*

*The cumulative deficit since 1976 is around $4 trillion. Most alarmists and car burners equate that with spending our grandchildren's future, that the U.S. has spent $4 trillion more than it produced, and our grandchildren will practically be in slavery to pay back our "hog"iness.*

*If this was just German beer or French wine that we were quaffing in mass quantities and running deficits to do it, I'd be a little nervous. But, no, the intellectual property we export and then reimport in finished goods is the type that makes us more productive. Computers, with our designs but Taiwan-made chips and Malaysia-assembled disk drives, run our corporate back offices. Similarly cre-*

*ated digital networks now deliver phone calls, and other systems deliver e-mail cheaper every year.*

*Looked at another way, foreigners made us $4 trillion of stuff, in exchange for a piece of paper with Ben Franklin's mug on it. But we get it all back. Charity? Nah. They buy a piece of debt signed by Alan Greenspan, promising to pay them interest and their principal back in 10 years. Or maybe a colorful stock certificate. So, either foreigners are suckers or there is some economic reason for these deficits.*

*We got most or all of the 4 trill back, chasing our profits. Do they now own the U.S.? Nah. The entire U.S. bond market is $19 trillion, stocks another $15 trillion and growing.*

*A not-so-well-kept secret that Wall Street has figured out: creating intellectual property is lucrative. Microsoft sells Windows for $50 with virtually no physical costs, just massive research and development costs. Even at the bottom of the bear market of 2002, Microsoft, with its 40% operating margins, was the second most valuable company in the U.S. GE, a giant hedge fund, was #1.*

*Money comes out of the woodwork to chase these kinds of returns. Wall Street is an essential conduit. Excess capital at our trading partners, the "beneficiaries" of our drooling gluttony, comes right back and invests in the U.S.*

*Economists measure GDP, Gross Domestic Product, and live and die by its direction. People who run money look at gross domestic profit, since that's all that really matters. The Dow trumps GDP—that sigh you just heard was industrial economists fainting into a heap on the floor.*

*It would take 40 companies the size of Microsoft making 1% operating margins to generate the return that Microsoft does on their intellectual property. That's a lot of factories in a lot of countries making stuff for us. No wonder the deficit is $4 trillion and Microsoft is worth more than most Continents. And the deficit is probably going to get larger, but as Alfred E. Newman would say, "What, U.S. worry?"*

• • •

*But don't we owe someone $4 trillion? Sort of, not really—aw, screw it, no. They can get their money back eventually, but wealth beyond those four big ones will be created in the U.S. if we put their money to work effectively. When capital sloshes around and chases high returns, much of it gets invested in our stock market. And unlike a passbook savings account at your local bank, there is no account statement that reads $4 trillion. Bean counters need solid beans to count; if they are smashed and stirred into a soup, no one really knows how many beans there are.*

*A million dollars invested into a company's stock over a week or a month can increase the value of that company by a hundred million dollars. It works both ways: a million dollars sold can decrease a stock's value by that or more as well. Dollars flowing into the U.S. are lost in the bean soup of the market, but their effect is to lower the cost of capital for great companies. The $4 trillion may have increased wealth by $7, 8 or 9 trillion. Who knows? Except to say that it increases wealth.*

*Economists may insist we are running a trade deficit, but in reality, we are running a margin surplus. In a world where money crosses borders faster than J-Lo goes through boyfriends, profits are all that matter. The margin or profit over cost of goods and services is the only true measure of trade. I will gladly trade you an idea I make $1 profit on for five widgets that you only make a nickel on. And I'll make that trade every day of the week.*

*As long as the U.S. focuses on intellectual property, perhaps we'll never have to pay the "debt" back. It will just be constantly rolled over and shrink in relative size as foreigners buy our intellectual property and chase our returns. In the long run, the dollar will probably rise in value. But who really cares what the dollar does—it's just an economic construct. Real wealth is created by profits, not cur-*

*rency printing presses. Currencies trade more on relative interest rates than anything else—this was the secret of the Soros and Tiger successes.*

*Prevailing industrial economic thought has trade balancing via exchange rates. If the U.S. is running deficits, the experts say, we should lower the value of our currency to make our goods more competitive on the world market, sell more of them and eventually bring trade back into balance. But that theory is flawed for intellectual property. Money is flowing in, but perhaps our stuff (companies, intellectual property, etc.) is too cheap!*

*Things are now backward. A PC maker has to buy Windows XP no matter what the exchange rate. If the dollar is rising, then it takes more Chinese yuan and more Thai baht and more euros to buy Windows. Lowering the dollar won't help Microsoft sell a single additional copy, since there is no substitute. A rising dollar might perversely shrink deficits as foreigners are forced to pony up more of their currency for our intellectual property and make our reward, those leather-clad BMWs cheaper—an upside-down J-curve.*

*According to the International Monetary Fund, in 1994, foreigners owned 11% of the total value of U.S. long-term securities. At the end of 2001, they owned 18.3%. Their share of stocks went from 7% to 12.4%. But the stock market, even at the bottom of a bear market, more than doubled in that same time period. So even though foreigners own more, the U.S. is wealthier. Isn't that the right end game? At some point, as low-profit industries move out or close altogether, U.S. margins will be high enough to make the economy cash-flow positive. We won't need the economist's phrase "kindness of strangers" anymore. No kindness here—just money chasing returns.*

*This may sound like voodoo economics, but only to those who see the world through the eyes of the Industrial Revolution. Economists live in Washington and New York, not Silicon Valley. Margins are making economists marginal.*

*If Toshiba wants to put some liquid crystal display and plastic around an Intel Pentium and Microsoft Windows, and sell it to me as a laptop,* let them. *In fact, they have to do it—it's their contribution to the world economy. The entire margin on PCs is around $400, $350 of which is split by Wintel (Microsoft and Intel) and other U.S. companies. If GM made the exact same laptops, they would cost $10,000 a pop, weigh 40 pounds and need a battery change every 3,000 miles.*

*If Sony wants to sell you a big honker, 60-inch diagonal comb filter DLP or LCOS cable-ready TV for practically no profit, should we stop them? We should instead encourage them. They go to the dark edges of western China, seeking out cheap labor to grow the tubes or assemble the flat panels and then move them to assembly plants all around the South China Sea. Why? Because it keeps Sony employees fully employed. Now you know why they bought a studio in Hollywood: anything to add value. But if you and me buying that Sony or Sharp TV means Japanese children can buy Kentucky Fried Chicken and go to Jim Carrey's next movie, and upgrade Windows 98 to Windows ME to Windows XP, so be it. Jerry Lewis will tell you—do it for the children.*

*But never underestimate the ability of policy makers to stick with oxymoronic conventional wisdom. Even if the dollar stays where it is and we go to $6 trillion in trade deficits, our stock and bond markets might be worth $50, $60, $70 trillion, double or triple today's value, run up by margin chasers. Just about everything about this margin surplus model is upside down.*

*The modern U.S. has farm bills and textile quotas and on and off steel tariffs like the British Corn Laws, not to mention late-model-car flamers. How dumb. Because of our margin surpluses, big trade deficits are our just dessert. These foreign-made consumer items are our gold. Let them*

> *flow. Tariffs, quotas and subsidies will return us to an industrial age. No thanks. Foreigners sweat and toil to make our physical delights, in exchange for our intellectual output. It doesn't get any better than this.*

So, Mr. Zed—there it is.

A paradox? Yes! Investing where others *can't know,* unless they stand on their heads.

That is my edge—someone tell Jack Nash.

I know it sounds wrong, counterintuitive, like eating your spinach, but for Americans in an intellectual property era, we all just have to suck it up and toodle around in our Mercedes with Corinthian leather. And drink French wine and watch the biggest-ass Japanese TVs we can afford. And wear clothes made in Ghana. Someone has to help those in other countries to be able to afford our ideas. Whatever dollars we send them will come back like a boomerang to buy our high-margin stuff—the fifth season of *The Sopranos* on DVD to the next release of code to run Cisco routers, or maybe they'll just buy our stocks. Who cares—there are great investments to find either way. That is the big waterfall. This works for all intellectual property, but I'm sticking with things that scale.

Warning. Even the name intellectual property is a paradox. It wrongly implies you can own something and have wealth. It's not true. Intellectual property means constantly improving on something to continue to generate high margins—else the market price collapses. None of this stuff is static; it constantly evolves.

Microsoft doesn't sell DOS, their original disk operating system, anymore, even though that was their key piece of intellectual property. It's worthless today. But their process of invention and innovation, even if it is painfully slow, is enormously valuable because of its 99% gross margins. Their only material costs are CDs and a thin manual. Even after spending billions on research, they make 50% operating margins and can afford to spend more each and every year on research. Nothing static about it. Wealth is a process. If I learned nothing else from running money, that is it.

Running money is supposed to be unemotional. Get conviction

on things others don't or can't know about and find future returns. But the stock market is also a force of change. It is the embodiment of Adam Smith's invisible hand. It funds growth and starves dying businesses and pushes progress. Not always, I suppose, but enough. With intellectual property and the margin surplus the U.S. is running, the stock market plays a key role in balancing payments and currencies and how the world now works. In an odd way, being a player in the stock market is a form of activism, albeit indirect and invisible activism, in pushing a model that increases living standards.

But it's hard to be unemotional for long. It's about ideas that affect people. It's about finding waterfalls that create massive growth and monster markets and change for the better to the status quo.

One hundred thousand or more people running money all day, every day, most staring at their screens, doing trades, providing access to capital, sloshing capital around. Whether we realize it or not, we are all driving progress, not individually, but collectively. Adam Smith's invisible hand? If you like. That's what a stock market does. But in this postindustrial, intellectual property world, it's more like Doug Engelbart's visible hands, clasped together, rising up, scaling knowledge, augmenting humans.

## > > > *Ghana a Goner*

This virtuous model of the margin surplus creating jobs and a middle class in the developing world at the same time it increases wealth in the U.S. and other intellectual property economies is pretty counterintuitive. But most things that work are counterintuitive, or dare I say, a paradox, at least at first.

I wanted to bounce this idea off anyone who would listen to see if there were holes in my logic. It's hard to stay unemotional.

"Yes, but the more successful a country is, the lower their inhabitants score on the Steen-Seligman Happiness Index, so what's the point?" and so finished the diatribe by a short guy with a funny beard.

I had leaned over to my friend who sucked me into this dreadful meeting and asked, "Who is this bozo?"

"A Harvard professor," she answered.

"Jeez," I moaned under my breath.

"The what quotient?" I asked the professor.

"Stress is a terrible by-product of the Industrial Revolution."

"So is a doubling of life expectancy."

"Yes, but we are just stressful for much longer."

"And who scores high on the Stream Happiness thing?"

"Ghana."

It was time to test out my margin surplus theory. I was stuck in the basement of an Indian restaurant in the bowels of lower Manhattan, with several professors who hoped to save the world.

"The industrial era is over, at least in the U.S., and now we have the opportunity to bring countries like Ghana into the developed world." I figured that might make an interesting conversation starter, changing the subject from happiness quotients.

"Yes, of course," said the learned Harvard man.

"You see, the world economy is now built on U.S. intellectual property, our chip designs, software, pharmaceuticals, heck, even movies and music."

"That's right," he said.

"We export IP to countries who put plastic around them and sell them back to us in exchange for dollars that they hold in Treasury bills, so we don't have to. We can invest in high-margin companies instead."

"I lost you," the prof said. He had an uncomfortable, pained look on his face. I thought it might be because he wasn't used to admitting he couldn't follow an argument, but then I remembered how crass it is to talk money or stocks with university types.

"If Ghana or any other of these other desolate countries run by kleptocrats would just leverage their low labor costs and learn how to make, oh, I don't know, DVD players or how to assemble chips or whatever, then their employment would skyrocket, a middle class would develop, a new generation could afford to be educated and they would eventually begin creating some of their own intellectual property. They've gotta start with low-margin products, build up reserves of dollars and a banking system, maybe even a stock market. Before you know it, they're watching *Seinfeld* reruns. Then, over time, they might contribute intellectual property of their own and see margins go up and move up the value chain."

"I'm not sure it will work."

"Ask Taiwan, Singapore, Malaysia, Vietnam—they can fill in the details. Even the Commies in China will sing its praises."

"I've heard this suggestion before. Look, I do a lot of consulting for Ghana."

"Wasn't Shirley Temple the ambassador there?" I asked.

"Well, yes. And, you know, they are connected to Jamaica. For a long time the slave trade ran directly from the shores of Ghana to Jamaica."

"To staff the sugar plantations," I said to keep him on his toes.

"Yes, well, Ghana is a very poor country. Twenty million inhabitants, most of them below the poverty line. Something like $2 per day average wages. Their government budget is about $500 million, almost all of it donated by foreign aid and U.N. programs. They are very interested in a way out of their poverty." The professor started getting agitated, rocking back and forth, almost trance-like, as if he was giving a lecture.

"But their labor force is their advantage," I said.

"Well, not how you think. We think we have found a way to bypass the industrial step and go directly to an intellectual property economy."

"Really? Is that even possible?"

"It turns out that people in Ghana are very musical."

"Like Jamaicans, I suppose."

"Their music is the key to their high scores on the Steen-Seligman Happiness Index. It has almost mystical qualities, very soothing to the soul." This is usually where I tune out, when the yoga talk starts, but I just had to hear his plans. I did order another drink, to improve my own happiness quotient.

"And?"

"Well, I go to Ghana several times a year, and what I have been recommending to their leaders is that rather than build factories, they work on leveraging their music."

"Leveraging?"

"Sure. They can export their low stress. Simply direct their music toward countries like the U.S. that have high levels of stress and low happiness quotients. The value of that kind of IP is huge."

"I suppose it worked on a small scale with Bob Marley, but what about the other 19.9999 million people?"

"It's a performance art."

"So we'll all have Ghanese musicians move in with us?" I had this bad image of a group with a harmonica and a steel drum playing "The Good Ship Lollipop" in my family room.

"Something like that. Your views on intellectual property are dead on, but the U.S. won't necessarily lead the way. This is the next battleground. The point is that industrialization is so impersonal and devastating to one's well-being that Ghana can consider alternate economic programs to enter what you call the developed world. Their stress-reducing music is probably more valuable than any chip or software."

"Have you run return-on-investment calculations?"

"Return on what? The numbers aren't important. This is revolutionary."

I made a note to myself to check in the morning to see if I could short an entire country—or an Ivy League institution. Hey, maybe I'm unemotional enough for this hedge fund stuff after all!

# Part VIII

# Epilogue

## > > > Close Fund

I know we put a five-year life on the fund, and I know we agreed to close it at the end of September, and I know it has been the smartest thing in the world to have forced redemptions and send money back every month to investors, and I know this market sucks and will probably stay sucky for some time as the mental damage from the bubble heals; but damn it, I was having second thoughts about ending it.

It was such a pain in the ass to raise money. We had busted our humps for five years to build a reputation with investors and with companies here in Silicon Valley. So, why throw all that away? Why close shop? Why give it all up? This is what I do.

Oh, yeah, now I remember. I haven't had a stress-free day in five years. I have puzzled out the future 24/7. I have conceptually fast-forwarded hundreds of soap operas until I could figure out how they might end. I feel like Jim Morrison of the Doors. "The future's uncertain and the end is always near," although no Budweiser on my corn flakes—not yet anyway.

You can't go to cash and ride it out. Investors insist you invest; they're paying you to invest, not sit on their money and collect interest. You can find stocks that work in bear markets, but not many. It was the smartest thing to do to get out to live to fight another day.

Our exit strategy was a little complicated by accounting and taxes. We can estimate pretty well how we did at the end of a month, to within maybe a tenth of a percentage point, but it usually took three or four more weeks to get real accurate numbers from the bean counters. Plus, we had a lot of individual investors, including

Fred and me, who didn't want cash back, because they would have to pay capital gains taxes. We were more interested in getting shares, tax-free, and then selling them if and when we wanted to.

So, we distributed all the cash we could to those who wanted cash on August 31 and then let the fund settle down for a month, and then when the accounting was done, we would distribute shares to everyone else sometime after September 30.

We did all the selling we needed to do all summer, mostly off the box, finishing at the end of August. I could sleep late in September.

On a Tuesday morning, I turned on the TV and flipped to CNBC in time to hear *Squawk Box* host Mark Haines say, "OK, this is no longer an accident. Two planes now have hit the World Trade Center buildings." Nancy and I hit the phones, calling friends who were nearby to make sure they were OK, and life became unreal. Performance and stocks and earnings and management all became incidental to White House press briefings and mini-obits in the *New York Times*. I recognized a few names of business acquaintances who perished, folks I had met once or twice. And I heard about brothers-in-law of friends, but no one in our close circle of family or friends.

Our decision to finish selling by August 31 was lucky. It wasn't so much that the markets went down after September 11, it was that the markets didn't even open for a week, in order to give the New York Stock Exchange time to get their act together. I found out that Instinet and the Island were ready to trade by 9:00 a.m. on September 12 at backup sites in Jersey City, but NASDAQ closed for as long as the NYSE needed—all markets were closed.

This might have bothered me more if I needed to get out, but we just held shares with no need to trade. Those shares took a beating, but who cares, we weren't selling, so they could do what they wanted. It hurt our performance, but so what, I was getting out of the business, not into it. We ended up down 5% for those nine months in 2001. Most other funds got annihilated—down 20–30–40%.

We averaged somewhere over 50% annual returns. We returned five or six times our original investors' money. I think we were in the top 10 of all hedge funds over our five years. But then again, 1996–2001 was not an ordinary stretch. Sometimes timing is everything!

And like that, I was out of the hedge fund business but not out of the investment business. I had learned too much. The quest for knowledge and understanding and working out the puzzle of the future was too ingrained into my psyche. I am still wide awake by 6:30 every morning, ready to face the news of the day. But now, I actually have time to think about the big picture, rather than sweat the details. It was going to take a while for the market to get out of its yo-yo pattern, so there was no better time to just think. But I was determined to figure out how all this nonsense really worked. I figured I will be back in the game at some point, but hopefully not in some dumpy office above an art supplies store or eight hours a day in my car, running between back-to-back-to-back meetings. Mr. Zed was right. I wanted to be a better investor for the next cycle, but somehow, now I need a better edge—an even bigger picture to be able to invest in.

## > > > The Tide Goes Out

Since we closed our fund, the market has been nothing but ugly. Packet switching was like an Iowa twister that leveled everything in its path. The business of switching telephone calls got shot in 2001 and died in 2002. CEOs from Bernie Ebbers at WorldCom and Gary Winnick at Global Crossing tried to revive the corpse of the old phone network with accounting tricks to buy themselves time to move to packets. Yup, Bob Metcalfe's technology helped create the accounting scandals in 2002.

The market dropping was like the tide going out, and all of a sudden, all the really butt-ugly bottom-feeding creatures that live in the tide pool were visible. Vibrant in the protection of the sea, they shrivel up and die in the sunlight, or are picked to shreds by passing seagulls (read, government bureaucrats) that feed off this garbage.

Oh, you know the names—Enron, WorldCom, Global Crossing, Quest, Adelphia, Tyco and HealthSouth. And what the heck, America Online, Lucent, Nortel were all guilty of either funny numbers or fudging the truth about how bad their business really was. Accounting firm Arthur Andersen lost their reputation on their Enron business, and after being found guilty as a firm, disappeared in a beat.

Wall Street analysts were conflicted and got caught recommending many of these bottom feeders to their clients all the way down. Mutual funds, which are priced once a day, were caught allowing insiders or outside hedge funds to make easy money arbitraging the stale price with a real-time value of their portfolios.

Damn, there are a lot of scumbags out there!

Did these folks all set out to cheat *me*? OK, to cheat me and every investor? I had a pile of dough to generate returns from. Did some CEOs, in some form or another, lie to keep me interested in their story, prop up their stock and buy time to fix their problems? And did Wall Street have a hand in it, with analysts telling me to buy? (Not that I listened to them, I knew their game.) Nope—it was my fault, your fault, all investors' fault. In the end, if you are running money, you have only yourself to blame. You get paid to seek out returns. You could have seen the fraud if you looked hard enough. You have to study people too, not just technology and numbers.

As an investor, these are the hardest lessons to learn. But it's not just numbers and products. Like technology, stocks are about people too. The force of technology's change affects people who are more than happy to keep things the same. But it's not over. Over time, those same packets that destroyed the phone network will wrestle control away from monopolies and media moguls, who cling to the dying exclusivity of their pipeline. TV and radio broadcasts, telephone wires, cable, DBS satellite, even CD and DVD sales in stores, are all pipelines up for grabs, to be crushed by "packetized" competition. Even sticky regulations proffering favored status to the incumbents can only slow, not stop, packets' deadly path of destruction. As an investor, timing is everything, but this is one of those trends you want to hop on and ride rather than fight against.

The tide going out ripped through the hedge fund world too. Remember the High Watermark? It caused the death of hundreds of hedge funds. Many funds were long and wrong in 2000, 2001 and especially in 2002, some down 30–50%. If you are down 50%, you have to go up 100% to get back to the High Watermark before you can charge the 20% of gains incentive fee. In other words, you are working for free, there is no incentive for your staff, and so you might as well shut the fund. This would have happened to us if we hadn't been sending money back for the last 18 months.

The best story floating around Silicon Valley was about Bowman Capital. Larry Bowman was a tech fund manager at Fidelity who moved out to the Valley to run a hedge fund at the start of the '90s. He ended up with billions in assets and huge success—enough to be one of the largest owners of vintage muscle cars in the country. Rumors had it that he was turned down by the town of Portola Valley for a permit to put an eighty-car garage under his house.

But that's not the story people were talking about in 2003. It was talk that Bowman was way under his High Watermark in his fund. So he called all of his investors and told them that he was going to return all of their money on December 31, 2002, and could they please send it all back on January 1, 2003, into a new fund that he was creating so that his High Watermark would then be reset and he could start earning his performance fee again. Simple enough. Except I heard that very few investors bothered to give the money back on January 1.

And other hedge funds? Tiger didn't last as a firm another 18 months after the yen-carry trade blew up. They missed the entire move in tech stocks; their only saving grace in 1999 was a huge position in US Air. It was a value stock, and Julian Robertson had bought it right. By May 2000, United Airlines had made a $60 cash bid for US Scare-lines. Tiger was sitting pretty, despite a tough year of withdrawals—$20 billion in assets dropped to about $6 billion as the Texan from the Institute of Pry-Vat Investors and his friends all ran for the hills. With the airline merger, Tiger showed a gain for 1999.

But Julian Robertson joined a long line of old dogs chasing fire hydrants. Once deregulated, airlines were protected by the complexity of their back offices. Anyone could refuel and fly a plane, but it took a special organization to sort the paper tickets. In fact, like United, you could buy other airlines and sort their tickets too, saving zillions.

But when technology ended the paper trail and e-tickets came of age, it wasn't the existing airlines that benefited. New players like Southwest and JetBlue could enter the business cheaply. A couple of million bucks in servers and broadband was all the back office they needed—the sorting tables were a thing of the past. It was like taking candy from a baby for these new guys to take market share from unionized United or US Air with their Vietnam-era pilots and aging battle-ax flight attendants.

Withdrawals were relentless, so Julian Robertson closed Tiger in March 2000, holding onto a few shares he thought would do well, like US Air.

US Airways filed for bankruptcy in August 2002, its stock a children's shoe size of 2 or 3 compared to the mature $60 United offered and withdrew.

Soros didn't fair much better. Back on April 28, 2000, news leaked out that the two top guys at Soros had left the firm. Stanley Druckenmiller, who ran the Soros Quantum fund with over $8 billion in it, and Nicholos Roditi, who ran the billion-dollar Quota fund, were out. Chasing returns, these guys apparently made huge investments in technology and Internet names in the second half of 1999 and got caught holding them. Soros had lost close to $3 billion since March 1, 2000.

And in a tragic coincidence, on that same April 28, 2000, a federal judge ruled that my favorite hot IPO, MP3.com, had violated copyright laws by creating a database of music downloadable off the Web. The stock dropped 4⅝, or 40%, to 7, on its way to 3. Goddamn, if Nick Moore wasn't right. M-P-Three! Never buy a stock with the price target in its name. MP3.com eventually hit zero, a long way from $60.

## > > > 747 Office

"Now what?" Mr. Zed wanted to know.

"Now what, what?" I evaded.

"So, you'll set up another fund soon?" he asked.

"Not yet," I answered. "At some point."

"Why wait? It seems like a great time, now."

"Because I'm not sure yet where the next waterfalls will come from."

"But you're never really sure," Mr. Zed reminded me.

"I know, but I've got to look under a lot more rocks in a lot more places with a lot more languages."

"Ah, I think I understand. The world is now smaller, but it takes a lot longer to see companies from a plane than from a car." Mr. Zed figured it out.

"I still think the best investments will be within a 10-mile radius of our old art supplies store in Palo Alto. It's just that I'll need to travel around the world to get the needed amount of conviction. I'm going to have to go to places like Ghana someday to figure this all out."

If there is one piece of denial in Silicon Valley, it's that the Internet really happened. Well, of course everyone knows that it happened. But the fact that so much of the ideas and code and chips and lasers and optics that made the Internet happen came from around here has provided a kind of bravado that everything new that is going to happen will come from Silicon Valley.

I think it will all roll up here, but piece parts will come from a lot of far-flung places. Things have spread out. Those soap operas

Fred warned me about are now happening in places I've never been to. I still don't think you can skip the industrial step; Mr. Haavaard is going to keep Ghana in poverty for too long, but at least they are thinking about intellectual property and its value.

To invest right, I've got to find the waterfalls for the new monster markets, and an office above an art supplies store in Palo Alto driving around in a car all day probably won't cut it anymore.

This is not to say I need to invest in Bangalore or Shanghai—probably the opposite. The margin surplus idea gives me enough comfort to invest in the U.S.—that's not the issue. The problem is finding the big explosive markets since the clues—the ideas that drive great investments—might come from a stilted or choppy conversation in Finland or Mumbai.

I want to find as many pieces of intellectual property as I can. And some are probably right in front of my eyes in an industrial park in San Jose next to a SpeeDee Oil Changer. But will I recognize it? I can't be sure anymore.

Should I move my family to China? Or is it the next Russia or Korea and about to blow up? Or is it India and tikka masala for dinner every night? Or Finland? Or, gasp, Ghana? Or worse, head to these places once a month? The idea of living on Singapore Airlines 747s or United Airlines 777s doesn't float my boat.

The answer is simple—I'm not sure. There is no way to be sure. Most of these places still seem stuck in that industrial mode—making stuff for us. But the more I look, the more I see these pockets of innovation: a group writing code for Symbian cell phones in Norway, architecting call centers in Bombay, designing a chip for Chinese set-top boxes in Guangzhou, rethinking the physics of nanoscale electronics in Tel Aviv. They may not amount to much, but I damn sure need to understand them before I invest in any technology, in Silicon Valley or anywhere else.

George Soros and Julian Robertson of Tiger had it easy. They analyzed central banks and politicians and figured out the direction of currencies. In an era of relatively stable currencies, the modern-day investor has to dig, early and often and everywhere. I'd still rather dig than get whacked by a runaway yen-carry trade.

Another cycle is coming. The drivers of it are still unclear.

Likely suspects are things like wireless data, on-command computing, nanotechnology, bioinformatics, genomic sorting—who the hell knows what it will be.

But this is what I do. Looking for the next barrier, the next piece of technology, the next waterfall and the next great, long-term investment. Sounds quaint.

I've come a long way from tripping across Homa Simpson dolls trying to raise money in Hong Kong. Or getting sweated on by desperate Koreans. Or driving around all day with Fred. Or getting thrown out of deals. Or yucking it up with Nick Moore.

But this is what I do.

Wealth really is a never-ending process. So is running money. You can't just walk away and ask about the meaning of life. It is my life—and all-consuming. I've just got to find the right time to get back in.

# > > > Acknowledgments

I'd like to thank Marion Maneker of HarperCollins for taking a ragtag collection of chapters, getting rid of most of them, bugging me for new ones and turning the mess into a real book. I sometimes felt like George S. Kaufman, who was playing pinochle backstage during a Marx Brothers performance of his play *Animal Crackers* when he paused, shook his head and said "Sorry, I thought I just heard an original line I wrote."

Edwin Tan and the rest of the folks at HarperCollins were extremely helpful throughout the process. So was my agent, Daniel Greenberg.

I want to thank Fred Kittler for being my partner in Velocity Capital through this bizarre journey and agreeing to let me tell this story. Nick Moore was critical in helping reconstruct the rollercoaster ride, and Rich Karlgaard provided needed insight when I got stuck. Michael Lewis gave me words of encouragement over the years and a path to follow.

I made a few friends suffer through early drafts—John Malloy, Stuart Litwin, Alex Balkanski and Eric Lamb—and each of them made important suggestions that I incorporated. Michael Dreyfus consulted on spatial considerations. I got revenge on my parents, Joan and Fred Kessler, who from age two always told me to do my best, by making them plow through more iterations of this book than anyone else.

My boys, Kyle, Kurt, Ryan and Brett, figured out when to leave me alone (rarely) and when Dad needed some distraction (always). Most importantly, I'd like to express my deep appreciation and love to my wife, Nancy, for encouraging me to pursue my dreams and helping to clear a path. She is my partner and real meaning of everything in life.

# > > > Index